Industrial Organisation and Innovation

NEW HORIZONS IN THE ECONOMICS OF INNOVATION

General Editor: Christopher Freeman, *Emeritus Professor of Science Policy, Science Policy Research Unit, University of Sussex, UK*

Technical innovation is vital to the competitive performance of firms and of nations and for the sustained growth of the world economy. The economics of innovation is an area that has expanded dramatically in recent years and this major series, edited by one of the most distinguished scholars in the field, contributes to the debate and advances in research in this most important area.

The main emphasis is on the development and application of new ideas. The series provides a forum for original research in technology, innovation systems and management, industrial organization, technological collaboration, knowledge and innovation, research and development, evolutionary theory and industrial strategy. International in its approach, the series includes some of the best theoretical and empirical work from both well-established researchers and the new generation of scholars.

Titles in the series include:

Foundations of the Economics of Innovation
Theory, Measurement and Practice
Hariolf Grupp

Industrial Organisation and Innovation
An International Study of the Software Industry
Salvatore Torrisi

The Theory of Innovation
Entrepreneurs, Technology and Strategy
Jon Sundbo

The Emergence and Growth of Biotechnology
Experiences in Industrialized and Developing Countries
Rohini Acharya

Industrial Organisation and Innovation

An International Study of the Software Industry

Salvatore Torrisi

Lecturer in Economics, C. Cattaneo University, Castellanza and Bocconi University, Milan, Italy

Preface by Keith Pavitt

NEW HORIZONS IN THE ECONOMICS OF INNOVATION

Edward Elgar
Cheltenham, UK • Northampton, MA, USA

Published by
Edward Elgar Publishing Limited
8 Lansdown Place
Cheltenham
Glos GL50 2HU
UK

Edward Elgar Publishing, Inc.
6 Market Street
Northampton
Massachusetts 01060
USA

A catalogue record for this book
is available from the British Library

Library of Congress Cataloguing in Publication Data

Torrisi, Salvatore
    Industrial organisation and innovation: an international study of
the software industry / Salvatore Torrisi.
        (New horizons in the economics of innovation
series)
        Includes bibliographical references and index.
        1. Computer software industry. 2. Computer software industry—
Technological innovations. 3. Industrial organization. I. Title.
II. Series: New horizons in the economics of innovation.
HD9696.63.A2T67 1998
        338.7'610053—dc21   98–24860
                                                            CIP

ISBN 1 85898 894 2

Printed and bound in Great Britain by
Biddles Ltd, Guildford and King's Lynn

To Iolanda

Contents

Tables

Acknowledgements

This work draws on a research project conducted during my D-Phil studies at the Science Policy Research Unit, University of Sussex. Keith Pavitt encouraged me to start this project. From the discussions with him I always received kindly provocations and frank opinions. I also benefited from criticism and suggestions from Tim Brady, Robin Mansell, Paul Quintas, and Nick von Tunzelmann.

With Franco Malerba I shared ideas and hours of work in trying to understand the economics of the computer and software industry. I also received great help from the workshops held at the University of Berkeley within a research project supported by the Alfred P. Sloan Foundation. In particular, I am indebted to Yasunori Baba, David Mowery, Edward Steinmueller and Shinji Takai and the other participants in these workshops.

I received many useful comments and stimulation during seminars, private discussions, and inteviews with Suma Atreje, Alberto Bazzan, Lorenzo Cassinelli, Gianni Cozzi, Luigi Della Bora, Alfonso Gambardella, Roberto Maglione, Luigi Marengo, Giuseppe Militello, Alina Rizzoni, Enzo Rullani, Roberto Simonetti, Sergio Vaccà, Carla Vegetti, and Antonello Zanfei.

Marco Giarratana, Laura Pontiggia, Iolanda Schiavone, and Alfredo Volontè provided invaluable research assistance in different stages of this research project.

I am grateful to Maria Schiavone and Fiona Hunter for reviewing the language style and an anonymous referee for a critical reading of parts of the book manuscript.

The Italian Ministry of University and Research (MURST), The National Research Council (CNR), and The European Commission, Human Capital and Mobility Programme, DGXII, gave financial support to this research project.

Salvatore Torrisi
Milan, 1998

Preface

One of the most difficult tasks for researchers in the social sciences is to measure and analyse accurately processes of radical change. Signals are incomplete and confusing, theoretical constructs are inadequate, and there are violent swings in fashion and interest. History remembers those scholars who in hindsight turn out to have got it right.

Dr Torrisi's book can, for the moment at least, be only a candidate for such notoriety. His subject is software, which has emerged in the past twenty years as a major (the major?) growth industry in the advanced countries of the world. Software is based on spectacular advances in the technologies underlying computers, components and communications, that have led to reduction by orders of magnitude in the costs of storing and transmitting information. Software technology is the knowledge of how systematically to manipulate and use this information. The demand for the products and services based on this knowledge has turned out to be very elastic in terms of price, something not anticipated by a pioneer, Thomas Watson Senior, the Head of IBM – who in the early days (1948) judged that all the world's information needs could be met with just five computers.

Since then, IBM and the rest of the world have learnt otherwise. Software has progressively emerged as a revolutionary new technology with multiple and expanding applications, stimulating the development of new academic disciplines like software engineering (sometimes and misleadingly called computer science), new institutional locations of technological development like the Systems Departments in business firms, new spheres of application in service activities like finance and distribution, and new heuristics for its development, given that manufacture (reproduction) is virtually costless.

Dr Torrisi's book is one of the first systematic and quantitative studies of the software industry. Given the difficulties of data collection, the purely descriptive dimension of his work is a major achievement. In particular, he shows that, like developments in mechanical technology, applications of software advances are pervasive, and a high proportion are untraded, being developed and applied by user firms themselves. He also shows that the two types of technology, systems software and application software, are complementary in application, but have very different product characteristics and competitive dynamics. Finally, he shows that developments in hardware and software technologies are also complementary, but with the latter becoming progressively unbundled from the former with the emergence of dedicated software firms.

Dr Torrisi goes well beyond description to analyse the development of the software industry in the light of theories of technical change. In doing so, he considerably deepens our understanding of the central importance of the processes of learning, and of what has come to be known as 'knowledge management', – for this major industry of the twenty-first century. Scholars of technical, economic and organisation change will owe him an intellectual debt for a long time to come.

Keith Pavitt
Science Policy Research Unit
University of Sussex
January 1998

1. Introduction

1. THE AIMS OF THE WORK

This book studies the industrial organisation of innovative activities in the computer software and services industry.

This knowledge-intensive activity shows important differences with respect to manufacturing and, to some extent, to the traditional service sectors. First, software products are intangible artefacts and a large share of software production is non traded: a significant amount of this production is undertaken by users or is embedded in electronic equipment. Second, because of the small importance of fabrication and the many overlaps between innovative activities, software development and software production, it is difficult to separate production from innovation or R&D activity. Finally, there are important economic differences between packaged software (for example, a personal computer word processor) and customised software and services. The former draws on increasing returns and network externalities, while the latter relies on the ability to meet specific users' needs and continuous interactions with customers. Overall, software is a special case of industrial design activity.

Despite its importance as a source of technical and organisational change for many other industries, the literature on the economics and management of software production is quite limited. This depends on the young age of software activities as a specialised industry and some peculiarities of this industry mentioned before. This study aims to analyse the patterns of product innovation, the internal competencies used in the innovative activities, the firms' external sources of technological change and the instruments for the protection of innovation. Moreover, this work seeks to provide a picture of the division of labour among software firms in the production and diffusion of knowledge.

In the last decades, most innovative efforts in this industry have aimed to improve the process and organisational technology. However, many software producers still use 'ad hoc' and craft techniques which contribute to low labour productivity and poor product quality. Like other intellectual activities, software production is difficult to codify, while its products are almost by definition a major source of knowledge codification for the modern economy. Why is the 'engineering' of software activities difficult? This work tries to answer this question by analysing the types of process innovations introduced by different types of software firms and the obstacles to the use of these innovations.

The empirical analysis illustrated in this work is based on a conceptual framework that takes into account the interactions between technical and organisational innovations at the firm level and focuses on the innovation process as a 'social construction' involving different types of institutions: firms endowed with different skills and producing a variety of products and services, users and academic research centres. Market selection, the evolution of technological opportunities and other institutional mechanisms (including public policies) influence the specialisation and the division of labour among these institutions. This issue is analysed by comparing the historical evolution of software activities in Europe and the United States.

This introduction provides a guide to the theoretical framework, the main research hypotheses underlying this work, its methodology and organisation.

2. THEORETICAL ARGUMENTS

This study draws on two strains of economic studies: the economic analysis of technological change and market structure and the management of innovative activities at the firm level.

In the economics of technical progress, an increasing emphasis has been given to the study of knowledge and the division of labour between different organisations in the production and use of this good.

The economics literature, drawing on previous studies in other disciplines, makes a distinction between two types of knowledge: general-abstract, codified knowledge and tacit, uncodifiable knowledge. The former is associated with science and the latter with technology. Knowledge can be incorporated in artefacts (for example, capital goods and organisations) or in the human mind. The economics literature suggests several definitions of person-embodied knowledge, including skills (codifiable and tacit), capabilities, expertise and know-how.

Some scholars have focused on tacit and uncodifiable knowledge in both scientific research and technological activities (Nelson 1962). The debate on the particular nature of knowledge (and information) and its economic implications has been spurred on by the seminal work of Arrow (1962a). This work focused on scientific knowledge as a public good, making the point that basic research deserves public support because of the low private appropriability of inventive benefits, the high uncertainty of scientific activities, and the lack of private incentives to undertake its production. Most later economic literature has extended the analysis of scientific knowledge as a public good to the study of technological knowledge (Dasgupta and Stoneman, 1987).

More recently, the economics literature has suggested that scientific, codified knowledge is not a pure public good. The fact that science is publicly accessible does not mean that the ability to evaluate, absorb and utilise it is also a public good. On the contrary, absorptive capabilities are a private good, as demonstrated by large industrial expenditures in basic research (Cohen and Levinthal, 1989; Rosenberg, 1990; and Pavitt, 1991a).

Another critical issue raised by the economics literature and economic history concerns the production and use of information. These activities show intertemporal economies of scale which are determined by various kinds of learning. Dynamic economies of scale generate cumulativeness and path-dependence. Small, unexpected events may have large and lasting effects on economy, by locking decision-makers into inefficient technologies (David, 1985; Arthur, 1989; Dosi et al., 1988; Malerba, 1992).

Moreover, the cognitive structure of individuals and organisations, and some characteristics of knowledge explain the localised nature of technological change (Stiglitz, 1987; Antonelli, 1995). Cumulativeness of change affects the trajectories of change at the firm level. The directions of R&D activities and the search for new knowledge at the firm level is bounded by the firm's past experience and its stock of knowledge (Teece, 1988; Pavitt, 1991b). This may give established firms some cumulative advantages towards newcomers, but also generates inertia by reducing the firm's ability to adapt to major breakthroughs. The economics literature and business history have showed that technological change may have 'competence-destroying' or 'competence-deepening' effects on incumbent firms (Tushman and Anderson, 1986). Few studies, however, have tried to measure the role played by different capabilities in the production and use of knowledge (Usher, 1971). Some economists have recently focused on the role played by organisational skills in this process. Particularly, Aoki (1986 and 1990) points out the importance of 'information processing and communicative capabilities' as a major source of rents. Teece et al. (1994) have pointed to the role played by organisational capabilities as a source of firms' sustained competitive advantage.

Other scholars have addressed the issue of how capabilities, particularly the technical ones, are developed by firms (Prahalad and Hamel, 1990; Jacobsson and Oskarsson, 1993). In particular, Patel and Pavitt (1994) observe that large firms develop complex products that require the integration of different technologies. The interdependence between these technologies force firms to accumulate diversified in-house competencies. Product complexity may also explain why a high degree of technological diversification does not elicit a similar degree of product diversification at the firm level. For instance, technological convergence forces firms working in different industries such as computers, telecommunications equipment, and consumer electronics, to accumulate a variety of in-house capabilities which are used to evaluate, absorb and combine different technologies embodied in their respective products. This may spur feature proliferation and the integration of functions once performed by distinct products developed in different industries (for example, television sets and computers). Although some of these products are now commercialised through the same distribution channels (for example, computer stores and general stores), many firms which have tried to produce a diversified array of consumer electronics, computers and telecommunications products have failed or have encountered major obstacles (Gambardella and Torrisi, 1998).

The process of competence accumulation is linked to the division of labour within and across firms. First, individuals and institutions facing the uncertainty of technological and economic change try to reduce their ignorance by developing routines and devices that may be effective even if there is no scientific understanding of the variables affecting their performance. On the other hand, firms rely increasingly on science and codified knowledge in their innovative activities and make use of sophisticated instruments and search methods (including computers and software). Some scholars argue that progress in computational facilities and instrumentation, along with the use of scientific methods in problem solving, will reduce the costs of information transfer and create new opportunities for an 'innovative division of labour' (Arora and Gambardella, 1994). Other scholars claim that the increasing diffusion of codified knowledge and scientific methods in industrial innovation and problem solving do not reduce the complexity of problem solving and the importance of tacit knowledge and 'craft'. This affects the division of labour in knowledge-intensive, problem-solving activities (Rosenberg, 1982; Kline and Rosenberg, 1986; Rosenbrock, 1988; Johannesson, 1988; von Hippel, 1990a).

Second, the division of labour is a major source of technical progress and competence accumulation. Since Adam Smith's *Wealth of Nation*'s, economists have asked what variables affect the specialisation and the division of labour within and among firms. In particular, Stigler (1951) explains the degree of specialisation or 'vertical disintegration' of upstream phases of production of given products to the extent of the market for these products. However, Rosenberg (1976) argues that the extension of the market for single final goods is not enough to explain the specialisation of activities such as the machine tool industry. Rosenberg submits that vertical disintegration of machinery from other downstream industries since the second half of the nineteenth century is explained by two factors: the traditional economies of scale at the level of the single firm and the external economies arising from 'technological convergence'. This process of convergence consisted in the use of common tools, skills and techniques in a large number of different manufacturing sectors. The widespread accumulation of mechanical engineering capabilities in different user sectors and the emergence of an industry specialised in machinery greatly contributed to the industrial progress in the period between the last two centuries. Another 'pervasive' technology, that is, ITC (information and communication technology), a key component of which is represented by software, is affecting the progress of modern economy. It is important to keep in mind the similarities and the differences with the experience of mechanical engineering. This work analyses the main forces that have contributed to the specialisation of computer software and services activities, technological convergence, rapid market growth, and institutional changes.

3. RESEARCH ISSUES AND QUESTIONS

There are several open issues raised by the literature and many suggestions for empirical research. This work aims to investigate the following issues.

1. In the computer and software industry there are many market segments and a variety of suppliers. To understand the current division of labour and the patterns of specialisation in this industry, we need to know what variables have affected the emergence of software development activities as an independent industry. This work analyses the historical evolution of software activities in order to explain the patterns of specialisation of this industry in the US and Europe. The analysis aims also to explain why US firms acquired a leadership in packaged software while European firms specialised in customised software and services. Moreover, I collected and analysed data on growth and restructuring operations concerning large US and European software firms during the period 1984–92. This analysis aims to highlight how the past evolution of the software industry in the US and Europe influences the recent corporate changes.

2. The vast empirical literature on the characteristics and the determinants of innovations aiming to test the 'Schumpeterian hypothesis' of a positive relationship between firm size (or market power) and inventive performance has not reached clear-cut conclusions. The differences across industries in the determinants of innovations shown by several studies, point out the importance of industry-specific characteristics of innovative activities, especially the nature of knowledge underlying these activities and the type of

competencies involved in the different stages of the innovative process. Case-studies are useful to understand inter-industry differences and differences across firms in the same industry. This study aims to provide some evidence of the inter-firm differences in the computer software and services industry. Because of the immateriality of software products and the weakness of legal protection, innovation in software activities is difficult to measure by the traditional indicators such as patents and even copyright. This work tries to compare the role played by technological and market opportunities in the introduction of different types of product innovations (major vs. minor innovations). In addition, I consider the differences across firms with different size and productive profiles in the propensity to introduce different types of product innovations, and to rely on different instruments for the protection of their innovations. This analysis aims to test the hypothesis according to which large firms benefit from 'appropriability' advantages compared with small firms. These advantages depend on a large internal market for innovations and internal financial resources for innovation. On the other hand, large established firms may have weaker incentives to introduce major product innovations compared with small, new firms. The large firms' weak commitment to major innovations rely on managers' risk aversion, weak individual incentives to innovate (due to excessive bureaucracy), and poor perception of new market opportunities.

3. Several scholars have emphasised that scientific and technological knowledge, as well as codified and tacit knowledge, interact with each other in complex ways. The increasing importance of science and instrumentation in industrial research shifts the frontier between tacit and codified knowledge towards the phases downstream of the innovation process, namely engineering, production, and marketing. In software activities the use of more formal, structured methods for software development (for example, CASE, computer-aided software engineering, tools and OOL, object-oriented languages), tacit knowledge and 'practical wisdom' (defined as the ability to mediate and integrate different sources of knowledge) becomes less important in programming operations, which become more codified and can be automated, while it is increasingly important in more complex and less divisible tasks, like users' needs specification, system analysis and system engineering. As observed by Charles Babbage over a century ago, codification and separation of tasks enable managers to assign more critical tasks to skilled persons. This implies that skilled human resources can be allocated to more complex tasks that require much 'wisdom', intuition and know-how. Also, the more efficient allocation of skilled resources to complex activities and the reduction of trial-and-error at the level of simpler operations may bring about a reduction of total costs and vertical disintegration of separable and codified activities. In the debate regarding the

balance between tacit and codified knowledge, an issue that is addressed by this work is not how much tacit knowledge is likely to resist the escalation of science, but what changes in the organisation of labour within firms and among firms are likely to occur as a result of an increasing use of general and codified knowledge in some stages of the innovative and productive process. In this work I investigate the changes in the degree of knowledge codification and division of labour that take place in software firms through the adoption of process innovations. A research question is whether the complexity and the difficulty of codifying software innovative activities makes any form of division of labour within firms impossible or whether 'new' flexible production techniques and engineering principles experienced in other manufacturing industries can be applied to these activities. Moreover, the differences among integrated hardware and software producers, large specialised software firms and small software firms are analysed. Integrated producers and large specialised software firms are likely to show a greater propensity to adopt software engineering techniques and a more formal division of labour compared with small firms. A more formal and automated development environment requires larger fixed costs that only large firms can afford. Moreover, unlike small firms, large software firms possess human and financial resources to try new techniques and re-train their programmers, system engineers and project managers. Finally, the software divisions of integrated firms may exploit the 'externalities' from in-house computer manufacturing divisions. This may explain why large hardware manufacturers, such as IBM and many of its Japanese counterparts, have pioneered the introduction of 'software factories' whose organisation emulates that of manufacturing ones. By contrast, specialised software firms may reveal a 'cultural' aversion towards production techniques drawing on the experience of manufacturing activities.

4. From a different point of view, the role played by codified (generic) and tacit (context-specific) knowledge in innovative activities can be analysed by focusing on the type of firm-specific capabilities involved in the innovative activities. It is important to acknowledge that the 'still modest literature on the role of firm-specific capabilities in affecting innovation raises the question of exactly what R&D-related capabilities matter for innovative activity and performance' (Cohen, 1995, p. 203). This work analyses firm capabilities by suggesting a theoretical model that studies the effects of different capabilities on a firm's propensity to set up links with external sources of technological change. I have classified the firm's innovative competencies into *general-purpose capabilities* (such as mathematical and computer science skills) and *context-specific capabilities* (such as the experience from the interactions with users). The former rely on a wider knowledge base as compared with the latter, which rely on a localised and

idiosyncratic base of knowledge. A research hypothesis tested in the empirical analysis is that general purpose capabilities make firms more able to exploit the opportunities arising from generic, codified sources of knowledge such as universities. By contrast, context-specific capabilities are likely to affect the firm's ability to exploit the opportunities arising from 'context-specific' external sources of technological change such as users. This hypothesis can be restated by asking whether there is a division of labour between different in-house capabilities in absorbing knowledge from (or interacting with) different types of external sources.

4. DATA AND RESEARCH METHODOLOGY

There are several indicators of technological change and innovative activities that have been developed in the economics and management of innovation, including R&D expenditures and patents. Other studies have relied on different types of approaches, including the collection of qualitative information through direct interviews. These approaches have both advantages and drawbacks. They can be used together in order to have a comprehensive picture of the innovative activities in specific industries or for inter-industry comparisons. Recent studies on innovation based on qualitative data and self-assessment have provided useful insights into the organisation of innovative activities of different industries (see Nelson and Levin, 1986; Levin et al., 1987). Although the data drawn from interviews and self-assessment should be interpreted carefully, especially in inter-industry comparisons, this methodology seems particularly effective when used to understand qualitative features of single industries. In sectoral analysis such as this the control of responses is made simpler by the possibility of carrying out in-depth analyses based on specialised literature and the possibility of resorting to the assessment of independent experts (for example, scientists, policy makers and market analysts).

Moreover, the characteristics of software technology make R&D and patents unreliable as indicators of innovative activities. This is one of the reasons why this work is based on qualitative data collected through interviews with software firms.

Few data on firms and the organisation of innovative process in the European computer software and services industry are publicly available. Despite the few case-studies on single product development and process innovation that have been published recently, there is no comprehensive survey that accounts for the main characteristics of innovative activities in software, including the characteristics of product and process innovations, the sources of firm's technological change, the instruments for the protection of innovation and the nature of innovative skills. The author has conducted a survey in 1990 with the aim of filling in part this gap in empirical analysis by collecting qualitative data on the innovative activities in the computer software and services producers located in Europe. These ordinal-level data were gathered through direct interviews with project managers of 51 firms located in Italy, the UK, France and Germany on the basis of a semi-structured questionnaire.

The author has worked on an extension and repetition of the survey that was carried out in 1993 within the EEC research project on 'Research and Technology Management in Enterprises: Issues for Community Policy', Monitor-SAST 8. The strict confidentiality required by the firms allow only a partial use of data from this survey. However, the overall similarity of results between the two surveys makes us comfortable about the validity of results discussed in this work, which is entirely based on the 1990 survey. Only a minor use of some results from the 1993 survey is made in order to include a few issues uncovered in the 1990 survey.

Moreover, the author has conducted another survey in 1997 on a set of firms interviewed in 1990. Although there are some differences between the two surveys, the main picture of innovative activities provided by 1990 survey remains quite unchanged.

Other data were obtained by classifying 912 growth and restructuring operations concerning 38 large software firms (19 European and 19 American) over the period between 1984 and 1992. The sample includes 8 firms that participated in the 1990 survey on innovation. Of these operations, 638 are inter-firm linkages – joint ventures, minority stakes, licensing agreements, other collaborative agreements, and mergers and acquisitions. The remaing 274 operations concern internal corporate restructuring, creation and shutdown of new subsidiaries, and other internal reorganisations (for example, the merger of two divisions and job cuts). These data have been collected from the Predicast's F&S Index of Corporate Change, US and Predicast's F&S Index International which is based on information drawn from press sources. Firms for which information are provided are classified by Predicast's according to their main business sector. The sample firms were classified under the SIC codes 7370 to 7379 (computer and data processing services). Each operation is also classified by Predicast's according to the SIC classification. These categorical data were then transformed into count data (number of operations of given categories) to be processed. This database was developed by the author as part of a larger data set within the project on 'The Economics of Scientific and Technological Research in Europe' under the EEC Human Capital and Mobility Programme.

5. OUTLINE OF THE BOOK

This work is organised as follows. Chapter 2 presents a survey of the economics literature on technological change and the role of knowledge as an economic good. This survey aims to provide a theoretical framework and to lay down some basic concepts that will be used in later chapters. However, this work tries to avoid a sharp separation between theory and empirical analysis. Therefore, some theoretical issues that are more directly related to specific topics of our empirical analysis are further developed in different chapters.

Chapter 3 introduces the economics of software production. It also analyses the recent evolution of the world software market by focusing on products and suppliers. Chapter 4 illustrates the historical evolution of this industry, highlighting the main changes in the technology and organisation of innovative activities since the early development of the electronic computer industry. The chapter focuses on a set of variables that, as mentioned above, have affected the evolution of market structure and the division of labour among firms. Finally, the chapter analyses the process of software firms' growth and restructuring.

Chapter 5 discusses the pattern of product and process innovations emerging from survey data. The first part of the chapter checks whether hypotheses suggested in the literature on technological change are confirmed by the data. The structure of the analysis illustrated in this chapter follows the research hypotheses mentioned above. The second part of the chapter aims to give a picture of the changes in the technologies and organisation used in software development activities. The analysis begins with a brief illustration of the organisation of software development activities according to a standard model that draws on principles taken from engineering, traditional microeconomics, and management science. The model represents an attempt to apply to software development the sequential organisation of innovative activities in distinct phases that has been experienced in other manufacturing industries, particularly in the US. This model has been used by some 'software factories' for measuring the effects of process innovations on the software production function. Moreover, the analysis focuses on recent changes of software production which draw on a 'developmental' or 'evolutionary' and 'object-oriented' approach to software production. Finally, I discuss the results of my empirical analysis. The characteristics of process innovations, the determinants, and obstacles to process innovations are discussed. The chapter ends by focusing on the differences among three categories of software firms in terms of their incentives (and ability) to make use of structured methods and tools for their innovative activities: innovative entrepreneurial firms, small established firms specialised in 'mature' market niches, and large software firms that offer a diversified range of software products and services.

Chapter 6 analyses the capabilities that are employed in innovative activities by the sample firms. The chapter distinguishes between different kinds of firms' innovative capabilities and external sources of innovation. Moreover, the chapter illustrates the relationship between internal competencies and external sources of innovation according to the hypotheses discussed above.

Chapter 7 summarises the main results of the empirical investigation considering them in the light of the theory.

2. Innovation and Knowledge-Intensive Production

1. INTRODUCTION

This chapter introduces ideas that economists have often taken from other scientific disciplines. Among these ideas, knowledge is probably the most widespread in the economics and management of innovation.

Knowledge designates different types of goods, the most important of which are science and technology. In the economics literature these two are used as if they were the same type of knowledge or, alternatively, as if they were two completely different types of institutions with different aims and rules of conduct. Few studies have tried to assess the linkages between these two institutions. Moreover, in the standard economics literature knowledge is considered as a pure public good. As a consequence, the market mechanism fails to convey a socially desirable level of resources to knowledge production and public intervention is needed. More recently, several studies have distinguished between codified-abstract knowledge ('know that') and tacit knowledge ('know how'), by pointing out that even scientific, abstract knowledge is not a pure public good.

The following sections compare different types of knowledge, embodied in products, techniques, skills and organisational routines. Some implications for the organisation of innovation within firms and among firms are also discussed. Obviously this is not a comprehensive survey of the literature since it aims to illustrate only the theoretical background of the empirical analysis conducted in the following chapters.

The chapter is organised as follows. Section 2 discusses some definitions of knowledge, information and skills. Section 3 focuses on the standard economics of knowledge and information. Section 4 discusses the process of knowledge production, while Section 5 analyses the 'division of knowledge' among organisations engaged in innovative activities. Section 6 closes the chapter.

2. KNOWLEDGE, INFORMATION, AND SKILLS

2.1. Codified knowledge, know-how, and skills

The economics of technological change usually distinguishes between general-abstract or codified knowledge and tacit knowledge.

General-abstract knowledge in the vocabulary of Gestalt psychology and philosophy of science is referred to as 'propositional knowledge' ('know that'), which is associated with the understanding of basic scientific principles and methods to acquire or learn other knowledge. General-abstract or basic knowledge is therefore an intermediate good that can be used for the production of both specific, applied knowledge and physical goods. For instance, the knowledge of Avogadro's number has useful applications in physical chemistry and the results of fundamental research in solid state physics have helped engineers and technicians to cope with different problems in electronics and computing. Recently, Kline and Rosenberg (1986) have defined general-abstract knowledge (or science) as an activity aiming for the 'creation, discovery, verification, collation, reorganisation, and dissemination of knowledge about physical, biological and social nature' (p. 287). General-abstract knowledge may be thought of as a kind of logical framework for combining and explaining information about diverse events with the objective of understanding the fundamental characteristics of these events and the linkages between them and observed regularities about the states of the world (Rosenberg, 1990).

Tacit knowledge or 'know-how' is also referred to as 'procedural knowledge' to mean that individuals know how to perform given tasks, or that they have the skills or the ability to solve a given problem. Technological knowledge and engineering are often identified with tacit knowledge. A fundamental difference between codified and tacit knowledge is that the latter allows firms to solve specific problems, even when there is no general understanding of the reasons why these problems arose or the optimal, rational methods for their solution. Skills or know-how are associated with the use of implicit routines or 'procedural rules' that cannot be easily transmitted across individuals and organisations via 'blue-prints', but can be transferred via learning, imitation and practical examples. At the level of individuals, tacit knowledge can be expressed as 'feelings which can be known only by experience, not described in words of prose' (Machlup, 1980, p. 36). The difficulty to articulate and transfer tacit knowledge makes it 'context-specific', that is difficult to replicate beyond the experience of specific individuals, organisations, or applications.

The importance of tacit knowledge in the social sciences has been acknowledged quite recently: 'theorists have ... ignored the question what it is for someone to know how to perform tasks'.[1] Michael Polanyi (1962 and 1967) focused on the importance of tacit knowledge in human behaviour and analysed the association between tacit knowledge and skills. Most acts of skills require a 'subsidiary or instrumental knowledge' (tacit knowledge) as opposed to 'focal awareness' (explicit knowledge). For example, a pianist in performance has a 'subsidiary awareness' of his finger work because his 'focal awareness' is captured by the music. The subsidiary or tacit knowledge according to Polanyi (1967) cannot be made explicit: 'we know more than we can tell'.

Amongst scholars of the economics and management of innovation, Usher (1971), Nelson and Winter (1982), Rosenberg (1976), von Hippel (1990a) have studied the effects of tacit knowledge on firm behaviour and innovative activities. For instance, Nelson and Winter (1982) have identified tacit knowledge with competencies (or skills), which cannot be transmitted, as opposed to 'articulated' knowledge, which is transferable. Skills are defined as the capability of carrying out 'automatically' a sequence of co-ordinated actions to reach a given objective within a given context. The exercise of a skill usually implies some choices by the skilful individual, but the selection process is almost automatic (it belongs to the realm of 'subsidiary awareness'). Moreover, there is a trade-off between capability and deliberate choice. Capabilities or skills represent an important mechanism that reduces the costs of information elaboration and decision making (cf. Nelson and Winter, 1982).

However, the association between skills, or capabilities, and tacit knowledge is not simple. In general, skills imply both tacit knowledge and codified knowledge. For instance, all electronics engineers 'know that' there are some general principles of electricity from their academic studies but each of them shows a different ability to apply these principles to the development of specific electronic devices. Moreover, there are differences across different types of skills which depend on the type of knowledge on which these skills rely. We can distinguish between skills drawing mostly on general-abstract knowledge, such as the ability to build mathematical models, and skills drawing on the knowledge of particular contexts, such as the ability to develop software programs for specific user sectors. In Chapter 6, I refer to these two types of skills as respectively *general-purpose skills* and *context-specific skills*, assuming that they have different effects on the organisation of innovative activities at the firm level.

The concept of *skills* for individuals corresponds to that of routines for organisations. The behaviouristic approach to economics has studied the way individuals and organisations form their expectations and take decisions under conditions of uncertainty and 'bounded' or 'procedural rationality'.

1 Gilbert Ryle (1949), quoted in Machlup (1980), p. 30, note 3.

Like individuals, organisations cope with complexity and uncertainty by developing routines or procedures that are used to guide their behaviour and reduce informational costs. Decision makers rarely undertake global calculations or acquire all possible information to take decisions because the acquisition and elaboration of information is costly and processing capabilities are limited (Simon, 1972 and 1979).[2] But even if firms had an unlimited access to information and unlimited processing capabilities, they would not utilise all available information because of organisational inertia and 'cognitive dissonance'. The theory of 'cognitive dissonance', developed by social psychology, is based on three main propositions. First, people have preferences over states of the world but also in their beliefs about the states of the world. Second, people can manipulate their own beliefs by selecting sources of information that support their desired beliefs. Third, beliefs once chosen tend to persist over time (Akerlof and Dickens, 1982).[3] The main economic consequence of cognitive dissonance is that individual and firm behaviour cannot be predicted assuming 'rational expectations' and 'substantive rationality'. Cognitive dissonance gives an argument in favour of procedural rationality. It is worth noting that procedural rationality implies that suboptimal equilibria and routines persist over time. Individuals and firms do not react to *marginal variations* in the decision environment because of switching costs linked to the information acquisition-processing and to inertia arising from cognitive dissonance. The search for new routines and information is spurred only by *discrete changes* in the relevant variables, that is changes over critical thresholds.

Drawing on Simon's seminal work on procedural rationality, Nelson and Winter (1982) analyse the importance of bounded rationality and routines in innovative activities, including the decision to adopt a new technology or to change current managerial techniques. In particular, they focus on the use of heuristics, or high-level routines, which are principles or devices that are believed to shorten the average search to solution of technical or managerial problems. The use of heuristics in research activity and problem solving highlights the importance of the 'art of inventing' or the technology of research which is discussed more in detail later. Skills, routines, and heuristics are the 'memory' of the organisation, that is the locus of firm's

2 Besides the limited capacity to process information, the managerialist approach points out that firms are not global maximisers because of internal negotiations among different contrasting stakeholders.

3 A dynamic implication of cognitive dissonance is that individuals and firms monitor new information and beliefs in order to check whether these are coherent with their own beliefs. When the divergence between established beliefs and new information reaches some 'critical threshold', individuals and firms have to initiate a search of new or modified beliefs. Robin Mansell has brought to my attention this implication of cognitive dissonance. Nelson and Winter (1982) have inaugurated a line of research which takes into account procedural rationality in innovative activities, drawing on simulation modelling.

knowledge (Nelson and Winter, 1982, pp. 132–3).

Other studies have further explored the nature and organisation of knowledge by making the point that even scientific-abstract knowledge cannot be completely made explicit and codified in instructions or 'books of blueprints', but requires learning and experience. They also argue that there are strong complementarities between tacit and codified knowledge in scientific activity (Nelson, 1962, Pavitt, 1991a). A typical example of how tacit knowledge affects the behaviour of scientists is described by Nelson (1962) in a study of the invention of the transistor. The research team that invented the transistor at the AT&T's Bell Laboratories, under the direction of William Shockley, was managed according to an 'evolutionary' approach that is typical of scientific activities. Experience and co-operative learning within the research team helped to focus the research towards given directions and to select alternative research projects. The decentralisation of research activity also favoured trial-and-error activity and gave each scientist the possibility to follow, for a while, his/her own intuitions and feelings which could not always be expressed in 'words of prose' before some tangible result came out. This example has an important economic implication for tacit knowledge (and uncertainty) that I discuss later: the division of tasks of any economic activity (including research and development) cannot take 'a priori', centralised knowledge as given but requires a continuous interaction between prior and ex-post information. Particularly, in R&D activities, the ability to evaluate the most promising research trajectories at any given time is largely tacit and difficult to demonstrate to external supervisors.

2.2. Knowledge and information

The economics literature does not often distinguish between knowledge and information, as if there were not significant differences between knowledge and information from an economic point of view. In fact, there are some basic differences.

The mathematical theory of information and the theory of risky decisions, initiated by the seminal works of Shannon, Morgenstern and von Neumann, define information as freedom of choice in the selection of signals. Information increases with the number of signals and the number of possible alternative choices among signals. Information can be acquired to reduce ignorance or uncertainty over different 'states of the world', but it can also increase uncertainty when the recipient (receiver) does not know the language used by the supplier (transmitter).[4] More precisely, the recipient may need to possess some 'a priori' knowledge (for example, from theories or experience) that assigns unambiguous meanings to each signal, allowing the recipient to select the signals and make rational choices (Arrow, 1974). An example that clarifies the nature of this problem is suggested by von Hippel:

> artists seeking to generate computer art using fractals will not typically be aided by the transmission of a math program containing that information. The recipients must either get the information they seek in 'user friendly' form ... and/or the recipients must learn the additional information needed to obtain and operate the information base. (von Hippel, 1990a, p. 4)

This example helps to distinguish between knowledge as a stock variable and information as a flow variable. Information is generated by a process through which some signals flow iteratively from a supplier to a recipient. The content conveyed by these information flows may increase and modify the pre-existing stock of knowledge of the recipient, depending on the compatibility between the recipient and the supplier. The modified stock of knowledge may be different not only in quantity but in quality or structure: 'the new knowledge may simply be different from the old, and the difference need not be the same as the new information received' (Machlup, 1980, p. 57).

The probability that any given information modifies the stock of knowledge of a recipient depends on the form in which the content is organised. This can be codified or tacit, embedded in artefacts, persons or organisations. A piece of information may have a localised, organisation-specific meaning and, therefore, its use is limited to specific contexts. On the other hand, information may be codified and applied to many different contexts. This is the case of 'general-purpose technologies', such as the electric motor, mechanical engineering, and IT (information technology). These technologies are 'pervasive' (they can be used as an input in many different sectors), have a high potential for technological change, and represent a major source of productivity improvements for downstream sectors' innovative activities (Rosenberg, 1982; Bresnahan and Trajtenberg, 1995).

The relationships between the nature of knowledge (information) and the organisation of innovative activities are addressed in the following sections.

---

4 In the information theory elaborated by Claude Shannon, the amount of information I_i conveyed by an event i is inversely related to the probability p_i associated with that event, $- p_i \log p_i$, while the information associated with all possible events is $I = \Sigma^n_{i=1} p_i \log p_i$, where $\Sigma^n_{i=1} p_i = 1$. (Gotlieb, 1985, p. 113).

3. SCIENTIFIC AND TECHNOLOGICAL KNOWLEDGE

3.1. Knowledge as a public good

Most studies in the economics of innovation rely on the assumption that scientific knowledge is a public good.[5] These studies draw on the seminal work of Arrow (1962a) on the economics of basic research and are inspired by a normative preoccupation that can be summarised as follows:

- The time, costs, and outputs of knowledge production are subject to high risk and uncertainty;
- The production of this good is characterised by increasing returns to scale arising from indivisibilities (all production costs are virtually fixed costs);
- This good exhibits non-rival consumption: 'if a person gives another a piece of information it does not reduce the amount of information the first person possesses' (Dasgupta and Stoneman, p. 3, 1987). Thus, its marginal cost of production is virtually zero and any price different from zero is Pareto- inefficient;
- It is difficult for the producer of this good to exclude from consumption anyone who does not pay for it (non-escludability). This characteristic implies that the producer cannot appropriate all the economic benefits associated with the use of his/her product because of free-riding;
- Positive spillovers from knowledge production and free-riding reduce the private incentives to produce a socially desirable level of this good. Therefore, the market mechanism fails to convey a Pareto-optimal allocation of resources to the research activity;
- Market failure calls for public intervention, such as public research, financial support to industrial research and intellectual property right.[6]

Arrow's model rejects the Schumpeterian hypothesis according to which

---

5 For our purposes, in the following I do not distinguish technical inventions (or scientific discoveries) from their commercialisation (innovations).
6 The production of a public good by voluntary agreements, as an alternative to public support, is undermined by free riding.

market power increases the ex-ante incentives to innovation.[7] This model demonstrates that the incentive to introduce an innovation of a monopolist in the product market is smaller compared with that of a firm in a competitive market. Both, however, have a smaller incentive to innovate than the social planner. Arrow refers to process innovations. He acknowledges that in the case of markedly incremental innovations the monopolist's incentive overcomes that of the competitive firm because of its greater ability to appropriate ex-post the benefits of innovation (Arrow, 1962a, pp. 177-8). More recently, Reinganum (1983) has developed a patent race model to compare the incentive to innovate of a monopolist in the product market with that of an entrant. This model shows that the incumbent (monopolist) has a weaker incentive to innovate in the case of drastic innovations, because of a 'replacement effect' (the marginal productivity of R&D expenditure is inversely correlated to his initial profit).

Arrow's model and later studies suffer from different weaknesses concerning the description of the inventive process whose discussion goes beyond our goals (see Dasgupta and Stiglitz, 1980). Also, this stream of the literature often assumes that the social planner is perfectly informed and able to bring the production of knowledge to its socially optimal level through public research, intellectual property right, R&D subsidies and tax incentives.[8] This hypothesis is far from being realistic, as we discuss in Section 3.4.

Moreover, the hypothesis of scientific knowledge as a pure public good is debatable. Besides public subsidies and tax incentives, the main reason why firms 'do basic research with their own money' is that basic knowledge is not freely available 'off-the-shelf' to everyone once produced. Significant research efforts must be devoted to acquire the ability to understand, evaluate and utilise knowledge for specific uses. The accumulation of an 'absorptive capacity' is a costly activity that requires investments in human capital, that is, in researchers dedicated to basic research (see Cohen and Levinthal, 1989; Rosenberg, 1990; and Pavitt, 1991a). These researchers, in order to gain

7 The Schumpeterian hypothesis posits a positive relationship between monopoly power (or market concentration) and innovation activity. The position of Schumpeter is in fact more articulated. Schumpeter (1934, chapter 4) noticed that profits affect innovations in two ways. First, the expectations of future profits spur on entrepreneurs to introduce 'new combinations'. Secondly, previous 'entrepreneurial profits' are a financial source for future innovations. Later on, Schumpeter (1942) recognised that a rising share of innovations was produced by the R&D laboratories of large corporations, rather than being introduced by individual entrepreneurs. Many empirical studies have tried to test various versions of the 'Schumpeterian hypothesis' by using firm size as a proxy of monopoly power (see Cohen and Levin, 1989; and Cohen, 1995 for a survey).

8 Public support is typically financed by lump-sum taxes (the Pigovian solution) (see Dasgupta and Stoneman, 1987, and Stoneman, 1995).

access to the scientific community, have to observe the norms and rules of conduct of this community and set up linkages with researchers from other scientific institutions. Personal contacts (and sometimes geographical proximity) are important because some scientific knowledge is tacit, as discussed before.[9] Moreover, in-house scientific skills have to communicate with other skills within the same organisation, applied researchers, engineers, and technicians involved in the production stage, product managers and marketing forces. The systemic complexity of these interactions makes the access to outside generic knowledge difficult and costly. In Chapter 6 I discuss the relationships between firms' skills and the linkages with various external sources of innovation. These links can be thought of as investments to facilitate the absorption of different types of knowledge, from the most abstract-generic one (science) to the most context-specific one (knowledge of specific applications and users' needs). We also show that different internal skills may have different effect on firms' propensity to set up links with external sources of knowledge.

3.2. The relationships between science and technology

Most studies drawing on Arrow's seminal work have applied the public good argument to the production of technology. For example, Dasgupta points to some basic similarities between science and technology, by arguing that the private incentive mechanism for both scientists and technologists is that of races among rivals where 'as a very first approximation ... the winner ... takes all' (Dasgupta, 1987, p. 12).[10]

However, there are important differences between science and technology. Dasgupta and David (1986) give a useful explanation of some basic differences between science and technology in terms of the *institutions* that carry out scientific and technological research. Dasgupta and David argue that science and technology are two distinct social organisations with different collective norms, objectives and codes of conduct. Science treats knowledge as a 'public consumption good' and the social imperative of scientific organisation is full disclosure of research results. The rule of priority is an institution that gives a private incentive (reward) to scientists and stimulate full disclosure and diffusion of knowledge, thus providing a solution to the appropriability problem raised by Arrow. By contrast, technology is a social organisation that considers knowledge as a 'private capital good'. The private incentive mechanism for members of a technology

---

9 The importance of geographical proximity between industry and university research has been showed by Jaffe (1989).

10 Because of this similarity, the economics of science policy is similar, in Dasgupta's view, to that of technology policy, the differences being 'a matter only of degree ... not of substance' (Dasgupta, 1987, p. 12).

community are the private rents from the production of new knowledge. The most diffused incentive mechanism, the patent system, has some features of the reward system of the scientific community in that it gives an intellectual property right to the producer of a public good. But, as discussed before, the economic value of the asset (that is, the property right) is determined by the market and this reduces the diffusion of knowledge below the socially optimum level (Dasgupta and David, 1986).

Other scholars focus on differences related to the *output* of scientific and technological activity, by pointing out that, unlike scientific knowledge, technological knowledge is 'specific ... partly tacit (uncodifiable) and therefore difficult and costly to reproduce' (Pavitt, 1991a, p. 28). Technology is not simply applied science, as assumed by the so-called 'linear model' of research. The relationships between basic knowledge and applied knowledge are complex (Rosenberg, 1982; Kline and Rosenberg, 1986; and David, Mowery and Steinmueller, 1988). In particular, Kline and Rosenberg (1986) submit a theoretical framework ('the chain-linked model') that takes into account the complex interactions between science and technology in innovative activities in terms of both the outputs and the institutions that are involved in these activities. They argue that, contrary to common belief, most industrial innovation is not initiated by recent scientific discoveries. Kline and Rosenberg also argue that the innovative activity aiming at technical innovations can be viewed as a problem-solving activity initiated by the following typical question: 'Do I know a current device that will do the job?' The search aiming to solve a given technical problem is an 'evolutionary' process based on a simple economic principle that consists of using first the stock of existing science or heuristics to solve a given problem. Only when the existing stock of scientific or technical knowledge cannot answer the questions posed by the innovator, does he/she start 'the much more costly and time-consuming process of mission-oriented research' (Kline and Rosenberg, 1986, p. 291). There are also several examples of technological changes which have occurred even without a sound understanding of the underlying scientific principles.[11]

Another indirect but important channel of interactions between science and technology is university training of industrial scientists and engineers. Recent studies in the UK and in the United States show that academic training, research methods and skills are more important to industrial innovation as compared with the direct transmission of new scientific knowledge (compare Irvine and Martin, 1980, and Nelson and Levin, 1986).

11 As noted by Rosenberg (1982), 'even today ... we routinely fly in airplanes the optimal designs of which are achieved by fairly ad hoc, trial-and-error processes because there are no theories of turbulence or compressibility adequate to determine optimal configuration in advance' (p. 143).

Finally, a link between science and technology is represented by the inventions of scientific instrumentation by scientists and their subsequent adoption by industrial researchers. In some cases, such as the telescope and the microscope, technological advances have anticipated or greatly facilitated scientific research (Rosenberg, 1976).

3.3. Increasing returns, cumulativeness, and organisation of research

An important characteristic of knowledge production is 'cumulative causation' or 'path-dependence', that is the possibility that small events at a given time have major effects on the long-run evolution of a specific technological trajectory (David, 1985, Arthur, 1989). The economic impact of these effects depend on intertemporal increasing returns arising from the production and use of knowledge. Increasing returns are linked to learning, economies of scale, and network externalities.[12] An apparently small and unexpected event that creates a contingent advantage for a given technological alternative may lock-in an industry or an economic system into inefficient solutions and lock-out superior alternatives (which yields larger benefits in the long run). For instance, a labour shortage may spur firms to adopt a capital-intensive technology. However, when the labour shortage is eliminated, the economy can find it difficult to turn back to the old technology because increasing returns generate high switching costs (Stiglitz, 1987, p. 134). A famous historical example that illustrates the economic implications of path-dependence and the amplified effects of small events is the QWERTY typewriter keyboard. QWERTY became a market standard and locked-out the alternative, superior technology (Dvorak typewriter keyboard) because of a quite fortuitous lead in the early stage of diffusion of typewriters (David, 1985).

Cumulativeness and irreversibility in the production and use of knowledge have been studied by historians and economists of technological change. For instance, the concepts of 'natural trajectories' by Nelson and Winter (1982), 'technological paradigms' by Dosi (1982) and 'techno-economic paradigms' by Freeman and Perez (1988) point at cumulativeness and dynamic economies as mechanisms that impress precise trajectories on technological change.

---

12 There are several types of network externalities. To simplify, positive network externalities take place when the value of a good increases for a user with the number of users that adopt the same good or compatible goods. Externalities may be direct, as in the case of telephone network users sharing a common software program (and other fixed costs). They are indirect when complementary products can be supplied because of increasing returns to scale in production (for example, the large number of PC-compatible personal computers makes attractive the development of applications that run on these computers). On this issue, see Farrell and Saloner (1985) and Katz and Shapiro (1986).

Cumulativeness and the emergence of technological trajectories help decision-makers to focus their research and to forecast future technological advances. However, firms and policy makers are often forced to take myopic decisions, which aim to make local improvements but do not guarantee global optimality. With few exceptions, technological trajectories are usually known only 'ex post'. Important decisions are made by firms and policy makers during the process of selection of alternative trajectories under conditions of imperfect information. Moreover, cumulativeness amplifies the negative effects of wrong decisions. The early allocation of resources by firms or policy makers to an inferior technical standard is a case in point.

However, firms and policy makers are not unarmed against ignorance and uncertainty. As mentioned above, firms build up conventional rules, heuristics and rules-of-thumb that have proved to be valid by experience and are influenced by their expectations, subjective 'visions', and beliefs. As mentioned above, problem solving and innovative activities are often based upon experience and trial-and-error, rather than science. Even in 'science-based' industries, like those based on electricity, practical experience of engineers and technicians often anticipates scientific knowledge. Moreover, various 'focusing devices' drive industrial research in certain directions. An important focusing device is given by technical bottlenecks and imbalances between complementary technologies or tasks of a production process (Rosenberg, 1976).

Recently, some scholars have shed light on the importance of experience, judgement, and tacit knowledge for technological activities. For instance, Rosenbrock (1988) has argued that the increasing use of science in engineering will not displace 'art' and tacit knowledge as basic features of this activity. Johannessen (1988) has argued that researchers engaged in artificial intelligence (knowledge-based systems used, for instance, for simulation) should take into account 'practical wisdom', 'craft', and tacit knowledge as opposed to knowledge expressed in the 'precise language of science'.[13]

On the other hand, one can observe that a large part of industrial R&D efforts are devoted to understanding, to learning 'how to learn' and/or to increasing the capability to absorb knowledge from external sources. Investments in general-abstract knowledge by firms may have positive effects on the productivity of applied research, increase the ability to select among different alternatives and focus the efforts on the most productive approaches. In other words, basic knowledge provides firms and applied researchers with general frameworks that reduce the costs of trial-and-error procedures (Nelson, 1982). Moreover, progress in managerial science and

13 'the tacit dimension of expert knowledge is, in many cases, more significant than the linguistic knowledge' (Johannessen, 1988, p. 287).

instrumentation (including computers and software), along with the use of scientific methods (that is, general-abstract knowledge), may create new opportunities for 'division of innovative labour' among different institutions and increase the efficiency of research (Arora and Gambardella, 1994).[14]

3.4. Implications for public policy

The vision of knowledge as a public good and R&D as a linear process have influenced the research policies, especially in the US, giving theoretical support to 'mission-oriented' programmes. The relationship between knowledge as a public good and the 'linear' model of R&D is not direct. If knowledge were a pure public good, once produced, any agent could have access to it through imitation, technological licensing (under a strong property right regime) or other channels. In the 'linear' model technological activities aim to the application of publicly available knowledge to specific uses. Public policies drawing on this model usually focus on research (knowledge production), rather than development and diffusion, assuming that these stages of the R&D process are less relevant from the policy-maker's point of view.

An important assumption of this approach, mentioned above, is that policy makers are perfectly informed and able to correct market failure by first-best policies. In fact, policy makers are also subject to 'failure' for the following reasons. First, policy makers are not perfectly informed about the characteristics of the market for knowledge (both on the supply and the demand side). Second, policy makers cannot perfectly foresee the consequences of their action on knowledge production because of the complex relationships between science and technology and the irreversibilities which amplify the negative effects of 'myopic' decisions. Finally, many instruments under the control of the policy makers prove to be inefficient ex-post, because of asymmetric information, adverse selection and moral hazard.

An example of first-best policy's failure is the patent system. Patents aim to correct the lack of private incentives to invest in inventive activities, to the benefit of dynamic efficiency (product variety). But they also allow an inventor to sell its knowledge at a price above the marginal cost and, therefore, give rise to under-utilisation (lack of diffusion) of knowledge. Moreover, a broad patent scope may inhibit subsequent incremental innovations. Recently, the economics literature has pointed out the trade-off between the social benefits from a wide patent scope (or duration), in terms of incentives to major innovations, and the opportunity-costs of strong

14 The economic implications of the use of science in industrial production are also discussed by Rullani and Vaccà (1987).

protection, in terms of lesser later improvements associated with imitation and 'inventing around' activities (Merges and Nelson, 1990). However, the optimal patent scope (and duration) is not known ex ante. A further consequence of the patent system is represented by the 'external diseconomies of common pool' arising from the patent race, that is the possibility of over-investment in R&D and duplication of research efforts (see Dasgupta and Stiglitz, 1980).

Another example which clarifies the failure of first best policies concerns the public support to specific technological standards. Government failure is particularly significant in the case of competition among technologies characterised by increasing returns, such as telecommunications and computers. As discussed before, the market mechanism does not guarantee the emergence of the best technology. Early public support of a specific technological alternative under imperfect information may also yield similar results, locking-out a superior technology. In these conditions policy makers can pursue second-best policies rather than first-best ones. They can foster the competition among alternative solutions (at the cost of some duplication of research efforts) in the early stages of a technology life cycle.

In general, second-best research and innovation policies take 'the constraints on the government as given and attempts to make gradual, piecemal improvements' (Itoh et al., 1991, p. 12). This approach is quite consistent with an 'evolutionary' vision of technological change as a process constrained by 'initial conditions' and bounded rationality of decision makers (including the policy makers). Moreover, the evolutionary approach takes into account the interactions among different institutions which belong to 'national innovation systems' (Dosi et al., 1988; Nelson, 1993).

4. THE ACCUMULATION OF KNOWLEDGE WITHIN FIRMS

4.1. Knowledge production and learning

Knowledge production is an economic process whose inputs are skills or capabilities, available knowledge and new information. The outputs of this process consist of modifications of the existing stock of knowledge, in the form of new products, new process technologies, and new organisational techniques.

The production of knowledge results from different activities, formal R&D activities, manufacturing, marketing, and interaction with other organisations. All these activities imply different types of learning, that is acquisition of new knowledge, capabilities or skills. Moreover, they are subject to different degrees of 'division of knowledge' within and across firms.[15]

Learning may occur as a consequence of production of goods and services (defined as 'learning by doing' by Arrow, 1962b) or during the use of technologies and methods ('learning by using' according to Rosenberg, 1982). Learning, particularly learning by doing and by using, is a source of tacit, idiosyncratic knowledge.

In the economics literature there are several attempts to model and measure learning processes. For example, learning curves, in the context of neoclassical production functions, relate the average costs of production (or maintenance) of a given plant to the years of production (or the cumulated output). Learning curves have been utilised to measure learning processes in several industries, particularly the aircraft industry (see Rosenberg, 1982, chapter 6). Moreover, learning processes have been studied with 'progress functions' or 'experience curves' that relate the reduction of average costs to technical progress embodied in capital goods and to disembodied technical progress (learning by doing and organisational change) (Malerba, 1992).

Individuals and firms may also improve their ability to learn through the study or the development of new products/processes, 'learning by studying' and 'learning by development' (Dutton and Thomas, 1985) or 'learning to learn' (Stiglitz, 1987). Learning to learn is thus the intentional result of formal R&D activities. Stiglitz has pointed out that 'experience in learning may increase one's productivity in learning. One learns to learn, at least partly in the process of learning itself' (Stiglitz, 1987, p. 130).

Learning sources may be internal or external (von Hippel, 1988; Dutton and Thomas, 1985; Rosenberg, 1982; Lundvall, 1988). Learning by imitation or learning by observing failures and mistakes made by lead innovators and competitors has been shown to be an important source of 'late comer' advantage, as in the case of the aircraft industry, where the American Boeing and Douglas have benefited from errors made by the early British employment of jet engines in commercial aircraft (Rosenberg, 1982). Moreover, firms learn and may 'invent around' technology embodied in capital goods and components and disembodied technology (for example, acquired through licensing). Cooperation with users, suppliers and universities is also an important source of knowledge in industries characterised by product complexity and multidisciplinarity of knowledge.

Learning processes are subject to increasing intertemporal returns to scale. Moreover, learning (including learning to learn) is localised.[16] As discussed above, the uncertainty surrounding knowledge production and bounded rationality spur decision makers to take myopic decisions, aiming for locally

15 The concept of 'division of knowledge' was introduced by von Hayek (1948).
16 This implication of localised technological change has been noticed by Stiglitz (1987). For a recent survey of the economics of localised technological change, see Antonelli (1995).

optimal solutions. Moreover, learning and progress of given techniques usually have limited spillovers to other techniques.[17] Large spillovers take place with particular technologies, like mechanical engineering and IT. The 'pervasiveness' of these technologies gives rise to 'technological convergence', as pointed out by Rosenberg (1976), that is the convergence of different industries in the use of a common set of techniques.

4.2. Capabilities and innovations

The objective of this section is to relate capabilities, as an input of knowledge production (and learning), with innovations, an output of this process.

A seminal work on the use of different types of skills in the production of knowledge is Usher's *Technical Change and Capital Formation*. Usher distinguishes between innate activities, acts of skill, and inventive acts of insight. Innate activities are defined as 'unlearned modes of actions that develop as responses to the structure of the organism or the biochemical processes that control its functions' (Usher, 1971, p. 46). Acts of skill are 'learned activities' that can be undertaken by technicians and engineers who possess the 'state-of-the art' technology in their routine activities. These acts are conducive to improvements and incremental innovations. Inventive acts of insight are defined as unlearned activities and give rise to 'new organisations of prior knowledge and experience'. These acts can be performed by both 'superior persons' and technicians during their normal activities (ibid., pp. 44 and 47). Sequences of different acts of insight result in inventions, which represent the synthesis of established knowledge with new knowledge. Even the generation of radically new knowledge ('primary inventions') is considered by Usher as a process of 'cumulative synthesis' rather than the isolated, heroic act of a superior individual. The social and cumulative dimension of change is clear when Usher describes the sequence of inventions that culminated in the conception of the steam engine. Usher disagrees with the distinction made by Schumpeter between invention and innovation.[18] The generation of new knowledge, in Usher's view, is a 'social contruction', a process that involves engineers, technicians and administrative staff working together in innovative firms. The separation between technicians–inventors and entrepreneurs–innovators does not allow

17 Technical progress in the traditional microeconomics is represented by a shift of the isoquant map. All techniques represented in each isoquant are assumed to be proportionally affected by technical progress. This implies that changes that affect a labour-intensive technique X are assumed to affect a capital-intensive technique Y in the same proportion.

18 In Schumpeter's view, inventions are irrelevant from an economic viewpoint until they are not introduced into the market and entrepreneurs (innovators) are not necessarily inventors (Schumpeter, 1934, chapter 2).

these interactions to be captured.[19]

As mentioned above, this process of social construction is affected by previous general-abstract knowledge and tacit knowledge which are combined with new knowledge and individual acts of insights. Organisational and managerial skills are complementary to technical skills in determining technological inventions and their commercial success.

4.3. The accumulation of technological capabilities

Usher and other scholars of technological change did not ask how capabilities are accumulated by the firms. Moreover, the traditional economics literature focused on technological change embodied in capital goods (see, for example, Kuznets, 1966, Salter, 1966). Relatively few theoretical and empirical studies have been directed to investments in intangible assets and disembodied technological change. As discussed above, the economics and management literature has recently recognised that the learning and competence of firms' technicians and managers are among the major sources of firms' technological change.[20]

Some scholars give some insights into the process through which firms build up technological and manufacturing capabilities in key technologies that give firms the ability to survive and grow in the long run by producing a diversified range of end products (Prahalad and Hamel, 1990). Firms build up their 'core competencies' (that is, technological competencies) to monitor technological change and develop their 'core products'. According to Prahalad and Hamel (1990) core competencies enable firms to coordinate different skills and technologies that are critical for their growth. Core products are defined as the 'physical embodiment of core competencies' (p. 83) and represent the building blocks of diverse end products. Therefore, in successful firms an apparently diversified portfolio of activities may be traced back to a coherent stock of competencies.

The technological complexity of many manufacturing activities forces firms to accumulate technical competencies in different technological fields, directly and indirectly related to their 'principal' or 'core products'. Particularly, 'general-purpose' technologies, like mechanical engineering, biotechnology and IT, become key inputs for the research and production activities of many different sectors. They have to be combined in different and often complex ways with other technologies to develop a wide range of products, systems and services.

19 This is what happens, according to Usher, in particular with 'secondary inventions', that is 'inventions which extend a known principle to a new field of use' (ibid., p. 54).
20 The importance of disembodied technical progress was also recognised in previous studies on human capital, a usual measure of which is the years of training/education for different types of skilled human resources (Becker, 1962).

Using different indicators of technological activities, Jacobsson and Oskarsson (1993) and Patel and Pavitt (1994) have studied the knowledge base of different industries to analyse this issue. Jacobsson and Oskarsson have used data on the educational background of engineers and scientists employed in the largest 25 Swedish industries in 1980 and 1989. Their analysis shows two main results. First, the technology base of most industries is diversified and many industries are 'multi-technology industries', as indicated by the number of engineering categories that each industry covers. Second, most industries make extensive use of mechanical and electronics engineers. This shows the pervasiveness of general-purpose technologies.

Patel and Pavitt (1994) have used US patent data of the world largest firms in different industries, obtaining results consistent with Jacobsson and Oskarsson's findings and previous studies (Granstrand and Sjolander, 1990). First, they show that large firms have a multidisciplinary technology base. Mechanical, chemical, and instrumentation engineering represent the most 'pervasive' competencies, while computing, materials and biotechnology competencies are increasingly being adopted in many different industries. Why do firms accumulate significant technical competencies outside their 'core business'? Patel and Pavitt (1994) find a positive and significant effect of firm size on technological diversification. Technological intensity, measured as patents per unit of sales, also shows a significant and positive effect on the dependent variable as well as of industry characteristics. Moreover, the need to integrate different technologies is an important determinant of technological diversification of large firms. Previous studies have produced evidence that the development of complex products requires the integration of different knowledge sources and that new technologies often do not completely replace old ones. For several decades electricity in manufacturing served to power central factory engines that in their turn transmitted energy to each machine through a mechanical system of transmission shafts and belts (see Freeman, Clark and Soete, 1982). More recently, the diffusion of another general-purpose technology, that is microelectronics, has increased systemic complexity of many products and services. In many downstream industries, from mechanical engineering to automobiles and telecommunications, firms have to accumulate competencies in microelectronics to develop their core products, thus diversifying their knowledge base. A similar effect is shown by biotechnology on various downstream industries including the chemical industry, pharmaceuticals, the food industry, and agriculture.

The second result that is worth noting for our purposes is the strong stability of firms' technological profiles and directions of search over time, as indicated by the strong positive correlation of the chemical, mechanical, electrical–electronic, transport and 'other' shares of total patenting between the periods 1969–84 and 1985–90. This result shows the importance of path-dependence of technological change and learning at the firm level. Nelson and Winter (1982), Teece (1988), Cantwell (1989), and Pavitt (1991b) have pointed out that, because of path-dependence, firms are likely to focus their research activity on areas that are close to their past experience.

Path-dependence of technological change at the firm level also may imply that current innovators have a higher probability of innovating as compared with non-innovators. On the other hand, however, path-dependence may generate a comparative disadvantage of large, established firms vs. new firms in terms of inertia or lack of incentives to introduce major innovations or 'competence-destroying' innovations   (Rothwell and Zegreld, 1982, Tushman and Anderson, 1986, and Swann and Gill, 1993). Major breakthroughs in the technological and economic environment may have contrasting effects on established firms. First, established firms may be displaced by new 'Schumpeterian' firms when new technological trajectories emerge. Second, established firms may survive a major breakthrough by reshaping their core competencies, searching for new skills and capabilities, and setting up external linkages with new firms. The possibilities to survive new technological trajectories for established firms depend on their technological background. In this respect, the accumulation of technological capabilities in fields outside their core business may give established firms the ability to anticipate and assimilate new technologies rapidly. For instance, during the 1950s and 1960s many large firms established in the electromechanical office equipment market, such as IBM (International Business Machines), Remington Rand and Underwood, had to face the market changes brought about by electronics. Only incumbents like IBM, which possessed a wide technological background and made an early commitment in electronics, survived.

4.4. Organisational capabilities

Organisations exist because 'individual's very limited capacity for acquiring and using information is a fixed factor in information processing' (Arrow, 1984, p. 170). As a consequence, firms develop an internal division of information and knowledge which gives rise to specialisation and accumulation of organisational capabilities. These capabilities are employed to reduce the costs of the information processing, to combine different types of knowledge, and to organise learning activities.

Like technological capabilities, organisational capabilities are firm-specific. In his analysis of the Japanese organisations (the 'participatory mode'), Aoki points out that 'the generation of informational rents is truly firm-specific in that employees' capacity to generate such rents is a collective one nurtured in the organisational framework and it cannot be embodied in, nor be portable by individual employees' (Aoki, 1990, p. 28).[21] Aoki analyses the advantages of a cooperative division of labour among the firm owners (who contribute the capital stock), the management (who develop and 'maintain' the organisational framework) and employees (who are endowed with expert productive skills and information processing capacities). He also discusses the characteristics of the division of knowledge between specific expertise ('expert skills'), that gives rise to 'productive rents', and 'information processing and communicative capacities' (organisational skills), that generate 'information rents'. Aoki argues that in the Japanese firms this division of labour is less marked than in their Anglo–American counterparts. Aoki draws on the distinction between 'specialised skills' and 'integrative skills' made by Koike (1987) and that between 'specialist' type vs. 'generalist' type of information skills made by Itoh (1987). In Japanese organisations the accumulation of capabilities is predominantly directed to the development of generalist or integrative type of skills. These skills are both able to cope with different contingencies (at the shop floor level and across shops) and to execute predefined tasks (at the shop floor level) (see Aoki, 1990, p. 30). Also, in the Japanese organisational approach the management (the 'central planning office') sets only a general analytical framework, allowing ad hoc and decentralised adaptation to environmental changes. More recently, this non-hierarchical approach has been adopted in European and US firms (for example, matrix organisations and multidisciplinary teams). Different approaches to the division of labour depend on 'task partitioning' choices aiming to reduce (or, alternatively, to take advantage of) interdependencies among different tasks. A sharp task partitioning, which is typical of the US management style, increases the specialisation or 'depth' of knowledge and skills at the cost of small 'breadth' (von Hippel, 1990b, p. 412). A division of labour centred on 'breadth' is close to the 'evolutionary' approach to problem solving and R&D discussed before. Some implications of this approach for production and innovative activities in software are discussed in Chapter 5.

Other studies have also showed the importance of firm-specific organisational capabilities. For example, Dunning (1988) has showed that firms increase their managerial capabilities by the experience arising from the coordination of transnational networks of technological activities and production. These organisational capabilities are difficult for competitors to imitate because they are embedded in the routines and experience of individuals within a specific firm. The success and growth of firms in dynamic industries can be explained by their ability to utilise and organise

21 For a discussion of the comparative efficiency of the Japanese and the American organisational modes see Aoki (1986).

different technologies for developing new products and creating new markets. Many successful Japanese firms have probably benefited from the organisational approach described above to exploit their competencies in microelectronics, product and process engineering by entering many different business sectors, from automobiles to computers, telecommunications, consumer electronics, and high definition TV.

The importance of organisational capabilities in innovative activities has been emphasised recently by Teece et al. (1994). They point out that coordinative and learning capabilities represent the main source of rent in the long run and the most 'distinctive' firm-specific features. Finally, these capabilities are cumulative, drawn on a variety of knowledge bases (with different degree of tacitness), and collective. They distinguish three types of organisational ability. First, there are 'allocative competencies' that give firms the ability to allocate financial and human resources among different R&D projects or product lines and the ability to price products and set up efficient incentive mechanisms. Second, there are transactional abilities that enable efficient decisions about their degree of vertical/lateral integration (make or buy decisions). Third, 'administrative competences' are utilised to devise efficient organisational structures and policies. According to these scholars, firms' competitive advantage in particular technological domains relies on their organisational capabilities that are utilised to coordinate different assets, including technical knowledge.

5. THE DIVISION OF KNOWLEDGE AMONG FIRMS

5.1. Division of labour and technological change

Since the *Wealth of Nations* of Adam Smith, the division of labour is considered by economists as one of the most important sources of productivity increase and technological progress. In Adam Smith's celebrated work, the advantages of division of labour arise from learning by doing ('increase of dexterity in every particular workman'), saving of time to switch from one task to another one ('the saving of time which is commonly lost in passing from one species of work to another') and inventions of tools and machinery that support each separated task ('the invention of a great number of machines which facilitate and abridge labour, and enable one man to do the work of many').[22] A further benefit of division of labour, made explicit by Charles Babbage, concerns the opportunity to employ workers endowed with different skills in different activities or operations:

22 Smith (1776), Vol. I, Chapter 1, p. 17.

the master manufacturer, by dividing the work to be executed into different processes, each requiring different degrees of skill and force, can purchase exactly the precise quantity of both which is necessary for each process; whereas if the whole work were executed by one workman, that person must possess sufficient skill to perform the most difficult, and sufficient strength to execute the most laborious, of the operations into which the art is divided. (Babbage, 1832, pp. 175–76).[23]

This observation lays some micro-foundations for the concept of comparative advantage. This principle can be seen in a dynamic fashion to take into account the positive interactions between skills and their employment in different activities or tasks. Any process of division of labour (specialisation) requires an initial set of diversified skills, but these skills evolve with experience and learning (as pointed out by Smith). Moreover, new skills may result from the division of labour and scientific or technological change. The latter stimulate the birth of new markets and spur on the formation of new 'talents'. This *virtuous circle* between skills, division of labour, and learning works as long as technological opportunities are significant and some selection mechanism takes place in the economic environment. The lack of technological opportunities and a weak (or excessive) selection environment may result in organisational slack and inefficiency. While much emphasis has been given to the negative effects of a weak selection (market) environment in the economic literature, relatively little analysis has focused on the effects of excessive momentum in selective mechanisms. Amongst the few studies on this issue, Hirschman (1970) notes that the management ability to react to the deterioration of product quality is a function of market selection. In a perfectly competitive market, silent consumers use 'exit' to signal their dissatisfaction with the quality of a given product. But the managerial reaction is not a positive monotonic function of the number of consumers' exits. Hirschman shows that an excess momentum in the exit process (which is likely to occur in perfectly competitive markets) probably results in a poor managerial reaction, because managers do not have enough time to initiate the search for new procedures. Consumers' loyalty (that is likely to take place in industries with market power) may smooth the reaction function. Loyal consumers use 'voice' first to signal their dissatisfaction and, only when quality deterioration persists, use 'exit'. The possibility to use 'voice' depends on the existence of good communication channels between consumers and managers. In the case of intermediate goods

23 Quoted by Rosenbrock (1990), p. 145. Adam Smith was not concerned about the allocation of different talents to different tasks because he was preoccupied with demonstrating that without the 'disposition to exchange' in human nature and 'co-operation of many thousands' (and the extent of the market) 'there could have been no such difference of employment as could alone give occasion to any great difference of talents' (Smith, 1776, Vol. I, Chapter 1, p. 23, and Chapter 2, pp. 28–9).

(for example, capital goods) these channels are usually well developed. In this case the selection mechanism is not the anonymous market, but a combination of market ('exit') and extra-market information flows ('voice'). From information channels and interactions with customers the producers draw the information needed to maintain and improve their products. Producers can also exploit these links to have access to new ideas from innovative users.

5.2. The determinants of division of labour and specialisation

Smith was aware of the opportunities for division of labour across firms and industries in the production of knowledge when he claimed that 'in the progress of society, philosophy or speculation becomes, like every other employment, the principal or sole trade and occupation of a particular class of citizens' (Smith, 1776, vol. I, ch. 1, pp. 21–2).

What are the variables that affect the division of labour in the production of knowledge? Modern economists have explained specialisation and division of labour among firms by focusing on two main variables: Smith's market extent and technological progress. In particular, Stigler (1951) has set forth the reasons why the market extent for individual final products results in 'vertical disintegration' and specialisation of upstream activities. Young industries internalise most phases of their production activities for several reasons, among which there is the lack of reliable supply of materials, components and machinery. By contrast, maturing industries rely on a larger market for their goods and externalisation of upstream activities becomes attainable. Thus, the economies of scale enjoyed by specialised suppliers depend on the market size for final products.[24]

More recently, Rosenberg has argued that the market size for a single final product explains only in part vertical disintegration and the division of labour between industries. In particular, Rosenberg tries to explain the degree of specialisation achieved by the American machine tool industry in the second half of the last century: 'individual firms producing nothing but milling machines would not have emerged in an economy where only firearms manufacturers employed milling machines' (Rosenberg, 1976, p. 17). Another reason why specialisation and vertical disintegration took place, according to Rosenberg, relies on 'technological convergence'. In the second half of the last century the skills and techniques for handling and shaping metals or for sewing fabrics became widespread among many different industries. Therefore the machine tool industry has enjoyed both Stigler's economies of scale and the Marshallian external economies arising from a widespread stock of knowledge (mechanical engineering). As Young

24 This point was previously raised by Young (1928). In particular, see p. 539.

observed several decades ago, the increasing returns associated with division of labour among industries are not simply the result of firm size: 'internal economies dissolve into the internal and external economies of the more highly specialised undertakings ... and are supplemented by new economies' (Young, 1928, p. 538).

The example of machinery highlights also a general characteristic of economic change, that is the circularity between technological change and market structure. The emergence of a new 'pervasive', general-purpose technology (mechanical engineering) increases the size of the market which in turn creates new opportunities for division of labour, and specialisation. Finally, the latter brings about further progress in the pervasive technology and, indirectly, in user industries.

The 'new industrial organisation' explains vertical disintegration and specialisation by diseconomies of scope (rather than economies of scale) across different stages of the same production chain or by the economies associated with the control of strategic assets (see Perry, 1989, and Holmstrom and Tirole, 1989).[25] Technological change is not taken into account in this literature.[26] Moreover, capabilities are not considered as firm-specific assets. The 'new-Schumpeterian' or 'evolutionary' perspective, by contrast, points out that a firm is a 'repository of productive knowledge' (Winter, 1993). The evolutionary theory also notes that the characteristics of knowledge and the cognitive limitations of firms shape the division of labour in innovative activities. For our purposes, these characteristics can be summarised as follows. First, there are sector-specific degrees of appropriability and levels of opportunity of technological advance. Second, there is the codifiability (or pervasiveness) of technological knowledge. Third, there is the variety of knowledge-base and search procedures; and, fourth, cumulativeness or irreversibility of change. Finally, there is the persistent variety and asymmetry among firms. This approach predicts that a low degree of vertical integration of innovative activities is likely to occur when there are high technological opportunities, low cumulativeness of change, high appropriability, and diffused innovative capabilities or technological pervasiveness (Dosi et al., 1988; Malerba and Orsenigo, 1996). The implications of knowledge characteristics for the division of labour in innovative activities have been explored by studies that focus on the relationship between in-house and external research activities. For example, Mowery (1983) has tested the hypothesis of complementarity between in-house and contract research by using archival data from three large

25 Similarly, horizontal integration is explained by economies of scope among horizontally related activities arising from the use of quasi-public inputs such as knowledge (see Panzar, 1989). An important application of the incomplete contract theory to vertical (and lateral) integration is provided by Grossman and Hart (1986).
26 One of the few exceptions is Holmstrom (1989).

independent American research organisations (Arthur D. Little, Battelle Institute and Mellon Institute) and their clients' in-house research laboratories during the period 1900–1940. For our purposes, this analysis has brought two interesting results. First, the size of in-house research laboratories in client firms (manufacturing firms) increased more rapidly than that in the independent laboratories. Second, two of these three research institutes (ADL and Mellon Institute) showed an increasing proportion of clients with in-house research facilities over the period. Moreover, the 'structural complementarity' between in-house and contract research was higher for the more complex and riskier research projects. These results indicate that the increasing in-house research commitment of industrial firms is a complement rather than a substitute for external sources of knowledge. Mowery explains these results through the need to possess internal ability to evaluate and exploit the services of external research channels. More recent studies have given further insights into the division of labour and interactions between internal and external search activities and capabilities. As mentioned before, Cohen and Levinthal (1989) and Rosenberg (1990) point out that firms' in-house research pursues two objectives. First is the introduction of new products and new processes, second is building up absorptive capabilities that enable firms to evaluate and 'invent around' external scientific and technological knowledge. More recently, Arora and Gambardella (1990) have studied the in-house research activities and the external links set up by large American pharmaceutical and chemical producers with different sources of scientific and technological knowledge. They give further theoretical justification and empirical support to the hypothesis of complementarity between internal and extra mural knowledge, showing that firms that carry out more in-house R&D are more likely to set up external linkages for the acquisition of knowledge. Malerba and Torrisi (1992) and Chapter 6 explore the association between internal innovative skills and external sources of technological change. My analysis shows that general-purpose capabilities and context-specific ones have different effects on the firms' propensity to set up links with external sources of innovation.

A final consideration arises from the more than proportional increase of in-house research compared with external research as reported by Mowery (1983). This evidence, according to Mowery, militates against the ineluctability of vertical disintegration predicted by Stigler. Mowery explains this finding as a result of several factors. First, there are the interdependencies between research and other activities (research output and manufacturing products are joint productions). Second there is the difficulty of codifing and separating complex research tasks from the rest of in-house research activity. Finally, there are problems arising from the contractual uncertainty as pointed out by the contractual and transaction cost theory.

In the same stream of analysis, von Hippel (1990a) focuses on the nature of knowledge (information) to predict the division of labour in problem solving and innovative activities. He analyses the implications of information 'stickiness' which depends on the costs of replication and transfer of information. These costs may overcome the economies arising from the application of information across different uses. When the degree of 'stickiness' is high, innovative activities tend to be concentrated and division of labour is limited. This analysis does not consider that the characteristics of information (its 'stickiness' or 'pervasiveness') are not independent of the institutional context where they take place.[27] As a matter of fact, the acquisition of new knowledge (the flow of information) is filtered by the 'visions', the beliefs, the 'culture', and the incentives structure of individuals and organisations.[28] Moreover, as discussed in section 3.3, information stickiness can be reduced by the use in innovative activities of scientific methods and instrumentation, such as computer simulation. The use of 'general' and transferable knowledge implies vertical disintegration and specialisation in innovative activities. The next chapter analyses the emergence of a specialised software industry in relation to the pervasiveness of software technology.

6. CONCLUSIONS

In the economics and management of innovation, an increasing emphasis is given to the study of knowledge, its sources and the division of labour between different organisations in the production and use of knowledge. Relatedly, this literature focuses on the analysis of competence accumulation at the firm level. However, there exist few theoretical models and indicators for understanding and measuring the variety of knowledge and skills types employed in innovative activities. Moreover, the relationships between in-house capabilities and external sources of innovation need further theoretical and empirical investigation. These issues are developed in the following chapters.

27 Von Hippel (1990a) assumes that information 'stickiness' is independent of the institutional contexts where information is produced and used. He also admits that this assumption is made for 'convenience' (p. 2).
28 Firms' 'visions' of technological change show significant effects on the evolution of technology and market structure, as pointed out by Swann and Gill (1993).

3. The Market for Software and Services

1. INTRODUCTION

During the 1980s, business practitioners and the specialised literature seemed to agree on the 'revolutionary' pace of technical progress in software technology and the rapid transformation of the way software was produced. In addition, the current specialised literature stresses the advent of object-oriented development languages and software automation tools, user-friendly interfaces, open systems, 'portability' of programs among different machines and operating systems, networks and multimedia. Some of these developments were given the same emphasis ten years ago or even before. For instance, the demand for open systems, which reduce users' dependence on incompatible proprietary standards, has been addressed to software producers since the early 1980s. Also, the first attempts to introduce modularity, automation, and engineering in software production were undertaken in the 1960s. As the concept of revolution implies radical and rapid change, we could say that software technology has not shown a revolutionary change, despite its radical effects on most economic sectors. A test of the gradual, cumulative changes in software technology and the underlying reasons are discussed later.

This chapter describes the basic economic characteristics of software production. There are both unique and general features that make software activity an interesting case study to compare with other manufacturing and service sectors. Moreover, the main market segments are presented and, finally, the current division of labour among different types of software producers is discussed. A detailed discussion of the division of labour in software production is justified by the overlaps between production and innovation in this industry.

2. IS SOFTWARE A SPECIAL CASE OF INNOVATION?

The International Standardisation Organisation (ISO) and the World Intellectual Property Organisation (WIPO) give similar definitions of computer software and services which can be summarised as follows. Software is the production of a structured set of instructions, procedures, programs, rules and documentation contained in any types of physical support (tapes, disks, electric circuits or film) with the aim of making possible the use of electronic data processing equipment (OECD, 1985).

Software activities deal with the codification of knowledge and information, the types of inputs and the outputs of these activities being virtually immaterial. The outputs can be delivered in the form of products (packaged programs and tailored or customised software) or as services (for example, access to application tools, consultancy and training services, and on-site programming services).

Software production shows some special features that make it a quite special activity in between the manufacturing industries and the service sector.

First, software development is an intellectual, labour-intensive activity, with negligible manufacturing costs. Software development is often described as a craft task that relies on the capabilities of 'individual creative, programmers' (Sommerville, 1982). In the case of software packages, the pure replication of the same product takes place only with later releases of software products (for example, word processing package). But even in this case, the replication activity, which corresponds to the production stage of manufacturing industries, shows virtually zero costs. Thus, software production costs are all fixed development costs. Once developed, the costs of fabricating a copy of a software program are almost negligible, except for the costs of packaging (magnetic support and manuals) and distribution. This explains why marketing and sales costs represent a large share of the total revenues of the largest packaged software vendors such as Microsoft (34 per cent), Oracle (44 per cent) and Sybase (52 per cent). By contrast, the personal computer manufacturers spend only 15 per cent of their revenues on marketing and sales activities. This has spurred many software producers to restructure their sales activities and rely on indirect channels (Semich, 1993, pp. 38–44). Thanks to Internet and electronic commerce, packaging and other sales costs are reduced and this produces further changes in the organisation of marketing and sales (Tucker, 1997)[1]. An important economic implication of this cost structure is that there are opportunities for increasing

---

1 For the purposes of this discussion I do not consider the maintenance costs, which are associated with the correction and improvement of software systems already installed.

returns to scale in the development of packaged software. However, these opportunities may not be exploited because software packages are in part public goods. This points to the importance of legal protection of innovation and other public support to industrial R&D in this sector.[2] As a matter of fact, one of the reasons why the US software industry has achieved world leadership in computer software and services is due to the comparatively early development of a domestic copyright system for software technology in 1980. Copyright helped the US software producers to exploit the economies of scale and scope arising from their large domestic market, by creating a powerful competitive advantage relative to the European and Japanese producers. Moreover, dynamic increasing returns reinforce this comparative advantage over time. Finally, network externalities arising from the complementarity between different software and hardware products (for example, microprocessors, operating systems and software applications) increase the size of the market and create further opportunities for increasing returns. These factors together explain a high market concentration. Similar to many hardware products, the market for software packages is characterised by relatively few global producers, most of which are Americans. For instance in operating systems, 'people are consolidating around a few vendors ... (IBM's) MVS at the top, (Microsoft's) Windows on the desktop, and (Microsoft's) Windows NT in the middle' (Tucker, 1997, p. 62).

The economics of customised software and services is different. The production of these goods shows relatively high marginal costs that depend on the difficulty of re-using users' specifications, designs, source codes and methodologies. Many software producers adopt production techniques and organisational arrangements that make possible only a low rate of re-use. Moreover, computer services require close and repeated interactions between production and consumption as it happens in other services. This makes it difficult to separate products from process (Miles, 1993). Furthermore, user–supplier interaction increases fixed costs, which are specific of a particular client or contract. Increasing returns to scale are also important in the case of customised software and services. But, unlike packaged software, the size of the project (contract), rather than the volume of production, is responsible for increasing returns to scale in the production of customised software and services. This explains a market structure characterised by a core of large multinational services suppliers such as EDS (Electronic Data Systems), Andersen Consulting and Cap Gemini, which are able to offer large, complex

2 Bresnahan and Trajtenberg (1995) have pointed out that a market economy cannot exploit the growth opportunities of 'general-purpose technologies', such as computers (and packaged software), because the production of these technologies is characterised by externalities which give rise to coordination problems between producers and users.

solutions for a large number of clients, and a fringe of smaller firms which focus on local markets and draw most of their revenues from customisation of software for few clients.

Second, more than other industrial activities, software production is almost by definition an innovative activity because it aims to produce new products or new ways of executing known tasks and functions. Of course, the degree of originality varies according to different types of software products. At one end there are nominally customised software programs and minor modifications of pre-existing software products that show a low degree of novelty. Most of these activities can be classified as routine or maintenance of existing systems. A large share of these activities is spurred by changes in users' requirements and hardware technology. This makes software systems similar to biological systems which adapt to environmental changes and 'learn' from experience. On the other end, there are cutting-edge software products like VisiCalc's electronic spreadsheet and unique programs or services created for single customers. Of course, in the case of services, innovation is not always dependent on technology.

Third, the absence of any manufacturing dimension in software activities affects the division of labour across firms and countries. In many engineering industries (like automobiles and chemicals), technology transfer may involve different separable activities, from factory planning and set-up of production facilities to manufacturing and training. By contrast, in the case of software, technology transfer takes place at the level of design know-how and training (Narasimhan, 1993; *Business Week*, 19 December 1994, p. 19). Moreover, the software design implies the combination of different software tools and components in large and complex systems. The absorption of this type of knowledge is particularly difficult and involves skilled manpower. This has not prevented large software firms from separating different phases of software design (for example analysis and design from codification). In the US and Japan, large software firms subcontract the least complex and routine activities (for example, programming) to foreign contractors (based in developing countries such as China and India). But some scholars have argued that a rigid division of labour may have negative effects on innovative performance because the software parts of an information system are much more interdependent and interact in more complex ways as compared with those of other industrial products (for example, an automobile) (Nakahara, 1993). An increasing division of labour within and across firms is likely to result from the use of object-oriented development techniques (Meyer, 1997).

Finally, another feature that makes this industry a quite special case is related to the difficulty of codifying the software development process and the uncertainty surrounding this process. Although uncertainty is a general feature of economic and technological activities, software activity shows specific forms of uncertainty. Like other 'experience goods', users cannot evaluate the quality of most software products before use, even in the case of relatively simple packaged software (for example, word processors). Also, and more importantly, neither users nor producers can easily predict the outcome of the development of packaged or customised software because it is intrinsically difficult to define clearly the problem to solve at the beginning or anticipate the outcome of learning by using and interactions between user and producer. Dan Brickling, co-developer of VisiCalc, the first electronic spreadsheet package, has partly expressed this type of uncertainty as follows: 'We try to build things ... and we really don't know what they are until we start to build them ... it is figuring out what we're trying to do that is hard.'[3] This uncertainty in problem specification affects software activities, making it difficult to codify and organise these activities. As discussed later in Chapter 4, software development is a continuous iterative process initiated by the specification of a specific problem. The efficiency of the development process benefits from an accurate initial specification but, as mentioned before, a complete ex-ante specification is structurally impossible in most cases because users' requirements will manifest themselves during the development and production activities. The uncertainty associated with users' needs, together with other factors illustrated previously, affects the division of tasks in software activities, which is of an 'evolutionary' or 'developmental' type, in that it evolves with the experience accumulated during each development project.

Despite the peculiarities discussed before, the software production shows some similarities with other industrial design activities, including mechanical engineering. For instance, an oil platform, a building or an aircraft design show complex interactions between components and complementary activities that make each product unique. Moreover, the 'evolutionary' approach to production and innovation which is required by software technology is not completely new to other problem-solving, intellectual activities (see Kline and Rosenberg, 1986, and von Hippel, 1990b). Industrial practitioners are aware of these similarities with other industrial design activities. John F. Schoch, General Partner of Asset Management Co. of the US, has made this point clear as follows: 'we have some wonderful arrogance in thinking that the world of software is so much different from mechanical engineering or the new biological and pharmaceutical disciplines. I, in fact, don't believe that is the case'.[4]

In summarising the issues so far discussed, similarities are found between the development of complex software products and industrial engineering

---

3 Quoted by National Research Council (1991), p. 45.
4 National Research Council (1991), p. 42.

activities. However, software technology shows certain features that make it an apparently unique activity, more similar to a purely intellectual activity than to manufacturing. Although many industries rely on knowledge as a production factor, few sectors can be properly defined as 'knowledge-intensive' as software activities.

3. THE SOFTWARE MARKET

3.1. Market segments

This work relies on a classification of software products adopted by the European Association of Manufacturers of Business Machines and Information Technology (EUROBIT)[5]. Following this classification, one can distinguish two broad classes of computer software goods: software packages (products) on the one hand, and customised software and services on the other. This classification includes software and services that are utilised to operate computers and other electronic data processing (EDP) equipment, including peripherals (for example, printers and monitors)[6]. Software embedded in electronics systems and sold as an indistinguishable part of these systems (for example, defence systems and consumer electronics products) is not included in this classification. Finally, software developed within user organisations is not accounted for in this analysis which focuses on traded software.

Software packages

Software packages (SIC 7372) include programs that are developed to execute cross-industry tasks (for example, scientific and technical calculations) or industry-specific tasks (for example the automation of operations in the bank and sector and retailing). Software packages include system software, programming languages, application tools and application solutions.

System software (or *basic software*) comprises operating systems and utilities. *Operating systems* are sets of programs that regulate the functionality of a computer system by linking the central processing unit

5 This classification was developed by International Data Corporation (IDC). Other IT market analysts, such as Gartner Group and Arthur D. Little, do not show significant difference in their classification of software products and suppliers.
6 More precisely, this work refers to computer software and services related to the installation, operation and maintenance of office equipment such as calculators, data processing equipment, 'other' office equipment, parts, photocopiers and sheet fed office printers.

(CPU) to computer peripherals, such as storage devices like RAM (random access memory) and ROM (read-only memory), monitors, printers and input/ouput devices (for example, keyboards and optical scanners). Operating systems translate programs developed in binary digit sequences of coded instructions (machine codes) into programme languages, that is, languages used by programmers to develop software products (applications and tools). Operating systems interface users and machines capabilities (for example memory and speed). Operating systems include LAN servers software, such as Novell's NetWare and Microsoft's Windows NT.

Utilities are programs managed by the operating system that are utilised for the maintenance and safety of programs, the conversion of programs from one language to another, and the organisation of information (i.e., sort and merge operations). They comprise compilers/assemblers, translators, sort/merge programs, screen generators and report generators, communication monitors and job accounting software. Recently, Internet software browsers, such as Netscape's Navigator and Microsoft's Explorer, have been introduced to extend the functions of traditional utilities.[7]

Programming languages and application tools play a role similar to that of machinery with respect to the manufacturing industry. Programming languages are the basic tools for the coding phase of software development in that they translate detailed design into instructions that are readable by the computer (machine code)[8]. Most of today's languages are improved versions of high-level, 'second' and 'third' generation languages developed between the 1950s and the 1970s (for example Cobol, FORTRAN, Basic, Pascal and C). 'Fourth' generation languages (for example, object-oriented languages such as Smalltalk and Java) were introduced during the 1980s and 1990s and are still at the early stages of their life cycle. *Application tools* are programs utilised by programmers to retrieve, process, and manage data and databases, and to develop application solutions (including databases). These tools range from spreadsheets (for example Lotus 1-2-3 and Microsoft's Excel) to database management systems, DBMS (for example, dBase, DB2 and Oracle). Most application tools incorporate programming languages (for example, Basic) that can be used by relatively unskilled programmers to develop simple applications. By contrast, CASE (computer-aided software

---

7 Internet is the world largest wide area network (WAN), that is a web of intranets or LANs.
8 The most elementary operations executed by a computer are the instruction set commands that are written in binary code, the only code readable by a computer's CPU (central processing unit). An example of instruction set commands are those that govern the transfer of data from memory (for example, hard disk or random access memory, RAM) to a specific location in the CPU ('register'). The format of the instructions is machine-specific, that is, it varies across different types of computers. The sequence of coded instructions is called machine code. The early stored programme computers were programmed in machine code and this made it difficult to modify the stored programmes.

engineering) tools (for example Index Technology's Excelerator and Nantucket Software's Clipper) require skilled programmers, and are used for automating specific programming phases (for example coding and testing). The same is true for 'object-oriented' tools such as Powersoft's Powerbuilder and Next Computer's Nextstep (more on these tools in Chapter 4).

Application solutions (applications) can be classified as follows: first, *cross-industry applications*, that include several types of standard packages, like payroll/personnel management, accounting, word processing and other office automation programs); second, *industry-specific applications*, that are developed to meet the requirements of particular sectors such as automobiles, banks and the financial sector, and transportation.

Customised (or bespoke) software and computer services

This market segment (SIC 7370, excluding 7372) includes a variety of software activities. First, there is the provision of software systems developed for medium-sized customers called *turn-key systems*. These systems are usually made up of both software and hardware. Second, are *system integration* services.

This activity aims at the integration of different hardware and software products from different vendors into complex systems for specific large customers, mainly in finance/insurance, manufacturing, and government sectors.

The remaining services are *bureau* or *professional services* and EDP (electronic data processing) services, including 'ad-hoc' customised software, consulting, professional training and maintenance, problem solving, transaction processing and on-line information services.

Finally, *systems and network operations management* include various services such as facility management and outsourcing. In this category of services there are EDI (Electronic Document Interchange), electronic-mail and other Internet services, and hardware maintenance and support services. Due to the increasing integration of intra-net (LAN) and inter-net (wide area network), the distinction between system management (or management information system, MIS) and network management is blurring.

3.2. Software and other information technology markets

Western Europe is the world largest market for IT after the US market. However, its share of the world market has decreased since 1992, while that of the US has increased significantly (Table 3.1).

Table 3.1 World market for information technology (IT)

	Largest OECD markets for IT [a]			
	1992		1996	
	Value	%	Value	%
US	152.52	35.43	285.75	41.36
Japan	75.03	17.43	116.84	16.91
West Eur.	157.44	36.57	187.96	27.21
RoW	45.51	11.57	100.33	14.52
Total	430.50	100	690.88	100
	Western European IT market by product type			
	1992		1996	
	Value	%	Value	%
Hardware	73.80	47.24	83.82	44.37
Soft. & Serv.	65.19	41.73	86.13	45.60
Hard. Mainten.	17.22	11.02	18.92	10.01
Total IT	156.21	100	188.87	100

Sources: EITO (1993, 1997)

Notes
a.   IT includes office equipment, computer and datacom hardware, hardware maintenance and support, software and services. Values are expressed in US billion dollars at 1992 and 1996 constant exchange rates.

Computer software and services accounted for about 46 per cent of Western European IT market in 1996, while computer hardware and office equipment (excluding maintenance and support services) accounted for about 43 per cent. The share of software and services has increased since 1992, the year when this market segment represented about 42 per cent of Western European IT market (Table 3.1)[9]. The growth rate of software and services market has been higher than that of hardware products between 1996 and 1997 (9.5 per cent and 6.5 per cent respectively) (EITO, 1997, pp. 29–30). Moreover, software represents a considerable share of GDP in many developed countries, especially in the US and the UK. The diffusion of software is positively associated with that of personal computers and, more recently, with the access to the world wide web (measured by the number of Internet on-line users). For example, the Japanese backward position in the

9 IT as a whole represented about 47 per cent of Western European information and communications technology (ICT) market in 1996. The remaining share of ICT was accounted for by telecommunications and services equipment (EITO, 1997).

world market for software is linked to the little use of personal computers and the limited number of Internet users (Table 3.2). Moreover, as Table 3.3 shows, there is a negative relationship between mainframes as a share of the hardware market and packaged software as a share of the software market. In the US and UK the share of mainframes has dramatically declined during the period between 1987 and 1995. Over the same period packaged software has increased to over 40 per cent of the software market in these countries. By contrast, the Japanese market has maintained a strong dependence on large systems and customised software over the same period. Finally, the largest European markets, especially Germany and France, have become less dependent on large systems and customised software between 1987 and 1995. Previous studies have analysed the international patterns of diffusion of electronics technologies showing marked differences across countries. These differences are explained by country-specific sectoral composition of manufacturing and institutional factors (Arcangeli et al., 1991).

Packaged software accounted for 32.2 per cent of total Western European software and services market in 1989 while by 1996 they have risen to about 38 per cent of the market (see Table 3.4)[10]. The share of packaged software has increased as a consequence of a larger annual growth rate of personal computers and network software applications. Within the market for packaged software, the segments for application solutions and system software have a similar size (about $19 billion in 1996). However, software applications are expected to increase more rapidly as compared with system software and application tools between 1996 and 1998. This depends on the rising demand for integrated application solutions which include accounting, human resource management, manufacturing and so on. (EITO, 1997, p. 33 and table 34).

System integration and facility management (especially network management) are the most dynamic market segments among the computer services, while traditional bureau services and EDP services, the major computer services marketed in the 1960s, are expected to remain stable. Particularly, facility management, consulting and system integration represent an efficient external alternative when the users' in-house resources are not sufficient to cope with the complexity of large information systems and they are unable to find solutions for problems concerning general corporate management issues (cf. EITO, 1993, p. 138).

10 EITO estimates are based on the sales mix of the major software and computer services providers in 17 Western European countries (15 EU countries and 2 non-EU countries, Switzerland and Norway), irrespective of the country of origin of each provider. These data include the sales of integrated hardware and software producers and those of specialised software providers. It is unclear whether these data include some in-house software and services activities or embedded software, that is software that is sold as a part of hardware–software systems and included in the hardware sales.

Table 3.2 World software market and IT diffusion indicators

	Software [b] market		Software/ GDP	PCs/100 white collars	Internet users (thousand)
	Value [a]	%	%		
USA	145.47	42.39	1.87	104	37,208
Japan	52.76	15.37	1.08	24	3,259
RoW	39.78	11.59	–	–	9,319
West Eur.	105.09	30.62	1.14	88	18,376
Germany	26.03	7.58	1.07	99	4,123
France	19.93	5.80	1.24	76	4,571
UK	15.81	4.60	1.39	93	3,969
Italy	9.52	2.77	0.77	72	734
Total	343.10	100	–	–	68,162

Source: EITO (1997)

Notes

a.   Values are expressed in US billion dollars at 1996 constant exchange rates.

b.   Software and Services include hardware maintenance and support services.

3.3. Software and services producers

Over the past decades a quite clear division of labour among different software producers specialising in different types of activities has emerged in the US and Europe and, to a lesser extent, in Japan. The reasons behind this pattern of specialisation and the national differences are illustrated in Chapter 4. The main software producers can be classified as follows[11].

Integrated producers of hardware and software (hardware manufacturers) supply a variety of software products from operating systems to application solutions for office and factory automation and services. However, the bulk of integrated producers focused on system software over the 1970s and 1980s. In system software most hardware producers pursued a strategy of proprietary control in the past.

With the diffusion of personal computers and workstations over the 1980s,

11 Data on markets and firm strategies reported in this section are drawn from *Datamation* (1990, 1991, 1992, 1993 and 1997).

Table 3.3 IT Market segments in selected countries

Mainframes as a share of total hardware (%)		
Year	1987	1995
US	46.82	21.57
Japan	72.33	42.85
Germany	55.82	30.16
France	53.19	32.39
UK	53.41	27.74
Italy	66.11	44.64
Packaged software as a share of total software & services market (%)		
Year	1987	1995
US	31.85	36.93
Japan	18.34	23.66
Germany	28.03	39.55
France	22.07	31.75
UK	37.16	42.80
Italy	33.47	35.71

Source:OECD (1997)

Table 3.4 Western Europe software market segments

1996	Packaged software	Profess. services	EDP services	Network services	Hard. mainten.	Total
Value [a]	39.54	32.81	9.78	4.01	18.92	105.06
%	37.62	31.22	9.29	3.82	18.00	100.00
	Packaged software by hardware type [b]					
1992	Large scale	Mid-scale	Small scale	Single user		Total
Values	4.92	7.38	7.38	3.69		23.37
%	21.00	31.57	31.57	15.78		100.00

Sources: EITO (1997) and 1992 International Data Corporation's estimates

Notes
a.   Values are expressed in US billion dollars at 1992 and 1996 exchange rates.
b.   Large-scale computers include mainframes, such as IBM 3090 series, and supercomputers; medium-scale computers include systems such as IBM system/38s and DEC VAX 11/750; small-scale computers include minicomputers such as IBM system 36 and AS/400 and DEC PDP-11/3X; single user computers include workstations for scientific and technical applications, such as Sun's SPARC and DEC Alpha RISC workstations, and personal computers.

there was an increasing demand for compatibility, defined as the possibility of combining different types of software. This can be attained through standardised file formats (as in the Unix environment), standardised data structures (as in the Lisp, main list processing language, environment) or standardised user interfaces (as in the case of Windows, OS/2 and MacOS). More recently, the object-oriented approach achieves compatibility through standardised access protocols and 'abstract data types' (Meyer, 1997, p. 8). Compatibility is associated with 'interoperability' across different machines and 'portability' of software products across hardware and software environments or 'platforms' (hardware, operating systems and utilities)[12]. The rising request for compatibility and portability has spurred hardware manufacturers to adhere to voluntary committees such as those that support alternative versions of Unix operating system[13]. Unix was invented at the AT&T Bell Laboratories in 1969 as a multi-user operating system for scientific and technical applications on minicomputers. The introduction of workstations in the 1980s pioneered by Sun and MIPS has stimulated the diffusion of Unix on a larger scale. According to IDC's estimates, in 1989, only 9 per cent of computers shipped worldwide run Unix OS, against 26 per cent of Microsoft's DOS and IBM's S/370 (IDC 1990). More recently, Unix has become a world standard for web servers (68 per cent of web servers in 1995) (OECD, 1997). Other routes to compatibility are represented by the diffusion of 'de facto' standards like MS-DOS or Windows-Intel and bilateral agreements (for example, Apple's Macintosh and Microsoft's Windows). The convergence towards 'open' standard platforms and the declining prices of hardware have spurred hardware manufacturers on software solutions and services during the 1990s.

Independent software firms include producers of software packages and suppliers of services. *Software producers* offer a large set of software products that include 'cross-industry' packages (application solutions and applications tools such as text and image processing packages and CASE tools) and 'industry-specific' or 'vertical' packages (application solutions such as packages for client portfolio management and cash dispensers in the

12 Open systems aim to meet the demand for 'portability' of programmes and data between systems, 'consistency' (homogeneity of user interfaces), multiple tasking (running different operations on the same system at the same time) and 'multi-using' (different users connected on-line) (Fertig, 1985).

13 There are three voluntary committees which support different Unix versions. First, Unix International (UI), which includes AT&T, NEC, Fujitsu and Olivetti, supports AT&T's Unix V.4. Second, Open System Foundation (OSF) which includes IBM, Digital, Hewlett-Packard, Hitachi, Siemens and Bull, supports Carnegie Mellon's Mach and IBM's AIX. Finally, X/Open which was founded in 1984 with the aim to set a bridge between the two consortia. Besides Posix, the standard supported by the Institute of Electrical and Electronic Engineers (IEEE), X/Open promotes the diffusion of the Common Operating Software Environment (COSE) (Malerba, Torrisi and von Tunzelmann, 1991; *Financial Times*, 1994a).

banking sector, for logistics in industry transportation and retailing). As a consequence of the declining profits on hardware, several software houses with some hardware activity have recently abandoned all hardware activities (for example, Microsoft, Novell and Cadence).

Suppliers of professional services and system integration services include a variety of firms. Traditional suppliers of EDP (electronic data processing) services offer timesharing services and on-line access to databases, or to application tools. Suppliers of professional services are increasingly focusing on facility management (on the customer site), training and consulting. An important market segment for professional service suppliers is system integration and turnkey systems. These activities consist of the integration of software from different suppliers (for example accounting, payroll systems) for the requirements of specific customers. System integrators (and turn-key systems suppliers) also offer in-house customised software, training and consultancy services. Besides hardware manufacturers, some large traditional software and services suppliers have recently focused on system integration (for example, Ernst & Young, American Management, TRW and Computer Task Group in the US). Hardware and software distributors, including Original Equipment Manufacturers (OEMs) and Value Added Retailers (VARs), also may offer professional services and resell hardware and software packages by adding custom software and service. VARs have flourished thanks to the development of customised software for technical applications on minicomputers (for example, Digital's PDP-11/3X and IBM's System 36 and AS/400). More recently they have suffered from the increasing system integration activities by hardware manufacturers, although some hardware producers (for example, Tandy, Cray and Micropolis in the USA) have preferred VARs to OEM contracts as external sales channels. Like software package producers, many service suppliers have recently abandoned hardware activities. For instance, General Electric's hardware sales declined from 35 per cent of its total sales in 1990 to zero in 1992. A similar strategy has been adopted by Andersen Consulting and Sterling [14].

3.4. Vertical disintegration and division of labour

Software is a young industry which draws its origin from users' and hardware manufacturers' software divisions. Over time the market share

---

14 The shutdown of hardware activities by software and services firms in the last few years is also explained by market contraction and financial difficulties. However, the recovery after 1992 has not produced any significant change to this trend (*Datamation*, 1997). It is worth noting that there are few exceptions to this trend, the most striking of which is ASK Computer Systems, a software and services producer with about 14 per cent of its total sales in midrange computers (cf. *Datamation*, 1993, p. 111).

accounted for independent software firms has increased compared to that of users and hardware manufacturers.

Users' organisations, especially large firms, still produce a significant share of their software programs in–house. According to *Datamation* estimates, externally supplied software and services accounted for about 2 per cent of the total IT budget of American firms in 1978 as compared with about 10 per cent in 1982 (OECD, 1985). According to other estimates, in-house developed software accounted for about 60 per cent of software expenditures in the four largest European markets (Germany, France, the UK and Italy) as compared with 40 per cent of software packages and services acquired from external sources (IDC, 1990). Another research survey based on 1,354 users in the UK shows that the share of non traded software within total software expenditures varies with the type of hardware product. Internally developed software is large with minicomputers (27 per cent of users' total software budget) and mainframes (24 per cent) as compared with microcomputers (15 per cent) (Brady and Quintas, 1991). This is consistent with the importance of packaged, traded software in small servers and personal computers (Table 3.4).

Despite the importance of in-house software development, the Management Information Systems (MIS) departments of several large user organisations have begun to sell their products and services on the market and, in some cases, have spun off from their parent company. This process of vertical disintegration has taken place in the US (for example, General Motor's EDS and TRW's TRW Information Systems and Services) and Europe (for example, British Leyland/Rover's Istel in the UK, Enidata and Pirelli Informatica in Italy)[15]. More recently, outsourcing of consulting, training, system integration and customised software development has become a dominant strategy for most user organisations (Asbrand, 1997, p. 73).

The market share of hardware manufacturers varies with the type of software. According to IDC's estimates, hardware manufacturers passed from about 50 per cent of Western European market for packaged software in 1989 to less than 30 per cent in 1993. A similar division of labour between integrated hardware–software firms and specialised software firms is observed in the US market while in the Japanese market integrated firms retain a larger share of the market (about 37 per cent, see Table 3.5).

Tables 3.6 and 3.7 show the world largest software and services vendors classified by *Datamation*.

15 Istel spun off from British Leyland/Rover Group in June 1987 and was acquired by AT&T in September 1989 (cf. *Computer Weekly*, 1990, p. 228).

Table 3.5 Worldwide packaged software sales by vendor class

	US	Western Europe	Japan
Specialised firms	69.5	70.4	63.1
Hard manufacturers	30.5	29.3	36.9
Share of US firms	88.9	63.3	54.1

Source: IDC (1994)

As mentioned before, hardware manufacturers have recently tried to improve their position in the software market. For example, Digital Equipment Corporation (DEC) has dramatically increased the software and services share of its total revenues, from 17 per cent in 1992 to 53 per cent in 1996. Notice that during the 1980s DEC had reduced the software and services share of its revenues (which was 25 per cent in 1981). Hewlett-Packard is probably the most striking example of vertical disintegration during the 1980s and re-integration in subsequent years. Software and services represented 29 per cent of its revenues in 1981, 8 per cent in 1992, and 27 per cent in 1996. IBM represents an exception to the trend towards vertical disintegration of software and services during the 1980s. Its share of software and services increased steadily between 1981 and 1992, from 17 per cent to 28 per cent. Moreover, in 1996 IBM drew 47 per cent of its revenues from software and services. (*Datamation*, 1982, 1993 and 1997). The most extreme example of diversification from hardware to software is represented by US Mentor Graphics that has divested its hardware activities to focus on software and services (its software and services sales increased from 39 per cent in 1990 to 74 per cent in 1992). Also some European hardware firms are increasingly focusing their strategy on software and system integration. For example, ICL (Fujitsu) and Siemens-Nixdorf respectively drew 48 per cent and 45 per cent of their 1996 revenues from software and services, while Olivetti divested its computer (hardware) division in the same year to focus on computer and telecommunications services. The reasons for the hardware manufacturers' increasing commitment to software are quite clear. The rising importance of open standards has stimulated an increasing price competition among hardware manufacturers which has brought about a progressive reduction of their profits. The rapid relative growth of the software market has also led to a high profitability of software firms compared with that of computer firms. *Datamation* has compared three samples of firms selected from the world largest IT companies. The returns on sales of software firms passed from 12.4 per cent in 1988 to 10.1 per cent in 1992 while service firms' returns on sales remained stable (from 6.7 per cent to 6.3 per cent).

Table 3.6 Leading firms in packaged software

Firm	1984	Rank	1992	Rank	1996	Rank	Country
IBM	3,197	1	11,366	1	12,911	1	US
Hewlett-Packard	500	2	nc	nc	941	13	US
Unisys	408	3	712	12	573	nc	US
NEC	300	4	1,840	4	2,263	6	J
Digital	200	5	800	10	1,224	10	US
Fujitsu	200	5	3,525	2	4,754	4	J
Nixdorf	160	6	nc	nc	nc	nc	D
Lotus	157	7	810	9	nc	nc	US
Manag. Science	142	8	nc	nc	nc	nc	US
Microsoft	125	9	2,960	3	8,963	2	US
Comp. Associates	116	10	1,771	5	3,156	5	US
Hitachi	100	11	983	8	5,487	3	J
Bull	100	11	nc	nc	nc	nc	F
Olivetti	96	12	708	13	881	14	I
Ashton Tate	82	13	nc	nc	nc	nc	US
Siemens	39	14	1,058	6	1,010	12	D
Oracle	13	15	782	11	2,280	7	US
Novell	nc	nc	989	7	1,225	9	US
ICL	nc	nc	692	14	449	nc	UK
SAP	nc	nc	nc	nc	1,699	8	D
Lockheed Martin	nc	nc	nc	nc	1,120	11	USA

Sources: Datamation (1985, 1993, 1997)

Hardware firms showed a 10.5 per cent returns on sales ratio between 1988 and 1990 which fell to 3 per cent in 1992 (*Datamation*, 1993, pp. 12–15). The higher comparative returns have spurred hardware manufacturers to re-enter the software market. Some manufacturers have done it through mergers and acquisitions.

For instance, in 1995 IBM has acquired Lotus Development, one of the largest US producers of software packages.

Moreover, the reduced growth of the software market during the period 1992–94, and a lack of financial and managerial resources, pushed many software firms, especially in Europe, to find large capital partners. Istel was acquired by AT&T from British Leyland; Cap Gemini sold 34 per cent of its shares to Daimler-Benz Interservices (Debis); and, finally, Finsiel has tried to merge with Olivetti's software division[16].

Table 3.7 Leading firms in services

Firm	1984	Rank	1992	Rank	1996	Rank	Country
ADP	959	1	2,075	5	3,567	10	US
Control Data	931	2	nc	nc	nc	nc	US
TRW	825	3	1,800	8	nc	nc	US
GE	825	3	nc	nc	1,187	nc	US
EDS	786	4	4,273	2	14,441	2	US
Comp. Sciences	710	5	2,474	3	5,400	5	US
Mc Donnell	608	6	nc	nc	nc	nc	US
Unisys	289	7	1,336	10	3,949	9	US
NCR	285	8	nc	nc	nc	nc	US
Boeing	260	9	nc	nc	nc	nc	US
Cap Gemini S.	206	10	1,893	7	4,104	8	F
IBM	200	11	6,410	1	22,784	1	US
General Instrum.	193	12	nc	nc	nc	nc	US
Quotron System	189	13	nc	nc	nc	nc	US
Xerox	180	14	nc	nc	2,033	nc	US
Andersen Consult.	nc	nc	2,445	4	4,877	6	US
Fujitsu	nc	nc	1,913	6	4,160	7	J
Digital	nc	nc	1,570	9	5,988	4	US
NTT	nc	nc	1,248	11	2,200	nc	J
First Data	nc	nc	1,205	12	nc	nc	US
AT&T	nc	nc	1,199	13	887	nc	US
Nomura	nc	nc	837	14	1,180	nc	J
Price Waterhouse	nc	nc	736	15	1,096	nc	US
Finsiel	nc	nc	633	16	800	nc	I
Hewlett-Packard	nc	nc	nc	nc	7,535	3	US

Sources: *Datamation* (1985, 1993, 1997)

However, the recent increased commitment of hardware manufacturers does not seem to bring about a re-integration of software activities by

16 The latter agreement has not been concluded for various reasons, including Olivetti's serious financial difficulties which culminated in the sale of its computer division.

hardware manufacturers, who face a strong competition from firms like Microsoft, Computer Associates and Andersen Consulting. These firms are not integrated in hardware manufacturing, which have strong service and organisational capabilities that are important to coordinate the activities of many subcontractors and to serve international markets. Moreover, as shown before, hardware firms are reducing their manufacturing activities to focus on software and services. Finally, most software firms have grown within the software sector or have diversified towards related activities (for example, telecommunication services), whereas they have not diversified into hardware. This suggests that there are not significant economies of scope between hardware and software justifying the integration of these activities.

New opportunities for economies of scope arise from the convergence between computer and telecommunication services. First, many traditional computer services firms are focusing on Internet as a new sales channel for their services and as a means to diversify their business (for example, EDS's Internet consulting and development services launched in 1996). Second, computer software producers are developing new products for Internet (such as Microsoft's Explorer browser and Active X software component for the Web). Finally, established telecommunications services suppliers are investing in computer communication services. For instance, MCI, a US leading long-distance telephone firm, acquired SHL Systemhouse (system integration) in 1995 and formed MCI Systemhouse (Asbrand, 1997).

The division of labour in the software activities illustrated in this section results from a process of industrial evolution that has been shaped by institutional, technological and economic factors. This process is described in the following chapter.

4. CONCLUSIONS

During the 1980s an independent software industry emerged. In this period, hardware firms accounted for a declining share of the software market, especially in the US and Europe, while specialised software and service firms increased their market share. The progressive reduction of profits from hardware sales and the rising importance of open standards over recent years have spurred hardware firms towards software and services. However, this process will not bring about a re-integration of software activities by large hardware manufacturers. In the late 1980s and early 1990s, these firms restructured their organisations and set up extensive networks of linkages with specialised suppliers of software products and services. Many established hardware manufacturers, such as IBM, DEC, Olivetti, ICL, Bull and Unisys, have increasingly focused on services (for example, system integration), for which they show some competitive advantage in terms of service networks and linkages with large customers. Hardware manufacturers show also organisational capabilities that are important to coordinate the activities of many subcontractors and to serve international markets. However, these firms have to face strong competition from large software firms, like Computer Associates and Oracle, which are also investing in this market segment. Hardware firms have also to face the competition of established consultants and system integrators, like Andersen Consulting, Arthur Young and Peat Marwick Management Consultants (KPMG), which have accumulated experience and reputation in these activities. Finally, traditional computer services providers are diversifying their activities and focusing on management consulting. For instance, in 1990 Lotus formed a consulting division and in 1993, Finsiel established a new consulting subsidiary that offers consulting services in the fields of strategy definition and revisions, organisation re-engineering, management of human resources, and technological management.

Therefore, the landscape is radically different from that of the early developments of the computer and software industry. The oligopolistic core of this industry seems quite differentiated, with a variety of producers endowed with different capabilities and comparative advantages.

The organisation of software activities and the pattern of firm specialisation vary across different national systems. Europe has lagged behind the US in the development of an independent software industry for reasons that are discussed in the next chapter. Moreover, the European software firms have specialised in customised software and computer services. At the same time, the share of packaged software in the European software market has increased quite slowly compared with the US market. These differences are explained by the different rate of diffusion of small computers which make use of packaged software. Although the differences between the European and the US markets have blurred during the 1990s, the US firms still hold their world leadership in software packaged. The persistence of US leadership points out the importance of cumulativeness arising from increasing returns to scale and network externalities.

4. The Evolution of Industry Structure, Industrial Policies and Firm Strategies

1. INTRODUCTION

This chapter aims to explain the current organisation of the software industry in the light of the evolution of technology, markets, and institutions. More precisely, the changes of this industry over time are linked to the following factors.

First, the evolution of complementary technological trajectories, particularly that of semiconductors and computers.

Second, certain intrinsic characteristics of software technology, especially its pervasiveness and adaptability to a variety of specific needs that have created opportunities for vertical disintegration and new entries.

Third, the evolution of the market conditions (market size and segmentation) and the accumulation of technical capabilities by users.

Finally, specific institutional conditions and public policies that have affected the rate of technological change and the division of labour in the software industry.

In the following pages the historical evolution of the software activities is described, from the early in–house development during the 1940s and 1950s to the emergence and development of an independent software industry during the 1970s and 1980s.

The story summarised in this chapter takes into account some differences between the US and the European software industry, including their patterns of specialisation. These differences are explained by the different combination of the factors mentioned above in these two areas.

Finally, I analyse the restructuring and growth operations of large US European software firms in the period between 1984–92. This analysis aims to show whether the differences between US and European firms discussed previously reflect upon their recent growth and restructuring strategies.

2. THE HISTORICAL EVOLUTION OF SOFTWARE ACTIVITIES

2.1. The main stages of the historical evolution

Our analysis focuses on four phases of the software industry evolution. The first phase, between the 1940s and mid-1950s, is dominated by electromechanical machines for business calculations and the first electronic computers for scientific computation.

The second phase, between the late 1950s and the early 1960s, is linked to the developments of the second generation of computers based on the transistor, the introduction of general-purpose computers and the first generation of minicomputers (for relatively small-scale technical and scientific calculations).

The third phase, between mid-1960s and the late 1970s, is characterised by the development of integrated circuits and the take off of an independent software industry.

The last phase is dominated by the consequences of microprocessor invention, the later diffusion of personal computers, and the introduction of new distributed computing architectures, like personal computer networks and client–server networks, and by Internet's take off.

Table 4.1 summarises the main steps of the historical evolution of computer and software activities.

2.2. The early developments of hard-wired software: 1940s–mid 1950s

The importance of computer technology and the interdependencies between hardware and software were strong well before the first digital electronic computer, the ENIAC (electronic computer integrator and calculator), was developed by Presper Eckert and John Mauchly at the Moore School of Engineering, University of Pennsylvania, in 1946. The idea of a 'programming system' was first experimented the beginning of the last century by Joseph Jacquard, who implemented the punched card system for the silk-weaving looms of his factory at Lyon. Jacquard's 'perforated belt' became the 'analytical design' for the Charles Babbage's 'mill' device and Hermann Hollerith's numerical card. During the period between 1822 and 1835, Charles Babbage developed the 'difference engine' or 'analytical engine' to be used in mathematical operations (for example, trigonometric functions). The 'difference engine' was equipped with a device called mill, a logical and arithmetical unit that used cards for the control of a 'repeating apparatus' (a set of sequential operations), corresponding to a modern software program (developed by Ada Lovelace, see Chapuis and Joel, 1990,

Table 4.1 The phases of the historical evolution of software activities

	Advances in Hardware Technology	Advances in Software Technology	Changes in Organisation of Software
1940s mid 1950s	1st computer generation (vacuum tube)	1st subroutine library (EDSAC project, 1950)	
	Electronic computers for scientific and military applications		
	Electromechanical Machines for business calculations	1st compiler (Manchester Mark I project,1952)	Users and universities take part in the development of early operating systems and develop their own application solutions
	Transistor (1947)	1st higher level language (Fortran, 1954)	
	1st stored program computer (1949)		
	Microprogramming (1951)	1st batch operating system (Whirlwind Project, 1954)	
End 1950s early 1960s	2nd computer generation (general purposes and based on transistors)	1st assembler (SHARE IBM, 1956)	Operating systems developed by hardware producers
		1st multiprogramming operating system (1960)	
	1st minicomputer (1960)	Cobol language(1960)	Applications developed by users
		Lisp, AI list processing language (1960)	MIT Conference on software engineering (1961)
		1st general purpose time sharing systems (1962)	
	Local area network (1964)	Real-time scientific and technical applications for commercial users	

III.1). Unlike Babbage's machine, in Hollerith's numerical card the 'program' was read by electric sensors. Developed in 1880 at the US Bureau of Census, the Hollerith machine enjoyed a significant commercial success and in 1896 Hollerith left the Bureau of Census to set up the Tabulating Machine Co. that, after a merger in 1911, became the Tabulating Recording Co. (TRC) and, in 1924, took the name of International Business Machines (IBM).

Table 4.1 (continued)

	Advances in Hardware Technology	Advances in Software Technology	Changes in Organisation of Software
Mid1960s mid 1970s	3rd computer generation based on integrated circuits (semiconductors)	Basic language (1965)	NATO Conference on software engineering (1968)
		2nd generation time-sharing systems (1966)	Unbundling (1969)
	Microprocessor (1971)	Pascal language (1970)	Emergence and growth of an independent software industry
		C language(1973)	
		Data base management systems	'Software factories'
			'Chief Programmer Team'
		Real–time applications for commercial use	
		Diffusion of Unix operating systems	
End 1970s to present	4th computer generation based on very large-scale integrated circuits	Software applications and tools for PC	Management Information Systems (MIS)
	Personal computers workstations	Scientific and technical applications in small firms	Hardware manifacturers re-enter the software business
	RISC (reduced instructions set computing) architectures	Proliferation of new business applications	System integration
		Relational database management systems	Facility management
	PC local area networks client–server networks	Object-oriented languages	
			Groupware
	Internet	Multimedia	Outsourcing

Sources: Bohem (1981), Gotlieb (1985), Flamm (1988), Friedman (1989), Cusumano (1991).

During the 1940s and 1950s, several electronic computers were developed for scientific and military applications. In 1943 'Colossus' was developed, a computer with electronic and electromechanical components, at Bletchley Park in the UK, and in 1945 ENIAC was invented in the US. Despite its similarities with Colossus, ENIAC is considered as the first electronic digital computer (Flamm, 1988, pp. 39 and 47). Based on vacuum-tube (valves) and punched-card, ENIAC was developed for the US Army. The first stored-program computer, EDVAC, was developed in 1946 at the University of Pennsylvania by a research group that included Eckert, Mauchly and von Neumann. In 1949 the second stored-program electronic digital computer, EDSAC (Electronic Discrete Sequential Automatic Computer), was developed at Cambridge University in the UK, and was followed by MARK I (based on cathode ray tube memory and magnetic drum memory devices), developed at the University of Manchester between 1948 and 1949.[1] The first application of the magnetic core memory was WHIRLWIND at the MIT in 1951 (Friedman, 1989, p. 70). The development of these stored–program computers was characterised by the crucial role played by the universities and the defence sector (particularly in the US). For instance, the US Air Force during the 1950s supported the SAGE (semi-automatic ground enviroment) which was developed at MIT Lincoln Laboratory's for air-defence systems.

University and Defence projects also gave rise to many spin-offs. These firms were managed by scientists–entrepreneurs in an academic, informal style. Users were also mainly scientists and engineers who had a good knowledge of the computer systems and programming capabilities. Most users developed their own software programs. For instance, during the early 1950s ERA (Engineering Research Associates) sold its magnetic drum computer to the US Defence Agencies without any operating system or even a programming manual (see Dorfman, 1987, p. 48). In that period the community of software (and computers) developers was a quite homogeneous one. Although software developers were scientists and engineers belonging to different organisations with distinct aims and norms of conduct (that is, universities, government agencies and industrial research laboratories), they shared a *common set of rules of conduct, visions and beliefs*, developed a common language through continuous personal, informal contacts, and together laid the foundations for a new scientific and, more importantly, a new engineering discipline and industry. This community of computer and software developers, working in different institutions but interconnected by a network of informal linkages, played a role similar to the Scientific and Technical Societies of the Industrial Revolution, by favouring

[1] Another computer, jointly developed by MIT and IBM in 1945, was also called MARK I (Friedman, 1989, note 2, p. 97 and Flamm, 1988, p. 8). All these computers are classified as *first-generation* computers in that they use vacuum tubes (valves) as electronic switches for regulating (allowing or stopping) the transmission of electrical pulses. The *second-generation* of computers, introduced late in the 1950s, made use of discrete transistors as electronic switches, while the *third-generation* of computers, developed in the 1960s, adopted integrated circuits (that is, transistors integrated into silicon semiconductors chips). *Fourth-generation* computers, based on very large-scale integrated circuits, have spread between the 1970s and the 1980s.

the accumulation of specialised knowledge and creating many technological opportunities for new firms that entered the market in that period.

Parallel to the development of the electronic computers for scientific applications, the first generation of electronic computers for business applications followed quite different trajectories driven by the needs of a variety of business customers. Business computers like the UNIVAC I (developed by Eckert and Mauchly in 1951), were the inheritors of the electromechanical tabulating machines (for example, Hollerith's machine) and thus focused on relatively simple calculations on large numbers. Compared with scientific calculations, commercial applications did not require much accuracy. Because of this trade-off between accuracy and quantity of data elaborations, the computers of that period were divided into specific categories: machines for scientific applications and business computers.

2.3. The leading role of hardware manufacturers and users: late 1950s to early 1960

General-purpose computers for both technical and business applications were developed by the early 1960s (Friedman, 1989, p. 71). During this period, commercial users gave important inputs to the development of software, particularly operating systems and applications. The first operating system (called 'monitor') was developed at the General Motors Research Laboratories for the IBM 701 in 1955. Later, in 1959, General Motors and North American Aviation developed the SHARE operating systems for an IBM 704, which was distributed by SHARE (the IBM users group) (Flamm, 1988, Appendix, tab. A.4). During the late 1950s many original operating systems or adaptations of existing operating systems were developed by users also outside the SHARE users' group (Friedman, 1989, p. 75). These operating systems were based on the batch processing technique.[2]

Users and universities also gave financial and technical support to the development of the early programming languages. For instance, Fortran language (formula translation) was developed by John Backus from IBM in 1954 with the support of SHARE group, and Cobol (common business orientated language) was developed in 1959 under the sponsorship of the US Department of Defence (see Flamm, ibid.; and Friedman, p. 79). As mentioned before, during the 1950s, the defence agencies provided support to computer hardware and software projects such as SAGE. This programme included large-scale software development which brought about SAGE

---

[2] With the batch processing technique, the central processing unit (CPU) executes different programs in sequence by means of a batch monitor (operating system). Sets of tasks are grouped together in an input batch on tape.

special purpose time sharing operating system in 1957 (Flamm, 1988, tab. A.4).

From the early 1960s computer manufacturers began to develop systematically the operating systems for their machines. The rising complexity of the applications and the high rate of technological change made it increasingly difficult for the users to develop their operating systems. Besides the operating systems, computer manufacturers began to develop software tools which were relatively easy to use and enabled users to create their own applications.

The development of 'natural' tools for software development represents an important trajectory in software technology. During the 1950s, assembler programs were developed to simplify the programming activities. An assembler program translates instructions written in assembler language (whose syntax of mnemonic codes includes words like 'ADD' and 'SUB') by the programmer (source program) into binary code instructions readable by the machine (object program). Assembler languages are now called 'low-level' languages because they represent the first step of a process of progressive abstraction of programming activities from the machine code. Despite their great utility in terms of programming errors and time reduction, assembler languages are machine-specific like the machine code. Each new machine requires its own assembler. Moreover, assemblers are 'machine-oriented' in that their vocabulary and syntax correspond strictly to the sequence of the coded instruction. 'Higher level' languages, like Fortran, Cobol and RPG (Report Program Generator) were developed during the period under examination to overcome the limitations of assemblers. A high-level language provides programmers with a more 'natural' syntax and vocabulary that is closer to the application environment than to the machine code. Higher level languages and compilers make programming easier and faster but are less efficient in the use of the machine capacity (see Friedman, 1989, pp. 77 onwards).

The development of programs by users is responsible for locking these users into their machines because the programs were not 'portable' (did not run on other machines). Computer manufacturers thus had a strong incentive to provide users with development tools. On the other hand, the availability of tools, which were relatively easy to use, reduced the costs of in-house development of application software and delayed turning to the services of specialised software suppliers (Steinmueller, 1996, p. 23).

The development of application software was spurred by the introduction of minicomputers pioneered by DEC's (Digital Equipment Corporation) PDP–1 in 1960. This machine, the first commercial interactive computer, was followed by the PDP–8 in 1965. These machines targeted real-time scientific and technical applications for commercial users (for example, industrial automation). Their cost and performance were low compared with general-purpose computers and for this reason they were accessible to new, smaller users.[3]

The particular emphasis given to the complementarities with computer hardware technology in this discussion is justified by the fact that advances in computer technology have often anticipated and strongly affected the organisation of software innovative activities. According to some scholars, however, the costs, the capacity and the reliability of hardware affected the evolution of computers and software technology only until the mid-1960s. Since then, and until the early 1980s, software-specific constraints have emerged in the form of programmers' low productivity and the difficulties with the efficient management of complex system development. Finally, the present stage of software and computer industry evolution is dominated by user satisfaction constraints that highlight the importance of quality management, users' needs specification, and client servicing (Friedman, 1989). This approach to the historical evolution of software technology is useful because it points to the increasing complexity of software technology compared with hardware and the marked social dimension of software development shown by quality management and the interactions with users. However, major breakthroughs in hardware technology continued to influence the evolution of software activities through the 1970s and the 1980s. Moreover, this approach does not take explicitly into account other institutional and economic variables that have played a crucial role in the evolution of software activities.

2.4. The emergence of an independent industry: mid-1960 to late 1970s

The evolution of computer and software activities during this period and the following years was influenced by three major breakthroughs: the introduction of semiconductor integrated circuits between 1964 and 1965, the invention of the microprocessor by Intel in 1971 and the new marketing practice, introduced by IBM in 1969 ('unbundling'), consisting of pricing software and services separately from hardware.

The invention of integrated circuits during the 1960s started a trajectory of increasing integration of circuitry on semiconductor chips that resulted in large-scale integration circuits (LSI) and very large-scale integrated (VLSI) circuits during the 1970s. These advances have greatly affected computer performance and the organisation of information resources allowing a marked reduction in computer size and better price/performance ratios. During the period between 1960 and 1980 the number of circuits per chip doubled every

---

[3] Minicomputer distributed architecture allowed the decentralisation of computing among different computers of different sizes and pioneered networked computing.

year and the price of integrated circuits fell from about 50 thousand dollars in 1960 to one dollar in 1970 (cf. Flamm, 1988).

The organisation of computer resources has benefited from the extensive use of microprogramming. This was invented by Maurice Wilkes in 1951 at Cambridge University but was first used in business computers in 1965 in IBM's System 360. Microprogramming made it possible to store complex sets of instructions in the hardware. Its introduction was allowed by the improvements in core memory speed and its effects were boosted by the introduction of the microprocessor late in the 1970s. Many different microcodes were developed for single microprocessors to replace pre-existing specialised software programs (Dorfman, 1987, Flamm, 1988). Moreover, the technical progress in hardware has stimulated changes in software technology such as the invention of time-sharing, multiprogramming operating systems, and many software development tools.[4]

During this period, software programs became progressively complex and represented an increasing share of IT budgets. It was estimated that in the US Air Force software costs as a share of total IT costs rose from about 20 per cent in 1955 to 50 per cent in 1965, and to 70 per cent in 1970 (Bohem, 1973).

The increasing costs of software in this period are in part explained by the demand for new applications and the users' difficulty to exploit the capacity of computers (Steinmueller, 1996). Some scholars also focus on the increasing costs of software development due to some 'bottlenecks' in the organisation of this activity. Late deliveries of systems, escalating costs, and failed software projects were due probably to the lack of system developers' competencies to cope with increasing software complexity (Naur and Randall, 1969). These bottlenecks re-focused the R&D activities of hardware manufacturers towards software technology. The diffusion of high-level languages, utilities and applications generators such as on-line monitors and database management systems has mostly resulted from these research efforts. Moreover, the complexity of programs and the variety of applications have affected the take-off of an independent software industry and the development of packaged software products (Friedman, 1989, p. 100).

The establishment of an increasing number of independent software producers has also been spurred by the 'unbundling' of software sales from hardware. This practice was started by the market leader, IBM, for reasons

---

[4] Multiprogramming is an important advance in operating systems that was introduced early in the 1960s. Multiprogramming enables the computer CPU to switch from one program to another. Multiprogramming operating systems evolved in multiprocessors operating systems with the introduction of multiprocessing architectures (cf. Flamm, 1988, Tab. 4.A).

that remain debatable.[5] The separation of software sales and prices from hardware was also adopted by the market followers.[6] The unbundling had direct consequences for the suppliers of time-sharing services, such as General Electric (GE), Electronic Data System (EDS), Automatic Data Processing (ADP) and McDonnell Douglas, and producers of software packages for centralised mainframes, such as Computer Sciences Corporation. The US software and services industry was very fragmented at that time, with IBM still in a dominant position and a quite large number of smaller firms that accounted for about half this market.[7] Market fragmentation concerned the production of software for general-purpose systems and for decentralised data processing based on minicomputers.

Minicomputers were poorly equipped with software and services. During the 1970s Digital's machines were sold through networks of independent systems houses that packaged the CPU by adding peripherals and application software on the basis of OEM (original equipment manufacturing) contracts (see Dorfman, 1987). The role played by independent system houses in the development of software applications for minicomputers in this period is similar to that played by service bureau firms like McDonnell Douglas and ADP, that supplied time-sharing services and developed application software on mainframes for small firms.

Moreover, all application software developed for a single minicomputer usually targeted specific technical or scientific applications. This generated many small market niches for specialised applications on minicomputers. The variety of software packages has increased over time. According to Datapro estimates, the number of software packages for minicomputers and larger systems in the US market increased from about 5,000 in 1979 to 6,200 in 1982 while the suppliers rose from 900 to 2,000 (Gotlieb, 1985, p. 208).

---

[5] It is unclear whether IBM's unbundling announcement in 1969 aimed to prevent the negative consequences of litigation for antitrust violation started by CDC in 1968 or was the consequence of the increasing costs for software support services (see Steinmueller, 1996 for a deeper discussion of this topic).

[6] After an early period of turmoil, bringing about many start-ups, mergers and acquisitions and departures, the computer industry became an international oligopoly dominated by American manufacturers of general-purpose mainframes. By the mid-1970s, the market leader (IBM) and the followers, called 'BUNCH' (Burroughs, Univac/Sperry, NCR, Control Data Corporation and Honeywell), accounted for about 80 per cent of the world computer market (cf. Malerba, Torrisi and von Tunzelmann, 1991, pp. 96–7).

[7] The software and services market was worth about $2.5 billion in 1970 (50 per cent of annual sales of computers and peripherals). The estimated number of independent suppliers for that period varies between 1,500 and 2,800 firms with estimated average revenues of $350–700 thousand that may correspond to about 12 employees on average (Steinmueller, 1996, p. 27).

2.5. Personal computers and distributed networks: 1980s to present

The spread of personal computers over the 1980s has brought about a dramatic proliferation of software applications and independent suppliers both in the US and in Europe.

The variety of applications required by an increasingly large base of computers has reinforced the specialisation of independent software producers, created new 'windows of opportunity' and increased division of labour among software producers.

The market segmentation observed during the 1970s remained high during the 1980s with minicomputers and mainframes. But a major difference introduced by personal computers is represented by the large number of installed units. Moreover, the emergence of a market standard platform (computers and system software) for personal computers (that is, IBM PC and IBM-Microsoft's MS-DOS) in the US and Europe has created huge opportunities for economies of scale in the production of application solutions. The fast growth of packaged software firms such as Lotus (Lotus 1-2-3 spreadsheet), Microsoft (MS-DOS, Windows and Windows NT, Word and LAN Manager), Ashton-Tate (dBase) WordPerfect (WordPerfect and WordPerfect Presentations) and Novell (NetWare and UnixWare) has been driven by the 'portability' of their products on a large installed base of computers from different producers (IBM and the PC-compatible manufacturers). Portability of programs over a large installed base of personal computers gives rise to large network externalities that make convenient to users the adoption of software products that are compatible with complementary products such as computers (and operating systems) and peripherals (for example, printers).[8]

Positive externalities accelerate the market selection mechanism by orienting demand towards a few 'dominant designs'. In the case of the software industry, network externalities may have reinforced the 'comparative advantages' of specialised suppliers of packaged software over time, against hardware manufacturers and in-house development by users, generating dynamic returns to scale. To take advantage of these reinforcing mechanisms, most producers of personal computers have set up contractual linkages with co-specialised suppliers of software applications and tools as an alternative to in-house development (see Teece, 1986). A similar strategy was adopted by some manufacturers of workstations (that is, Sun Microsystems and MIPS), during the 1980s. These firms gave up their exclusive rights over their own RISC (reduced-instruction-set computing) microprocessor technology in order to spur the development of complementary products

---

[8] For an historical analysis of the role played by network externalities in the PC software industry, see Cottrell (1994).

(including software applications) by independent suppliers (Khazam and Mowery, 1996).

During the period under examination, new business applications came to the forefront of software activities; in particular, applications related to the use of information for strategic and management control functions (for example, decision-support systems and on-line database management systems). Due to the comparatively low costs of personal computers and workstations, most smaller users have added more sophisticated applications (for example, scientific and technical calculations) to their traditional management applications (for example payroll system). The diffusion of distributed computer architectures, like the client-server networks (based on personal computers or workstations), is also responsible for the diffusion of new packaged solutions (for example, advanced graphical applications) and the distribution of information processing within the organisations.[9]

The proliferation of applications and decentralised computing have given rise to new organisational problems, whose solution has concerned in-house management information systems (MIS) and, increasingly, external consultants and services suppliers. The traditional computer services changed over the 1980s as a result of the transformations described above. Many suppliers of time-sharing services (remote computing) have abandoned the market, while others have had to re-shape their business activities to offer more specialised and value-added services such as system integration and professional services for 'vertical' markets (for example, for the retailing and bank sectors). System integration has become an emerging activity along with consulting, training and facility management services (for example, General Electric's increasing involvement in valued-added services like EDI).

The diffusion of Internet during the 1990s has spurred (and has been favoured by) the development of new programming languages such as HTML (Hyper Text Mark-up Language) and Java. It is worth noting that the diffusion of Internet affects user organisations (and their MIS) and market structure. Only a few years ago some sectoral experts believed that 'customers are switching from mainframes and minicomputers ... to networks of powerful PCs' (*The Economist*, 2 December 1994, p. 71). However, the complexity of intranet–internet management is pointing out the advantages of large servers (mainframes) and the associated software: 'the Web (is) by definition a server-dominated environment. Simple economies of scale mean that the bigger the server, the cheaper the service. And there are no servers bigger than mainframes' (Tucker, 1997, p. 61). This mainframes vindication

---

[9] A client–server network is based on distributed computing power that resides in different personal computers or workstations with specialised tasks. For instance, a workstation can work as a server of a set of personal computers (clients) for advanced graphical applications.

has important implications for the software market structure, in that it pushes large users to centralise IT system management (at the level of large servers) and smaller ones to outsource services such as network management.

Moreover, the rising importance of new object-oriented software engineering tools is creating opportunities for new entry and specialisation. For instance, graphical user interfaces (GUIs) such as Microsoft's Visual Basic and Powersoft's Powerbuilder have stimulated the development of many third-party compatible components (modules of code that can be bought and combined by the developer for specific functions such as image compression or advanced numerical analysis).

3. THE EVOLUTION OF THE EUROPEAN SOFTWARE INDUSTRY

3.1. The specialisation of the European firms

The supply of software and services in Europe is quite fragmented, with over 13,000 firms specialising in a variety of small market niches (EEC, 1991). The European market for packaged software is dominated by US products. In 1991 the European firms had a 16 per cent share of the world production of packaged software, against a 41 per cent European share of world consumption. By contrast, American producers accounted for 87 per cent of the world packaged software market against a US demand as large as 40 per cent of world demand (EITO, 1993). Moreover, US firms accounted for about 63 per cent of the Western European packaged software market in 1993 (see Chapter 3, Table 3.5).

The largest European producers specialise in customised software and computer services.[10] Also most smaller firms develop software tailored for specific customers or customise US software packages. Furthermore, European firms draw most of their revenues from their domestic markets, with the majority of small firms specialising in regional markets. Except for a few cases discussed later, European software and service firms rely on their domestic markets. For instance, over 80 per cent of SD-Scicon's revenues and 96 per cent of Finsiel's revenues came from their respective national markets in 1989, while only 49 per cent of Microsoft's revenues and 52 per cent of Oracle's revenues came from the domestic market (*Datamation*, 1990).

Few European firms have developed software packages that have enjoyed commercial success on an international scale. Considering the rising share of

---

[10] For instance, the French Cap Gemini, the Italian Finsiel, the Anglo–French Sema Group and the British SD–Scicon (which was acquired by EDS of the US in 1991).

the market for packaged software compared with customised software and services, and the growing international competition in services, the future performance of the European software industry appears unclear.

More recently, a few European firms have specialised in software packages. Most of these firms specialise in market niches such as object-oriented compilers (for example, the French Business Objects and ILOG), 3-dimension development tools for videogames and scientific simulation (for example, the British Oxford Molecular and Superscape), and multimedia software applications (for example, EMME Interactive of France). Few established European producers of software packages have grown international such as SAP of Germany and Baan of the Netherlands (integrated business software programs for accounting, finance, manufacturing and other applications). (*Business Week*, 6 May 1996, pp. 34–8). In particular, the SAP story shows many similarities with US innovative firms such as Oracle or Microsoft. Founded by a group of former IBM's software engineers in 1972, it drew on a new product concept consisting in the integration of compatible standard business modules (accounting, manufacturing and other application solutions). This company combines strong R&D efforts (25 per cent of total revenues) with aggressive marketing capabilities. Moreover, it has set up a network of strategic alliances with the leading computer manufacturers and other software firms such as Oracle, Informix and Arthur Andersen. As a result, SAP has gained a leading position in the world market for client–server application software (60 per cent market share).

3.2. The evolution of the largest national systems

This section seeks to explain the specialisation and performance of the European software industry discussed previously. The main explanatory factors are the strength of the local computer hardware industry, the size of the market and the evolution of public policies. The combination of these factors is analysed in each of the four largest European countries. The next section compares Europe as a whole with the US.

Germany

During the 1930s and 1940s, Germany accumulated significant scientific competencies and technical experience in electronics, magnetism and programming languages. During the Second World War, Konrad Zuse, of the University of Berlin, developed a series of electromechanical computers for military use.

The first national R&D projects in the field of computers benefited from the works of German universities and bridging institutions such as Berlin University and the Max Plank Institut (Gottingen University). Other academic institutions involved in early scientific research were the Munich Institute of Technology, the Institute for Practical Mathematics at Darmstadt, and the Technische Hocshule at Berlin (Flamm, 1988, p. 160, note 70).

After the war, a group of German scientists involved in computer science developed distinctive competencies in software, particularly structured programming, algorithm languages (for mathematical computation), and semantic theory of programming languages (Flamm, 1988, p. 161). In 1955, Zuse founded a company specialising in computers for scientific applications. In 1964 this firm was sold to Brown Boveri, and in 1967 it was acquired by Siemens which thus became the largest German computer hardware manufacturer.

Late in the 1960s, few German firms remained in the computer market, after several abandoned this business (for example, Standard Elektrik in 1964).

In 1968 Nixdorf entered the market by specialising in small minicomputers. At that time the US minicomputer firms had not reached a significant market position in Europe, and this favoured the rapid growth of Nixdorf. In 1989, with the takeover of Nixdorf, Siemens acquired a diversified knowledge base in computers and software. Although the acquision of Nixdorf has produced serious managerial problems, Siemens-Nixdorf became the leading European producer of software. More recently, it has been overtaken by SAP, a software firm which represents an interesting case of European success in packaged software.[11] The German market for software packages is relatively concentrated compared with that of services (see Table 4.2).

The German government has begun to actively support the computer industry since the late 1960s, when the first *Informationstecknick* (data processing) Programme was launched for the period 1967/69. A second *Informationstecknick* Programme was implemented for the years 1969/75, followed by a third one (1976/79).

Unlike the French and the UK programs, Germany's programs focused on the development of scientific and technical competence at the university level. Moreover, besides the support given to Siemens, the Third *Informationstecknick* Programme opened a window of opportunity to the second national firm, Nixdorf, which has developed capabilities in software applications and services.

---

[11] In 1996 Siemens reported revenues of $1,029 million from software, while SAP reported $1,699 million (*Datamation*, 1997).

Table 4.2 Market concentration in the largest European markets (1995)

		Germany	France	UK	Italy
	Hardware	10.6	19.6	16.9	25.2
Leader	Packages	6.5	7.4	4.8	5.0
	Services	4.5	4.7	4.9	9.1
	Hardware	41.7	57.0	60.3	54.8
Top 10	Packages	22.0	20.9	16.0	15.0
	Services	13.0	18.6	31.0	20.9

Sources: EITO (1996, 1997)

During the 1980s, Germany launched a new *Informationstechnik* Programme (1984–88), which explicitly focused on software. This program draws on the *diffusion-oriented* approach of the German industrial technology policy, which aims to the accumulation of competencies and technology diffusion. A major instrument of these policies is represented by the national education system, which shows a marked involvement in applied science and technical training. Moreover, German universities play a significant role in the diffusion of knowledge by setting up links with firms, and providing consulting services to smaller firms, under the promotion of local and federal Governments.

France

In France, unlike Germany, research in the field of computer science received military support only after the Second World War. The first French electronic computer was developed in 1953 by Societé d'Electroniques et d'Automatisme (SEA) for the French Ministere des Armes. Moreover, French universities had been less involved in computer science as compared with the German and the British universities.

The French government has adopted a *mission–oriented* approach, by providing significant financial support to industrial R&D in the electronic sector since the 1950s. In 1963 about 60 per cent of R&D expenditure in the French electronics industry was financed by public programmes. A coherent public campaign in the computer sector was implemented in the second half of the 1960s with the first 'Plan Calcul' (1967–71), which aimed to support a French 'national champion' – CII (Compagnie International pour l'Informatique). This was followed by a second and a third versions of the 'Plan Calcul' (1971–75 and 1976–80) which continued to support few French national champions. In 1983 the French government launched a mission-oriented program for electronics, the 'Plan pour la Filiere Electronique' (PAFE). Software was not taken explicitly into account, but it was included in different programs for microelectronics, telecommunications, professional and military electronics, and consumer electronics. As in previous French programs, PAFE sought to favour the restructuring of the national industry and to stimulate the competitiveness of the few national champions in the electronic industry.

In spite of the early and persistent government support, the French computer producers have shown declining performance. Bull, the French national leader, entered the computer market in the late 1950s and in 1958 launched the Gamma 3 ET computer to compete with the IBM 650 mainframe. The problems of Bull in facing the technological and commercial competition of American firms are emblematic of the difficulties experienced by newcomers who introduce products that do not differ substantially from that of the market leader. In 1964 Bull was acquired by General Electric who in 1970 sold its shares to Honeywell. In 1975 Honeywell-Bull and CII merged into a single company called CII-Honeywell-Bull. In 1987 Honeywell-Bull was created as a joint venture among Group Bull (22 per cent), Honeywell (42.5 per cent) and NEC (15 per cent). In 1989, Honeywell abandoned the computer sector and Groupe Bull took control of the joint venture. It is worth noting that the French government still has the control of Groupe Bull. Although, in spite of strong public support, Bull's performance has declined over time. In the last few years the company has made several attempts at restructuring. Moreover, it has increasingly focused on software and services and has invested in small computers for UNIX applications. Bull acquired Zenith IS division from US Zenith Electronics in 1990. However, the Zenith IS division showed a negative performance until 1996. This prompted Bull to sell Zenith Division to Packard Bell of the US (*Business Week*, February 19, 1996, p. 36).

The French software firms have specialised in computer services and system integration. However, the presence of foreign firms in the domestic market is less significant than in other European countries (for example, the UK) and the largest French service suppliers have been active on the international market as compared with other European firms. For instance, Cap Gemini Sogeti, the French market leader (over \$4.3 billion revenues, of which 95 per cent were from services in 1996), has grown through international acquisitions. As a result of this strategy, in 1996 Cap Gemini drew 52 per cent of its total revenues from various European markets and 14 per cent from the US market. The concentration of the domestic market for software and services is similar to that of Germany (Table 4.2). Bull was the second largest national producer of software and services ($2.2 billion) in 1996.

The UK

The UK is a typical example of early entry in the computer industry, followed by progressive decline. The UK scientific tradition in computer science dates back to the 1930s. Alan Turing, a British outstanding mathematician, in 1936 published a paper on the application of the electronics technology to the development of abstract logic machines, which drew on the studies of the mathematician Kurt Godel.[12] During the second world war Turing worked at Bletchley Park, the headquarter of the Foreign Office's Government Code and Cypher School, on decryption of German and Japanese military communication codes. As mentioned before, these studies resulted in the creation of 'Colossus' by 1943, a computer with characteristics similar to the ENIAC computer, developed two years later in the US. In 1945 Turing received financial support from the mathematical division of the National Physical Laboratory (NPL) for the development of a stored-program electronic computer. By 1946 a pilot version of this machine, called ACE (Automatic Computer Engine) was completed. Besides the NPL project, Cambridge and Manchester universities made considerable contributions to basic and applied research in computer science. The EDSAC project, mentioned above, was directed by Wilkes at Cambridge University. Wilkes in 1951 invented the concept of microprogramming. By 1949 Manchester University developed the Mark I, the first computer that used a magnetic drum memory (Turing took part in this project). During the 1950s there were eight British companies in the market, including Marconi, GEC, EMI, ICT, Elliot Brothers, Leo Computers and Ferranti. Particularly, Leo Computers was formed by J. Lyons, who pioneered the first British commercial applications (for example, bakery production monitoring in 1951 and payroll in 1954).[13] However, after some financial and managerial problems, most firms gradually withdrew from the industry and in 1968 ICL was formed as an intended 'national champion' by merging the computer activities of the early manufacturers. In 1968 ICL accounted for 41 per cent of the installed base of computers in the UK. In 1985 ICL's share fell to 31 per cent. In particular, ICL represented 15 per cent of total shipments of mainframes against 68 per cent of IBM (Kelly, 1987). In 1990 ICL was taken over by Fujitsu.

---

[12] Turing demonstrated the impossibility to prove by a mechanical process all the possible provable assertions (Flamm, 1988, p. 33).

[13] *Financial Times* (1994b), p. XIII.

The British universities represented an important source of new firms during the 1970s and 1980s. For instance, in 1984 30 per cent of founders of new firms (in all sectors) in Cambridgeshire were formerly employed as researchers in academic institutions, including the Computer Aided Design Centre and the Computer Science Laboratory of Cambridge University (Kelly, 1987). Another source of new firms is the network of informal links and the influence of 'role models' in particular industrial districts. The 'Cambridge University Club' (later renamed Cambridge Technology Association), an informal network of local computer executives founded in 1979, is a case in point. These technical societies cultivated the 'mythology of entrepreneurship' by drawing on models of successful entrepreneurs such as Clive Sinclair (Sinclair Research), Christopher Curry and Hermann Hauser (Acorn Computers), and Alan Sugar (Amstrad) (Kelly, 1987). However, the scale of entry and the growth of new firms were poor compared with the US experience. Most new entrants have left the market, including Amstrad and Sinclair.

British computer firms suffered from the small domestic market, a lack of coordination of publicly-supported R&D projects and excessive focus on few national champions. The British Government gave financial support to the early R&D efforts in the field of computer technology. The ACE project was backed by the NPL, the Mark I project (Manchester University) by the Ministry of Defence and the Royal Society, and the EDSAC project by Cambridge University (it also received the support of Lyons catering firm).[14] It is possible that the British computer industry could have benefited from a stronger coordination (if not the merger) of these concurrent projects. But some technological competition and experimentation are expected (and probably necessary) at this stage of the industry lifecycle. However, the focus on a few national champions during the 1960s and 1970s did not favour the entry of new firms and reduced technological competition and experimentation. ICL had received public support since its inception. The British government kept a stake in ICL until 1979 (Kelly, 1987, p. 74). Moreover, the government supported ICL's R&D expenditure until 1982. Finally, ICL received the support of public procurement policies. In 1970 the House of Commons recommended 'buying from British firms wherever reasonably possible'. Early in the 1980s the UK government ended the practice of preferential treatment to UK suppliers and began an 'open tender' procurement policy (Kelly, 1987).

The main government support to software technology has arisen from the 'Small Engineering Firms Investment Scheme' (1982) and Alvey Program (1983–88), which has stimulated inter-firm collaboration, pre-competitive research, and the involvement of universities. Software was explicitly

[14] Flamm (1988), p. 140.

included in areas such as 'Intelligent Knowledge Based Systems', 'Software Engineering', and 'Man-Machine Interface'.[15] Similar to the French Programs, the Alvey Program suffered from a mission-oriented vision, which has not proved to be effective in avoiding the declining performance by UK producers of hardware (cf. Georghiou et al., 1991; Grindley, 1996). Although the Alvey Program failed to lead to significant commercial results, it has stimulated cooperation between industry and university, and has led to the accumulation of national competences and to some diffusion of structured methodologies for software development.

The weak national computer industry and the late public support to R&D in software together explain the development of a fragmented software and services industry and the strong presence of foreign firms in the domestic market. In 1989, four out of the largest ten software vendors were domestic firms (Hoskyns, Thorn-EMI Software, SD-Scicon and Logica). In addition, over the last years many large British software firms have been taken over by foreign firms – for example Istel by AT&T (US) in 1989, SD-Scicon by EDS (US) in 1991, and Hoskyns by Cap Gemini (F) in 1990. After Thorn EMI Software left the software business, only Sema Group (UK-F) and Data Sciences remained among the largest ten software and services vendors in the UK. It is interesting to note that these firms are specialised in services, a market segment relatively concentrated in the UK – the largest ten firms accounted for 31 per cent of the domestic market in 1995 (see Table 4.2). ICL (Fujitsu) was the largest producers of software and services in 1996 ($2.3 billion), followed by Sema Group ($1.4 billion).[16]

Italy

Italy shows a quite different pattern of evolution as compared with other European countries. Unlike Germany and the UK, Italy has not developed an early academic background in computer science. Recently, the links between university and industry have improved in some regions. For instance, the Politecnico of Milan and the University of Milan have recently created a consortium (Cefriel) with local firms for the IT. Moreover, the national university system has not been a significant incubator of new Schumpeterian firms. More generally, few new firms have entered the market of computers. Olivetti, the largest Italian computer manufacturer until 1996, made an early entry (1959) into the computer business with the ELEA 9003, an electronic mainframe. A major financial crisis, arising from the acquisition of the American typewriter producer Underwood in 1959, the high R&D costs of

---

[15] Previous public support to software was given by the 'Software Products Scheme' (SPS) launched in 1973 and administered by the National Computer Centre (NCC) (Kelly, 1987).
[16] Grindley (1996).

electronic computers, and a strong 'electromechanical' corporate culture forced Olivetti to enter a joint venture with General Electric in 1964 and leave the computer industry in 1968. Late in the 1970s Olivetti re-entered the computer industry, and recently has devoted substantial resources to software and services.[17] Since the divestiture of its computer division, Olivetti has focused on computer and telecommunication services.

The discontinuous commitment to the computer sector by Olivetti, the virtual absence of public support until the 1980s, and the small size of the domestic market were among the main reasons for the poor performance of the Italian computer industry. The public support for electronics in Italy started in 1979 with the first 'Programma Finalizzato per l'Elettronica' (Targeted Electronics Programme) which was managed by Istituto Mobiliare Italiano (IMI) on behalf of the Ministry of the Scientific Research. The support of computer technology started as late as the 1980s, within the 'Fondo Speciale per la Ricerca Applicata', managed by IMI, the Ministry of Industry's 'Fondo Speciale Rotativo per la Ricerca Tecnologica' and the National Research Council (CNR)'s 'Progetto Finalizzato Informatica e Sistemi Paralleli' (Targeted Information Technology and Parallel Systems Project). In 1992 the Ministry of University and Scientific and Technological Research (MURST) launched a new 'Programma Nazionale di Ricerca per l'Informatica' (National Research Programme on Information Technologies). A major weakness of the public action over the 1980s and 1990s is the poor coordination among different programmes and institutions, despite some improvement in the last few years. Moreover, the process of projects definition and administration is slow, especially if compared with the rate of change of IT. For instance, the CNR's 'Progetto Finalizzato Informatica e Sistemi Paralleli' and the MURST's 'Programma Nazionale di Ricerca per l'Informatica' required about three years to take off. Moreover, for projects supported by the CNR, the average lag between the time of the application and that of the payment is 18 months. This lag put small firms at a disadvantage compared with their larger counterparts. The problem is serious considering that small firms are numerous in the Italian software market. There are about 4,000 IT suppliers in Italy. The services market segment shows a high concentration compared with other countries. The market leader (Olivetti) accounted for over 9 per cent of the market ($1.37 billion revenues from services) in 1996 (see Table 4.2).[18] Finsiel, with $800 million revenue from services in 1996, is the second largest local firm in the Italian market (and in the European one as well). This company drew about two-thirds of its revenues from the local and central government sector in 1989. The rest of the market is controlled by many small and medium-sized firms.

[17] Among the few studies on Olivetti's history see Kicherer (1990).

[18] Olivetti was the third largest European software producer in 1996 ($881 million revenue).

3.3. Why does Europe have a different specialisation from the US?

The main factors that make the evolution of the European software industry different from that of the US are the presence of a weak local computer industry, the fragmentation of the European markets, and a late, or inconsistent, public support to software given by the national governments.[19]

US software firms have exploited the externalities arising from interactions with local hardware manufacturers and the size of their domestic market to specialise in software packages and enter the European markets, thus pre-empting the entry of local producers. As a consequence, European firms have been pushed towards customised software and services, for which local firms have a potential advantage over foreign firms. However, few European firms have exploited this advantage to grow international.

As discussed previously, some European countries started early in the 1930s and 1940s to accumulate significant scientific and technical capabilities in computers. However, they have not been able to build on this early start for reasons discussed before. The weak performance of the European computer industry has affected the innovative performance and the pattern of specialisation of the European software producers. To grasp the importance of the linkages with hardware producers at the technological frontier, it is worth recalling that during the 1980s British firms gained access to the technical specifications of new hardware products one or two years later than American software houses (Ashworth, 1985). Most probably, the US software package firms have taken advantage of geographical proximity and continuous exchanges of knowledge with hardware leading producers.

The fragmentation of the European market compared with the US depends on linguistic and cultural barriers across countries. As discussed in Chapter 3 (Table 3.2), Germany, the largest European market, is only one-sixth the size of the US market and half the size of the Japanese one. Market fragmentation has hampered the exploitation of increasing returns to scale, which are particularly important in packaged software.

The direct contribution given by the US government to software innovations is less important than that directed towards hardware technology (Flamm, 1988, pp. 25–8). However, the US government support to the software industry is significant if compared with that of the largest European countries. As discussed earlier, the US public support to R&D in computers and software dates back to the 1940s. Public support to industrial R&D has continued thereafter (for example, in the form of tax incentives to R&D investment). Also, the public procurement policy in the US has allowed the

---

[19] A detailed analysis of these variables in a comparative perspective goes beyond the goals of this work. For a comparison of US, Western Europe and Japan see respectively Steinmueller (1996), Malerba and Torrisi (1996), and Baba, Takai and Mizuta (1996).

entry of new firms and a certain degree of technological experimentation, thus affecting the early development of a US software industry and its subsequent world leadership. Moreover, the widespread use of computers in the US public administration has reinforced the effect of a large, homogeneous domestic market on the take off of an independent software industry. As Table 4.3 shows, in terms of personal computers and terminals per employee, the US public administration had still a significant lead over the largest European administrations in 1993. It worth recalling that small computers mostly use packaged software (Chapter 3, Section 3.2).

Table 4.3 Number of PCs and terminals per 100 public administration
employees, 1993

US	Japan	Germany	France	UK	Italy
174.0	12.6	10.8	18.8	24.8	16.3

Source : OECD (1997)

Moreover, the US firms benefited from early legal protection of innovation. The copyright legislation was extended to software in 1980 (Software Amendment to the US copyright Act of 1976). Finally, during the 1980s, the US antitrust was relaxed to allow R&D collaborations (see, for example, the National Cooperative Research Act approved in 1984).

In Europe, as discussed in the previous section, the public policies have mostly focused on a few large 'national champions', with little or negligible resources devoted to stimulate new start-ups and to involve users. A major drawback of most European R&D projects is that they have sought to catch up with US firms in established market segments (for example, mainframes and semiconductors), whereas emerging technologies such as software have received attention only during the 1980s. The barriers aiming to protect 'national champions' have strengthened the segmentation of the European market.

Moreover, little efforts have been explicitly devoted to the accumulation of competencies at the firm level and the cooperation between industry and university, with the partial exception of Germany and the Alvey Programme in the UK. Even the national programs launched in the 1980s, explicitly oriented to software, have largely failed to improve the competitive performance of European software firms on an international scale and have not stimulated the establishment of European firms specialising in software packages. This depends also on the late development of legal protection of software innovation in Europe. The European Commission issued a directive concerning the application of copyright to software in 1991 and many

European countries followed the EU recommendations thereafter. But significant differences still persist across European countries, as discussed in Chapter 5.

National policies explicitly directed to software technology and independent software firms during the 1980s have been activated by the European Commission Programmes (especially, Esprit and Eureka) (EEC, 1992). However, even these programmes have focused more on hardware than software technologies. For instance, Esprit (European Strategic Programme for Research and Development of Information Technology) was set up by the European Commission in 1984. Esprit aimed at giving support to European SMEs in IT and at fostering the collaboration between industry and university. This programme has been criticised because of its excessive emphasis on chips, components and computers and a weak commitment to software (Evans, 1991).

4. FIRMS' GROWTH AND RESTRUCTURING: 1984–92

4.1. A comparison between US and European firms

This section analyses internal corporate changes (new subsidiaries and other reorganisations) and external links (mergers and acquisitions, minority stakes, joint ventures and other collaborative agreements) of 38 large European and US software firms during the period between 1984 and 1992. The analysis aims to illustrate to what extent the differences between the European and the US software industries discussed previously influence the recent patterns of growth and restructuring at the firm level. The firms analysed are facing a critical stage of the software industry evolution. Many sample firms have undergone major restructuring in the last years. In particular, several European firms have been taken over by other firms – for example, SD-Scicon, Istel and Hoskyns.

The 912 operations analysed were conducted by the sample firms during the period between 1984 and 1992. Of these operations 638 are *external linkages* – joint ventures (JV), minority stake, licensing agreements, others collaborative agreements, and mergers and acquisitions (M&As). There are 274 operations which refer to *internal corporate changes* – creation and shutdown of new subsidiaries, and other internal reorganisations (for example, the merger of two divisions, jobs cuts or improvements).

The sample firms were the 18 largest European and 20 US software and services firms operating in Europe in 1989. The sample includes the largest European firms in 1990, such as Cap Gemini Sogeti, Software AG and Finsiel, from six EU countries – France, Germany, Italy, Netherlands,

Sweden and UK. The European sample firms specialise in computer services, except for SAP and Software AG of Germany which specialise in packaged software. Finally, most US firms in the sample specialise in packaged software – only five sample firms specialise in computer services (see Tables 4.4 and 4.5). The growth and restructuring operations during the period between 1984 and 1992 confirm these patterns of specialisation (Torrisi, 1998).

The data on firms' growth have been collected from the Predicasts F&S database (see references), which relies on information drawn from press sources. Predicasts provides information about the partner(s), its nationality, and a brief description of the operation. On the basis on this qualitative information, a database was set up by counting the operations according to different categories (that is, partner's country, objective, business sector and so on).

4.2. Internal and external growth

Tables 4.4 and 4.5 show the total number of external linkages and new subsidiaries activated by the sample firms during the period 1984–92. Over this period, the 18 European firms included in the sample set up on average about 1.6 external linkages per year against about 2.2 of the 20 US firms. This difference is related to the different average size of the two groups of firms – there is a positive correlation between the number of links and the firm's size (OLS coefficient = 0.45; t = 4.50). There are no significant differences across firms with different specialisation in terms of the propensity to become involved in inter–firm in terms of the propensity to become involved in inter-firm linkages.[20]

Among the firms with a propensity significantly above the average there are both service providers, like Logica and Sema-Group, and firms specialised in software packages, like Novell and Ashton-Tate.

There are significant differences between European and US firms in terms of the geographical horizon of their linkages. About 63.3 per cent of the linkages set up by European firms involved foreign partners (either other European firms or non European ones), against 31.4 per cent of the linkages devised by US firms.

This can be easily explained by the large US domestic market compared with the fragmentation of the European market.

---

20 The chi-square test shows that there is not any significant association between firm's specialisation and external linkages. Chi-square statistics were also calculated for agreements, M&As and new subsidiaries. Finally, the chi-square test indicates no association between the nationality of the firm (European or US) and the variables mentioned before.

Table 4.4 Sales and growth operations of European firms

Firm	Revenues ($ mill.)[a]	External Links	New sub[b]	Home country	Core Business
CAP–Gemini.	889.20	51	18	F	Serv.
Finsiel	628.90	15	1	I	Serv.
SD–Scicon	431.50	11	1	UK	Serv.
Sligos	400.70	24	1	F	Serv.
Sema Group	378.60	36	0	UK	Serv.
Concept	288.20	7	0	F	Serv.
Datev	285.10	1	0	DE	Serv.
Hoskyns	277.10	17	0	UK	Serv.
GSI	267.00	4	1	F	Serv.
Programmator	259.10	2	0	S	Serv.
Volmac	256.50	7	0	NE	Serv.
Logica	225.40	32	7	UK	Serv.
Telesystems	212.00	13	0	F	Serv.
Thorn EMI	209.20	2	1	UK	Serv.
SAP	183.10	6	2	DE	Soft.
CGI	166.30	11	0	F	Serv.
Istel	166.20	10	1	UK	Serv.
Software AG	154.20	11	3	DE	Soft.
Total		260	36		

Notes

a.　　1989 or 1990 revenues.
b.　　New sub are new subsidiaries.

Moreover, some large US firms like Andersen Consulting and Microsoft have probably established long-term relationships with foreign partners before the period under examination.

Furthermore, for many European software firms external linkages have represented an important strategy for reaching a 'minimum' efficient scale that is required for competing with the larger US firms. Considering the limited size of the European national markets, international linkages enable local firms to increase the size of business activities.

Table 4.6 shows the evolution of different types of external links made by the European firms over the period in examination. Agreements (joint ventures, minority stakes, licensing agreements and other agreements) represent 60 per cent of total external operations, against 40 per cent of M&As.

Table 4.5 Sales and growth operations of US firms

Firm	Revenues ($ mill.) [a]	External Links	New sub [b]	Home country	Core Business
Microsoft	1323.00	67	9	US	Soft.
Computer Associated	1310.70	35	0	US	Soft.
Oracle	1002.00	11	12	US	Soft.
Lotus	664.00	49	11	US	Soft.
D&B Software	539.00	1	0	US	Soft.
Word Perfect	452.40	4	1	US	Soft.
McDonnell Douglas	398.00	20	3	US	Serv.
Novell	388.00	67	5	US	Soft.
Policy Management	272.00	3	0	US	Serv.
American Manag,	261.90	2	2	US	Serv.
ASK Computer Syst.	249.70	4	0	US	Soft.
SAS Instute	240.00	3	1	US	Soft.
Autodesk.	237.90	12	4	US	Soft.
Ashton–Tate	230.50	17	2	US	Soft.
Pansophic	228.80	14	0	US	Soft.
Cadence	178.00	15	2	US	Soft.
Mentor Graphic	170.00	21	6	US	Soft.
Computer Sciences	160.00	3	0	US	Serv.
Sterling Software	155.00	12	0	US	Soft.
Computer Service	na	18	1	US	Soft
Total		378	59		

Notes

a.   1989 or 1990 revenues.
b.   New Sub are new subsidiaries.

Total external operations have increased over this period, showing that the sample firms increasingly rely on external sources of technological and market-specific knowledge. US firms show a similar pattern of external growth. Compared with collaborative agreements, M&As have a strong impact on the firm's organisation, which has a limited ability to manage an increasing number of different business units.

Table 4.6 compares also the evolution of external linkages with that of internal corporate changes or restructuring (new subsidiaries, sale of subsidiaries, dismantling of operations and reorganisation of activities). Restructuring occurs jointly or as a response to external growth. Firms that grow by M&A and, to a less extent, agreements have to reorganise the scale and scope of their activities and may be prompted to modify their organisational structure. However, these organisational changes show a less regular trend than agreements and M&As over the same period, for reasons that include a less accurate diffusion of information in the press.

Finally, I have compared the evolution of external growth (M&As and agreements) with internal growth (new subsidiaries), which represents an important share of total internal corporate changes or restructuring discussed before. Both US and European firms have mostly centred their growth on external linkages rather than internal growth. This is explained by the need to reach a minimum efficient scale quickly. External linkages allow firms to increase the scale of their operations (particularly M&As) and to exploit the external economies of being part of a network of collaborative agreements.

4.3. The purposes of external linkages

Inter-firm linkages are the object of many empirical studies.[21] These linkages may be used to face two types of failure in the market for knowledge: the lack of private incentives to undertake innovations and the lack of capabilities complementary to innovative skills (for example, commercialisation capabilities). Accordingly, external linkages can be classified as *research-oriented linkages*, which mainly focus on the first type of market failure, and *market-oriented* or *complementary resource-seeking linkages*, aiming to cope with the second form of market imperfection. *Research-oriented linkages* may involve rival firms (for example, consortia for the definition of common standards or joint R&D agreements) or firms specialised in different stages of a technological 'filière'.

They allow firms to share the risks and the costs associated with the production of multidisciplinary, complex knowledge, thus increasing the private incentive to invest in R&D activities.

Moreover, they allow the acquisition of new technological capabilities whose in-house development would require a longer time and higher costs.

Market-oriented linkages are usually set up by firms that operate in different stages of a technological 'filière' (for example operating systems suppliers and turn-key systems developers) or in different regional markets.

They may provide access to complementary capabilities (for example, distribution capabilities) that cannot be acquired in the market (because of complex interdependencies between these capabilites and technological or production capabilities) and cannot be accumulated in-house for various reasons, including the time required for their accumulation.

These linkages may help to reduce a specific form of market failure, that is a socially insufficient production of assets complementary to R&D capabilities.

21 See, for example, Mowery (1988), Arora and Gambardella (1990), Malerba and Torrisi (1992), Hagedoorn (1993), Zanfei (1993), and Duysters (1996).

Table 4.6 External links and corporate change

	European firms			US firms		
	Operations	%	CAGR [b]	Operations	%	CAGR [b]
External links of which:	260	100.0	10.97	378	100	34.00
M&As	103	39.6	29.68	153	40.48	13.00
Agreements [a]	157	60.3	6.26	225	59.52	43.00
Corp. Change of which:	117	100.0	−6.76	157	100.00	−1.00
New subsid.	36	30.7	−14.99	59	37.58	−2.00
Sold subsid.	10	8.5	10.40	11	7.01	0.00
Disinvest.	30	25.6	−8.29	35	22.29	0.00
Reorgan.	41	35.0	9.05	52	33.12	8.88

Notes

a.   Agreements include joint ventures, minority stakes, licensing agreements and other agreements.

b.   Percentage annual compound growth rate 1984–92. The CAGR of sales of subsidiaries by European firms and disinvestments by US firms was calculated for the period 1985–92. The growth rate of the reorganisations by US firms was calculated for the period 1985–91.

This has important implications for innovators because the commercial success of an innovation depends on the supply of specialised and co-specialised inputs (Teece, 1986; Geroski, 1992). The access to complementary assets may take the form of M&As, minority stakes, joint ventures and other agreements, reflecting the importance of different factors (including economies of scale and scope, the degree of complex interdependencies among complementary knowledge and capabilities and appropriability conditions).[22]

Table 4.7 shows the main purposes of agreements and internal re-organisations. The operations have been grouped in accordance with the classification discussed earlier: operations that involve research and development activities (RESEARCH), operations that do not involve any R&D activity (MARKET) and purely financial operations (FINANCIAL).[23]

22 As discussed in Chapter 2, the economics literature has provided other explanations for the adoption of alternative organisation of economic activities which draw on transaction costs (Williamson, 1975).

23 MARKET operations may include commercial and production activities. RESEARCH operations may include production and commercial activities.

All these operations may involve competitors or firms located in different stages of this technological 'filière'.

Over 70 per cent of external operations signed by the European firms were *market-oriented*, against about 24 per cent of *research-oriented* operations involving R&D activities. The sample firms have signed market-oriented linkages to gain access to specialised commercial assets or service expertise, and new markets. The cross marketing deal between Sema Group and Finsiel signed in 1992 is a case in point. Active licencing agreements were also classified as market-oriented operations because they aim to find new markets for the licensor's technology. Examples of research-oriented linkages are the joint development of a videotext software package for IBM mainframes by Cap Gemini and IBM in 1984 and the acquisition of 80 per cent stakes of Technologies machine Art robot manufacturer by Cap Gemini in 1987.

The share of *research-oriented* operations is higher for the US firms as compared with the European firms (34 per cent). This difference is probably due to the large number of US firms specialising in packaged software which show a comparatively high involvement in R&D activities. An insignificant share of total operations have a pure financial content (3 per cent and 1 per cent for the European and the US firms, respectively).

Overall, the difference in number between market and research operations was expected. A firm may aim to set up many external linkages with different partners to achieve economies of scale and scope in the extensive use of its knowledge and capabilities. By contrast, the number of potential research partners is limited by the distribution of scientific and technological capabilities across firms.

Moreover, a firm that looks for a research partner may want to focus on few firms endowed with the best scientific or technical capabilities available on the market.

These data indicate that through external linkages software firms aim to gain access to both general scientific or technological knowledge and to more context-specific knowledge (linked to particular markets, users and applications).

The software firms use different types of external links (from M&As to technological and co-operative agreements) along with internal investments (for example, new subsidiaries).

Different forms of coordination are adopted according to the purposes and competencies of the firms involved in the knowledge exchange and pooling. For example, Novell, a US company specialised in LAN operating systems (NetWare) in 1989 acquired another US firm with competencies in networking software, Excelan.

Table 4.7 External links and corporate change by purpose (1984–92)

	European firms							
	Research[a]		Market[b]		Financial		Total	
	%		%		%		%	
Total external links[c]	62	24	186	73	8	3	256	100
Corp.change[d]	17	14	73	61	29	25	119	100
	US firms							
	Research[a]		Market[b]		Financial		Total	
	%		%		%		%	
Total external links[c]	128	34	246	65	2	1	376	100
Corp. change[d]	16	10	114	73	25	17	155	100

Notes
a. Research includes the links with a R&D content.
b. Market includes all links without any R&D content. Joint production agreements are included.
c. Total links include M&As, joint ventures, minority stakes, licensing agreements and other agreements. Eight links cannot be classified.
d. Corporate change includes new subsidiaries, sold subsidiaries, disinvestments and reorganisations. One operation cannot be classified.

Novell's NetWare gateway to IBM's SAA network architecture is based on Excelan expertise (*Datamation*, June 15, 1994, p. 76). The acquisition in this case is justified by the relatedness of the two firms' core businesses. A second example is that of Cap Gemini, a large French firm specialised in computer services which in 1990 jointly developed with Nynex International, a telecommunication services firm, a network control system for France Telecom. The complementary capability of these firms and the fact that telecommunication services were outside Cap Gemini's main business may explain the choice of an agreement as an alternative to M&A. By contrast, Cap Gemini has resorted to M&As and minority stakes to gain access to the resources of software firms such as Volmac, Programmator, Hoskyns and Sema Group, whose activities fall within Cap Gemini's core business.

A similar share of the operations classified as internal restructuring has a MARKET content for the European and the US firms (61 per cent and 73 per cent of total internal restructuring operations, respectively), confirming the importance of commercialisation activities in this industry and the linkages between internal growth and internal restructuring. Unlike external operations, a large share of internal restructuring operations shows a financial dimension, particularly for the European firms (25 per cent of total operations against 17 per cent of the US firms) (see Table 4.6). This category of internal restructuring includes equity issues to finance firms' expansion, management acquisitions of share capital etc. For instance, in 1984 Cap Gemini announced that 37.5 per cent of its stake would be acquired by the company management. Notice that, besides the management and other company stockholders, operations with a financial object often involve external institutions. For instance, in 1987 Cap Gemini was acquired for 8 per cent of its stakes by Financiere Suez.

5. CONCLUSIONS

The organisation of software has progressively evolved from an activity carried out by hardware manufacturers and highly trained users (scientists and engineers) into an industrial design activity with a clearer division of tasks among integrated hardware and software producers, independent software and services providers, and users.

Among the variables which have influenced this evolution, there is 'unbundling' of software sales from those of computers announced by IBM in 1969 which was spurred by the US antitrust regulation. This institutional innovation created 'windows of opportunity' for new software developers and, at the same time, it shows how specific institutional conditions and policy approaches may affect the direction of change, by introducing irreversible, cumulative processes that lock organisations and countries into specific technologies and patterns of specialisation.

Other factors analysed in this chapter are the pervasiveness of software technology, the externalities arising from technological progress in hardware, and the size of the market.

The organisation of software activities and the pattern of firm specialisation are influenced by the specific characteristics of different national systems. In Europe a considerable market fragmentation, due to linguistic and cultural differences across countries, the absence of a strong local computer industry, and the late support of European governments for software technology has caused the development of an independent software industry to slow down. Moreover, these factors are responsible for the specialisation of the European firms in customised software and computer services.

To further develop the comparison between US and European software firms, I have collected data on growth and restructuring operations concerning 38 large software firms during the period 1984–92. The analysis shows that both US and European software firms underwent major restructuring during this period, through M&As, collaborative alliances and internal corporate reorganisations. This process of corporate change aimed to increase the scale of firm's operations, either directly (through new subsidiaries and M&As) or indirectly (through inter-firm agreements). The importance of external growth (M&As and agreements) compared with internal growth (new subsidiaries) can be explained by the rapid change that characterises the software industry. After a period of internal growth, led by technological innovation, most sample firms reached a point where further internal growth would have been subject to decreasing returns. External growth was an efficient alternative to internal growth because it enabled software firms to grow more rapidly by acquiring existing complementary, technological, and marketing capabilities. Thus, to exploit the opportunities for increasing returns to scale arising from a rapid market growth, software firms combined their internal resources and capabilities with external ones.

There are some differences between US and European firms which reflect country-specific and firms-specific factors. First, European firms relied more on international operations compared with their US counterparts. This depends on the limited size of their domestic markets. Second, US firms showed a larger share of research-oriented operations compared with European firms. This reflects the specialisation of US firms in software packages, whose production is more R&D-intensive compared with customised software and services.

5. Product and Process Innovation in Software Activities

1. INTRODUCTION

Innovation in software and services accounts for an increasing share of R&D activities carried out in the service sector overall and in the manufacturing sector. For instance, a survey of R&D activities in Canada shows that in 1993 software accounted for 24 per cent of total R&D expenditure in manufacturing and 56 per cent in services. Another survey conducted in the Netherlands indicates that in 1994 about 23 per cent of total business enterprise R&D expenditure (OECD, 1997) was accounted for by software R&D. Moreover, within the IT and communications (ITC) sectors, software firms play an important role as R&D performers. In 1995 five of the world's ten largest ITC firms by R&D intensity were software producers (only one, SAP, was European) (OECD, 1997).

Studies of the economics and management of innovation have mostly concentrated the organisation of R&D in manufacturing. With few exceptions, there is little evidence of innovation in services, particularly in software and computer services. This chapter tries to fill this gap in the literature in part by providing a picture of innovative activities in software firms located in Europe.

My analysis of this issue was stimulated by the following questions. What does R&D mean in software activities? How can we distinguish product from process innovation in this industry? What forces drive these innovations? How has software production evolved over time in comparison with production in manufacturing?

The OECD's 'Frascati Manual' for the measurement of technological innovation included R&D in software in 1993 for the first time. Software development activities are classified as R&D activities if they depend on the development of a scientific and/or technological advance, and aim to 'resolve scientific and/or technological uncertainty on a systematic basis' (OECD, 1997, p. 62). Other software activities, aiming to improve programs already in the public domain (for example, customisation of software packages for local needs), to introduce new functionality to existing products, and to prepare user documentation, are not qualified as R&D. However, innovation is a multi-dimensional activity which includes R&D and other activities, including those described above, which are needed to bring an invention to the market. As noticed by Freeman, 'research and inventive activities are only a small proportion of this very wide complex of 'knowledge industries' (Freeman, 1982, p. 5).

This chapter focuses on innovation in general, rather than on pure R&D activities. It distinguishes radical or major product (services) innovations from minor or incremental product innovations. Moreover, I analyse process innovations in software, that is, the use of new methods and techniques to develop existing or new software products and services. In the past, this distinction was difficult because most software producers used craft 'ad hoc' techniques to develop new products. Furthermore, the interaction between production and use of software (and especially services) blurs the distinction between product and process innovation in software (what is a new product for the supplier is a new process for the user). However, there has been an increasing concern about the software development techniques and project management in the last decades. Particularly since the 1980s, the increasing number of software users, spurred by the diffusion of personal computers and networks, and the rising complexity of applications required, have highlighted the need to improve the organisation of software development activities, including quality and time management. Some scholars and business practitioners have pointed to the existence of a 'software crisis' or a 'software bottleneck' (in terms of poor productivity of programmers and high development costs) as a consequence of the difficulty faced by software producers to meet the demand for new complex applications and to cope with the high rate of change of hardware technology (Bohem, 1981; Moad, 1990; Garber, 1993). 'Software crisis' has stimulated a debate in the community of software engineers and spurred the emergence of a distinct submarket for development techniques (programming languages, compilers, CASE tools, integrated development environments and so on).

The distinction between product and process innovation in software, together with the rising focus on process technology, is not unexpected if one recalls the predictions in the product life cycle model. With the maturation of technologies and industries, the focus on innovation shifts 'naturally' from radical product innovations to process innovations and standardisation of production. The production process evolves from a fluid and flexible job shop activity in the early, exploratory stage of the industry life cycle into an integrated and linear one in the mature stage (Utterback and Abernathy, 1975). This model seems to fit the evolution of the automobile industry and other ones such as typewriters, automobile tyres, televisions, and penicillin. However, there are other industries, such as petrochemicals, zippers, X-ray, and ATM (automatic teller machines), whose evolution does not conform to the product life cycle model (Klepper, 1997). Moreover, criticisms have been directed to this model by scholars who have studied innovations in the service sector (cf. Barras, 1986). Although this work does not aim to test the validity of this theory, it is worth noting that the historical evolution of the software industry brings mixed evidence on this issue. Software development activities have been characterised by continuous product improvements since the early development of electronic computers in the 1950s and 1960s. Some major product innovations have been introduced in these years as well as in the later stages of the industry life cycle. For instance, in the 1980s personal computers spurred significant innovations in operating systems (for example, Mac OS, MS-DOS and Windows) and application software (VisiCalc, Lotus 1-2-3 and Dbase). In the 1990s there has been another wave of new software products, including network operating systems (Netware and Windows NT) and Internet browsers (for example, Netscape and Explorer). Thus the distribution of product innovations over time does not conform to that predicted by the life cycle model. Moreover, in the software industry there are several product submarkets. In some market segments a 'dominant design' has emerged (for example, personal computer and mainframe operating systems), as predicted by the product life cycle model. In other segments, however, several market standards have co-evolved over time (for example, programming languages and operating systems for minicomputers and RISC workstations).

Finally, 'exogenous' shocks, such as advances of hardware technology and 'unbundling' of software sales by hardware manufacturers, have given rise to both new software products, for example, graphical user interfaces and database management systems, and process innovations, for example, new development tools and programming languages. Thus process innovations and product innovations have co-evolved rather than evolved one after another.

Process innovations in software have been characterised by many attempts at applying engineering principles experienced in manufacturing industries to the development of new programming tools (Naur and Randall, 1969, Bohem, 1981). Since the late 1960s and the 1970s, some large computer and software producers in the US and Japan have established the first 'software factories', as an application of engineering principles to software development. The Japanese experience with software factories, like similar experience in other manufacturing sectors, is an example of process innovations co-evolving with incremental product innovations. Japanese integrated hardware and software producers, like Fujitsu, Toshiba, NEC and

Hitachi, pursued 'strategic management and integration' of software development as a way to achieve economies of scope, and to increase productivity and flexibility. The Japanese software factories were set up to produce large, unique or nominally differentiated programs for large customers, rather than new mass-market packages (Cusumano, 1991).[1] This also contrasts with the product life cycle model, which predicts that process innovations are associated with standard product design and large scale production.

However, except for a few large 'software factories', the spreading of rigorous software engineering and management techniques in the US and Europe has been quite slow until recently. This chapter analyses the causes of the difficult evolution of the software industry from a job shop, craft activity into an engineering discipline. Also, the pattern of product innovations is compared to the characteristics of process innovations. Finally, the chapter analyses the differences among firms of different size and specialisation in innovative activities.

The structure of the chapter is as follow. Section 2 illustrates the data and research methodology. Section 3 discusses the characteristics of product innovations, their determinants and the instruments for the protection of innovation. Section 4 focuses on process innovations in software and discusses some implications for the division of labour across firms. Section 5 closes the chapter.

2. DESCRIPTION OF DATA AND RESEARCH METHODOLOGY

Only a few data on the organisation of innovation in the European computer software and services industry are publicly available. Even though some case-studies on development and process innovation for single software products were published in the past, there are no surveys of innovative activities of European software firms that take into account the main characteristics of innovative activities. Moreover, the specific characteristics of software technology, such as its immateriality and the interactions between production and consumption, make the use of R&D and patents data not fully reliable as indicators of innovative activities. Moreover, data on copyright are difficult to use because in Europe the copyright legislation has been extended to software only recently.

The author conducted a survey in 1990, by collecting qualitative data on

---

1 In 1990 customised software accounted for about 84 per cent of the total software market in Japan (Baba, Takai and Mizuta, 1994).

innovative activities in computer software and services producers located in Europe. The survey includes questions on the types of product and process innovations undertaken, the instruments for the protection of innovation, the sources of technological change, the obstacles to the adoption of innovations, and the kind of skills utilised in the innovative activities.

Data were gathered through direct interviews with project managers (also called 'project leaders' or 'chief programmers') of 51 firms located in Italy, the UK, France, and Germany on the basis of a semi–structured questionnaire.[2]

The geographical coverage of European countries is skewed in favour of Italy and the UK. Twenty five firms were Italian and 18 were British; three were French and one was German. Among the remaining firms one was Japanese and three were from the US.

The sample firms were classified according to the following taxonomy:

a) Integrated hardware and software producers (firms producing both computer systems and software) (HW in the following tables). The software departments of eight firms were included in this class.

b) Independent software producers (SW). These are firms specialised in computer products (packages). There are 24 in this category of firms. These firms include two independent producers of system software (operating systems and utilities) and five firms specialising in development tools, including CASE (computer-aided software engineering tools), IPSE (integrated project-support environments) tools and artificial intelligence tools specialised suppliers tools (for example, expert systems tools like Knowledge-Base Tools).

c) Suppliers of professional services, customised software and system integration services. There are 19 of these firms in the survey.

Although users were not directly interviewed, some firms in this survey have spun-off from users (either in the bank and financial sector or the manufacturing sector).

The sample includes the largest European software producers (for example Cap Gemini, Finsiel, Sema Group, SD-Scicon, Logica, Concept and Software AG) and hardware manufacturers (Olivetti, Bull, ICL-STC) in 1989.[3] The American IBM, Lotus and Andersen Consulting and the Japanese Hitachi were also included in the sample because of their significant software activity in Europe. The firm distribution by size is illustrated in Table 5.1.

---

2 Some preliminary interviews were conducted by two researchers, while the bulk of the firms were interviewed by a single interviewer.
3 In the 1990s some of these firms have been subject to major corporate restructuring. Some have been acquired by other firms (for example, SD–Scicon, see Chapter 4).

Table 5.1 Surveyed firms by size

Classes of revenue	Revenue ($m 1989)	
	Firms	%
Up to 1 million	5	9.80
Above 1 to 10 millions	6	11.80
Above 10 and up to 50	19	37.30
Above 50 and up to 1000	13	25.50
Above 1000 millions	8	15.70
Total	51	100.00

Classes of employees	Number of employeers	
	Firms	%
Under 20	4	7.80
20 and under 99	4	7.80
100 and under 199	8	15.70
200 and under 499	14	27.45
500 and over	13	25.50
n.a.	8	15.70
Total	51	100.00

Source: annual reports and inteviews

The survey did not aim to cover either all the market segments or the most innovative ones (for example the defence-oriented aerospace industry). On the contrary, the purpose of the survey was to give a qualitative picture of the organisation of innovative activities in firms that represent the bulk of computer software and services in Europe. As mentioned above, the sample includes the largest European software houses and system integrators, some of which have carried out projects for the defense and space sectors (for example, Ferranti, Logica, Sema Group and SD-Scicon). However, a larger sample of firms that include a wider range of software suppliers should not significantly affect the main findings of this research analysis.

The structure of the questionnaire is illustrated in Appendix A. In most cases, interviewees were asked to give a score from 1 (= not important) to five (= very important) to variables that characterise the technological activities of their firms. In other cases they were asked to choose between two possible responses (yes/no). Finally, some questions were open to discussion.

The presentation of the research results in the following sections is based on mean scores. Modal scores and other statistics were also calculated to study the distribution of responses. Non parametric statistics, such as chi-square, were also calculated to test the independence of responses between integrated hardware-software firms and specialised software firms, between different size classes and between other samples of firms. The chi-square statistic and the p-values or significance level of the null hypothesis are presented in the tables.[4] The association among variables has been analysed by ordered logit regressions.

In 1997 the author conducted follow-up interviews with ten firms included in the 1990's sample. The new survey relies on the same questionnarie used in 1990, except for a few new questions regarding issues emerging recently in the specialised literature, such as the use of 'groupware' (or team development software) and Internet in software development activities. The main picture of innovative activities provided by the 1990's survey remains quite unchanged. Some differences emerged are discussed in the following pages. However, the differences in mean scores between 1990 and 1997 overall are not statistically significant.[5]

The author has also worked on an extension and repetition of the 1990's survey. This extension was carried out during the period between 1992 and 1993 within the research project 'Research and Technology Management in Enterprises: Issues for Community Policy', Monitor-SAST 8 (EC DGXII). Project managers of 65 firms in nine countries (Germany, France, UK, Italy, Netherlands, Spain, Belgium, Portugal, and Greece) were interviewed.[6] The overall similarity of results between the two surveys makes us comfortable about the validity of results discussed in this work, which is entirely based on the 1990 and 1997 surveys.

4. Nonparametric tests do not require any restrictive assumption concerning the population (for example, normal distribution or known standard deviation). The chi-square test of independence is a nonparametric test widely used with ordinal-level data. The small size of the sample has often required the correction of chi-square values by Yate's correction for continuity.

5 The chi-square test was calculated to compare the mean scores of ten firms in 1990 and 1997. Appendix B shows the mean scores of these firms in the two years.

6 A CEC report that summarises the main results of the 1993 survey is available (cf. Malerba and Torrisi, 1993).

3. NATURE AND DETERMINANTS OF PRODUCT INNOVATIONS

3.1. The research hypotheses

Hypothesis 1. There are industry-specific factors that make incremental product innovations particularly important in software innovative activities.

Scholars of industrial innovation agree that technological change is characterised by long periods of 'slow history' or 'normal' advances, during which inventions tend to accumulate incrementally along quite predictable 'trajectories' within the frontier set by 'technological' or 'techno-economic' paradigms (Nelson and Winter, 1982; Dosi, 1982; Freeman and Perez, 1988). Empirical evidence gives substantial support to this idea, as reported by several industrial studies. In summarising the results of some of these studies, Utterback has noted that 'many innovations of great commercial significance are of relatively low-cost, incremental type, the result largely of continuous development efforts' (Utterback, 1974, p. 30). Moreover, Pavitt has estimated that 'about three-quarters of all expenditures on industrial R&D is on "D", and an equivalent sum is spent on testing and manufacturing start up' (Pavitt, 1984, p. 348). These activities are by definition incremental in nature.

There are specific factors that concur in determining a pattern of incremental product innovation in the software industry. First, the market for software products is very fragmented, except for mass software packages such as operating systems and word processors, where major product innovations have emerged over time. This fragmentation is particularly strong in the European market because of linguistic, cultural, legal and institutional differences across countries as compared with the American market. This could explain why most major innovations, particularly software packages, were developed for this market. As discussed in Chapter 4, the large and homogeneous domestic market has enabled the US producers to spread the high costs of product R&D over a large client base, thus giving rise to increasing returns to scale. Other factors, like 'user sophistication' and geographical proximity to leading hardware manufacturers, are also important in explaining the US performance in radical innovations.

Second, the software industry is a labour-intensive activity and technical progress is mainly embodied in the experience and skills of system engineers and programmers. Thus, the rate of technological change is constrained by the time required for system engineers and programmers to learn new methods and techniques. Also, the learning process is slowed down by bounded rationality and idiosyncrasy.

Third, a significant part of the output of this industry consists of professional services and complex systems. These activities are typically customer-oriented, and imply complex interactions between users and producers. Recent studies in sectors such as flight simulation systems have shown that continuous technological change is explained by product complexity and the need to adapt continuously to users' requirements (Miller et al., 1993). As a matter of fact, few single services can be classified as major innovations. For instance, facility management was a significant service innovation when it was first introduced in the 1970s, and it has also changed through years. More recently, a significant share of facility management services is accounted for by intranet and internet management, such as electronic mail and electronic document interchange (see Chapter 4). However, the fundamental idea underlying facility management services has not changed significantly over time. More importantly, this idea has become widespread and no firm can claim any right over it.[7] As a consequence, it is difficult to distinguish the fundamental idea (major innovation) underlying a new service from the array of incremental subsequent developments of the same idea.

Hypothesis 2. Market opportunities and technological opportunities have different effects on major and minor product innovations.

There are several economic, technological and institutional forces driving product innovations, a detailed analysis of which goes beyond the scope of this work. For our purposes it is enough to recall that empirical studies on various sectors do not lead to any strong conclusive evidence on this issue (see Kamien and Schwartz, 1982; Cohen and Levin, 1989). From an historical and theoretical point of view, Rosenberg (1982) and Kline and Rosenberg (1986) have shown that technological and market opportunities (or imperatives) converge in affecting the direction and the timing of innovation. More recently, further empirical evidence on the role of technological opportunities has been produced by several studies. For instance, the Yale University's survey on innovation in 130 US manufacturing industries sought to measure different types of technological opportunities (both endogenous and exogenous to each industry) (cf. Levin et al., 1987). Using a similar methodology, this study aims to show how different perceived opportunities or imperatives have different effects on different types of product innovations. Another way of putting it is to ask whether technical opportunities and market opportunities play a different role in major and in minor innovations. As market and technological opportunities cannot be observed directly, I used as proxies two determinants of product

---

7 This shows that the difficulty to define product innovation in services depends, to a large extent, on the intrinsic difficulty to protect innovation.

innovations. The opportunity (need) to adapt to changes in hardware technology is a fairly good proxy of technological opportunities in this industry while the opportunity to enter a new market is almost by definition a proxy of market opportunities.[8]

Advances in hardware technology (electronic components and computer systems) have been so rapid compared with software that their potentialities are probably far to be fully exploited. However, the trajectories of change of hardware technology are quite predictable.

Thus software firms can anticipate the technological opportunities arising from hardware and adapt their products incrementally. Nowadays, a major source of radical change for software firms is the convergence of telecommunications, computers and consumer electronics.

However, the most critical aspect of this process of convergence is associated to market differences and software, rather than hardware technology (technological opportunities). Technological convergence is a process which started early in the 1980s with digitalisation of telephone networks, the development of computer-based communication and, more recently, the development of client–server computer architectures. The convergence of markets is a recent process, constrained by differences across users and distribution channels (Gambardella and Torrisi, 1998). The emergence of 'multimedia' markets depends mostly on the convergence of distribution channels and technological change of software. As a matter of fact, many recent Internet-based multimedia services rely on the combination of traditional telephone networks and client–server computer architectures.

The developers of Internet-based software and services are thus exploiting technological opportunities of hardware technologies that have remained partly unexploited for a quite long time.

Many product innovations in software arise from the flexibility or adaptability of software technology to differentiated, new users' needs. Thus, it is possible that new market opportunities stimulate the introduction of major product innovations (new products for a new type of demand). Most likely, new market opportunities will be perceived as an important source of major product innovations for software firms also in the future, because the convergence of many new markets will increase the possibility of experimentation and combination of different technologies to meet new users' needs.

Hypothesis 3. The declining uncertainty surrounding legal protection of software innovation and the diffusion of software packages spur software

8 To enter a new market, a firm may use established products/services or modifications of products already in existence (which correspond to my definition of minor innovations) as an alternative to new products for a new type of demand (radical product innovations).

firms to rely on copyright.

A specific factor that can influence product innovation is the appropriability of innovation, that is the conditions affecting the probability that an innovator can reap the potential benefits from its own innovation. The economic literature relates the appropriability regimes to the nature of public good of the innovative output (Arrow, 1962a). The empirical analysis has also indicated the importance of alternative means of appropriability. In particular, Levin et al. (1987) have highlighted the importance of dynamic factors in the appropriation of innovation, such as lead time (first-mover advantages) and continuous innovation, secrecy, and control of complementary capabilities (for example, marketing). The effectiveness of dynamic apppropriability relies on the Schumpeterian assumption that innovators by doing R&D learn how to exploit their own innovations better than imitators (incomplete R&D externalities). Dynamic appropriability is particularly important in technologies for which legal protection is difficult.

Because of software immateriality, it is difficult to disentangle innovative and protectable expressions of original ideas (for example a sequence of 'icons' specific to a graphical user interface) from unprotectable ideas (for example, the underlying lines of code and algorithms, more properly treated as literary works or industrial art). Copyright (protection of creative expressions) is largely preferred to the patent system (protection of novel processes and products) in software. A survey sponsored by the Massachussetts Software Institute in 1989 showed that about 75 per cent of respondents relied on trade secret law, only 25 per cent relied on copyright, and a minority used patents (8 per cent) (National Reserch Council, 1991). However, the use of copyright in software is relatively new, especially in Europe. This system was introduced after the US Copyright Act of 1976 and the Software Amendment of 1980. Europe has lagged behind in the extension of copyright to software. The European Commission issued a directive concerning the application of copyright to software in 1991 and many European countries have assimilated the EU recommendations thereafter. For instance, in Italy a law for software was approved in 1992. But significant differences still persist across European countries. For example, France grants 25 years' protection for copyright against 50 years' protection for most countries that have subscribed to the Berne Convention for the Protection of Literal and Artistic Property in 1988.

The uncertainty surrounding legal protection in this industry in the 1980s and, to a lesser extent, in the 1990s, has affected even large firms like IBM, which, in general, possess the capability to enforce legal protection. By the mid-1980s, IBM adopted a standard practice of delivering software products without a source code. According to Peter Schneider of IBM, this practice aimed to create a 'safety net – namely, going to object code only and more restrictive contract terms and conditions', and was justified as a 'reaction to become more secretive because of the uncertainty of the legal system' (National Research Council, 1991, p. 75).

My analysis aims to evaluate the importance of legal protection in European software firms as compared with other instruments of protection such as lead time and continuous product improvements. The increasing diffusion of software packages and the decreasing uncertainty of legal protection should spur software firms to use copyright as an instrument for the protection of innovation along with other instruments.

Hypothesis 4. Firm size and firm specialisation influence the patterns of product innovation

Many attempts at testing the Schumpeterian hypothesis of a positive relationship between firm size (or market power) and innovation indicate that there are marked differences across sectors and technological regimes (Kamien and Schwartz, 1982; Cohen and Levin, 1989; Cohen, 1995). More recently, Cohen and Klepper (1992) have argued that large firms have greater incentives to engage in R&D activities for which they have 'appropriability advantages' *vis-à-vis* small firms. These advantages are strong when knowledge is less tradeable, in 'disembodied forms', as in the case of process innovations and software innovations. Under these conditions, large firms' comparative advantage relies on the possibility to spread the costs of R&D over their own revenues. Cohen and Klepper provide a novel explanation of the fact that the average productivity of R&D, measured by the number of patents or innovations per dollar of R&D expenditures, is lower for larger firms (Mansfield, 1968; Pavitt et al., 1987). In contrast with the previous literature, Cohen and Klepper consider this stylised fact, together with the observed positive correlation between firm size and R&D efforts, as an indicator of private and social advantages of large firms in R&D activities. They argue that large firms spend more in R&D compared with smaller firms because the greater expected returns from a given level of R&D (which are conditioned by their ex ante output) offset the effects of the diminishing returns to R&D. This indicates that they have a comparative advantage in performing R&D activities rather than a disadvantage (Cohen and Klepper, 1992, pp. 793–4).

As software innovations are generally difficult to protect, large firms should have greater incentives to engage in product innovations, compared with smaller firms. However, the incentives arising from knowledge tacitness and weak appropriability in this case may be counterbalanced by knowledge disadvantages and inefficiencies in the management of innovation. The variety of applications and product submarkets in this industry may give small firms a comparative advantage arising from specialisation, speed of response to users' needs and flexible division of labour (Mansfield, 1968; Rothwell, 1983). Also, large firms may have comparative advantages in the commercialisation of innovations that should lead them to adopt a 'wait-and-see' or 'fast follower' strategy.

Moreover, the possession of internal financial resources enables large firms to acquire minority stakes in innovative startups or engage corporate venture capital with the objective of monitoring technological areas outside their own competencies.[9] The incentives for large firms (including integrated hardware–software firms) to get involved in radical innovations depend on the interaction between appropriability advantages and flexibility disadvantages.

The differences between large and small firms with respect to the use of different appropriability mechanisms are likely to be more marked compared with the incentives to innovate. Large firms usually possess a greater ability to enforce legal protection. Thus, despite the uncertainty of legal protection, large firms are expected to have a relatively larger propensity to use copyright.

3.2. The empirical results

Before going to the main empirical results, some clarifications are useful.

The meaning of 'product' innovation varies across the firms surveyed. In the case of firms belonging to the services group, the scores are given for service innovations, while the other firms responded for product innovations (application solutions, tools and so on). Moreover, the distinction between major and incremental product innovations proposed in this work draws on the classification provided by OECD (1992). According to OECD ('Oslo Manual'), major product innovations include both products embodying radically new technologies and products which rely on the combination of existing technologies for new uses. Incremental product innovations include significant improvements of existing products – except for minor design or presentation changes which are classified as product differentiation. More recently, Eurostat (1995) has broadened the definition of product (service) innovation in the service sector, accounting for the difficulty of separating minor product innovations from product differentiation in this sector.[10]

---

9 The stake in a new firm on the technological frontier represents an option to purchase. Depending on the market evolution of the asset, the holder will or will not take up the option.
10 An Italian pilot survey in the service sector suggests to include technology in the definition of innovation or to link innovation to 'a substantial investment in knowledge, or activities aimed at increasing the technological capabilities of firms' (Evangelista and Sirilli, 1995, p. 212).

Interviewees were asked to give a score from 1 (= not relevant) to 5 (= very relevant) to their latest product innovations classified according to the categories reported in Table 5.2. The distinction among these types of innovations was checked by examples of software products that, in the opinion of the respondent, belong to each category. A fairly strong convergence of opinion resulted with regard to most product innovations.

Table 5.2 Variables description

Characteristic of product/service innovation	
NEWPROD	New product for a new type of demand
NEWFEAT	New feature for products already in existence
ENHANCE	Enhancement of existing features
STAND	Adaptation to new platforms and new standards
Determinants of product/service innovation	
NEWMARK	Opportunity to enter a new market
ADAPTA	Adaptation to progress of hardware technology
QUALIT	Need to improve quality and reliability of products
DIFFER	Need to differentiate current products
Instruments for the protection of innovation	
LEGAL	Legal protection (copyright, patents etc.)
SECRET	Industrial secret
LEAD	Get to market first with an innovation
IMPROV	Continuous improvements
COOPAC	Cooperation with or acquisition of firms
PERSON	Presence or hiring of specialized personnel
SALES	1989 revenues
DHW	Dummy for hardware firms

Importance of incremental product innovations

The survey shows that minor innovations, improvements of existing features (feature proliferation) and continuous adaptation to new hardware/software standards represent important types of product innovations as compared with radical innovations for the sample firms overall (both integrated and specialised software firms).

Table 5.3 shows the means of scores for each class of firms. It seems to indicate that the differences across integrated hardware–software producers (HW) and specialised producers (SW) with respect to the strategy of product innovation are not statistically significant.

The follow-up interviews conducted in 1997 confirmed the importance of minor process innovations as compared with major product innovations. However, the latter have become more important compared to 1990. As illustrated in Appendix B, the mean scores of major innovations in 1997 is 3.4 (SD = 1.1).

Table 5.3 Characteristics of product/service innovation

	NEWPROD	NEWFEAT	ENHANCE	STAND
Total[a]	2.98	3.82	3.35	3.63
Std. Dvt.	1.26	0.99	1.11	1.18
HW[b]	2.71	3.71	3.57	4.29
SW[c]	3.02	3.83	3.30	3.51
Chi–square	0.08	0.01	0.00	0.04
p–value	0.76	0.39	1.00	0.83

Notes
a.   Means of scores from 1 = not relevant to 5 = very relevant.
b.   HW = firms which manufacture hardware and software systems.
c.   SW = firms specialised in software and services.

As discussed previously, these differences are not statistically significant. However, they probably indicate recent economic changes. First, the European market for software and services has become more globalised over the 1990s. As an indicator of this trend, one should consider that between 1982 and 1993 the number of employees in majority-owned European affiliates of US computer services firms increased from 7,000 to 54,200 (OECD, 1997, Table 4.1, p. 81).

This growth has raised the competition among software producers and spurred innovation in this industry. Second, the diffusion of client–server computer architectures and, more recently, the boasting of Internet's users have stimulated many new software products and services.

Differences between market and technological opportunities

The analysis of the determinants of product innovations aims to understand the problems that innovative activity is required to solve, and gives an indirect measure of the firms' incentives (or the perceived imperatives) to undertake product innovations.

As in the case of the characteristics of innovations, firms' managers were asked to give a score from 1 to 5 to some general determinants of product innovation.

Table 5.4 shows that integrated (HW) and specialised (SW) firms converge in terms of the importance assigned to product differentiation (DIFFER) and the need to improve product quality (QUALIT).

The follow-up interviews conducted in 1997 confirmed the relative importance of these determinants of product innovations.

Table 5.4 Determinants of product/service innovations

	NEWMARK	ADAPTA	QUALIT	DIFFER
Total[a]	3.15	3.36	3.75	3.62
Std. Dvt.	1.20	1.21	1.09	1.09
HW[b]	3.14	4.71	3.57	3.38
SW[c]	3.15	3.13	3.78	3.65
Chi–square	0.00	2.01	0.00	0.13
p–value	0.97	0.15	1.00	0.71

Notes
a.   Means of scores from 1 = not relevant to 5 = very relevant.
b.   HW = firms which manufacture hardware and software systems.
c.   SW = firms specialised in software and services.

They also show that market opportunities increase their importance (mean = 3.8, SD = 1.2). The latter may reflect the recent economic changes of the software industry illustrated above.

The second step of the analysis aims to see whether there are significant differences between determinants in their effects on different types of product innovations. Each type of product innovation (NEWPROD, NEWFEAT, ENHANCE, and STAND) was correlated with all determinants of product innovations (NEWMARK, ADAPTA, QUALIT and DIFFER) to control for multicollinearity among the five determinants of product innovations and possible association among different types of product innovation. The correlation matrix in showed in Appendix C, Table C.1.

Data used for this analysis are multivariate ordinal observations rating along a five-point semantic scale. This justifies the use of ordered logit models (Maddala, 1983; Agresti, 1990; Greene, 1997).

Appendix D discusses some characteristics of these models and the interpretation of estimated coefficients.

For the purposes of our analysis, the following ordered logit equations were estimated independently

$$\text{Radical} = f(\text{mkt, tech, z}) \qquad (5.1)$$
$$\text{Minor} = g(\text{mkt, tech, z}) \qquad (5.2)$$

where Radical and Minor are respectively radical product innovations (NEWPROD) and incremental product innovations (NEWFEAT or ENHANCE), mkt are new market opportunities (NEWMARK), tech are technological opportunities (ADAPTA), and z is a vector which includes firm size (SALES) and a dummy variable DHW. The latter accounts for the differences between integrated hardware–software firms and specialised software firms.

The results of the ordered logit regressions are reported in Tables 5.5 and 5.6. This analysis shows the following results.

Table 5.5 Ordered logit estimates for major product innovations (NEWPROD)

Variables	Estimates		
CONSTANT	−0.453	−0.407	−0.528
	(−0.513)[a]	(−0.472)	(−0.581)
NEWMARK	1.023	1.026	1.002
	(4.289)	(4.302)	(4.216)
ADAPTA	−0.400	−0.440	−0.374
	(−1.980)	(−1.958)	(−1.937)
DHW	–	0.421	–
		(0.587)	
SALES	–	–	0.003
			(0.646)
Log L	−62.871	−62.697	−62.529
Corr (π, π^*)	0.683	0.682	0.675
	(0.000)	(0.000)	(0.000)
Observations	48	48	48

Notes

a. Asymptotic *t*-values are in parentheses.

As expected, new market opportunities represent the major force driving major innovations in the sample examined, also when controlling for firm size and firm productive profile. Technological opportunities show a negative effect on major innovations (see Table 5.5). By contrast, new market opportunities show a negative effect on minor innovations while technological opportunities have a positive effect on the dependent variable (see Table 5.6).[11] Firms size and firm specialisation do not have any significant effect on the dependent variable.[12] These results confirm the hypothesis that the technological trajectories of hardware are perceived by software producers as quite predictable and thus represent a stimulus to

Table 5.6 Ordered logit estimates for minor product innovations (ENHANCE)

Variables	Estimates		
CONSTANT	2.847	2.834	2.808
	(2.899)[a]	(2.883)	(2.839)
NEWMARK	−0.553	−0.552	−0.562
	(−2.719)	(−2.715)	(−2.726)
ADAPTA	0.366	0.381	0.381
	(1.908)	(1.913)	(1.916)
DHW	−	−0.204	−
		(−0.290)	
SALES	−	−	0.000
			(0.294)
Log L	−65.998	−65.956	−65.956
Corr (π, π^*)	0.602	0.601	0.665
	(0.000)	(0.000)	(0.000)
Observations	48	48	48

Notes
a.   Asymptotic *t*-values are in parentheses.

introduce continuous changes in software products, rather than major product innovations.

On the other hand, new market opportunities disclose new avenues to develop products for new types of demands. This analysis helps to qualify rather precisely the different roles played by perceived technological and market opportunities on different types of product innovations. Both technological and market opportunities are important in affecting product innovation in software. However, they play a different role in this industry.

11 The estimated coefficients of a third logit equation (dependent variable NEWFEAT) are not statistically significant.
12 It is worth noting that the variables SALES and DHW are correlated (Pearson's coefficient = 0.45 and *p*-value = 0.001).

Legal protection and other instruments for the protection of innovation

As expected, legal protection is considered a weak instrument of appropriability by the surveyed firms, although HW firms give great importance to it. Table 5.7 shows that the difference between HW firms and the remaining firms (SW) is statistically significant with respect to legal protection. HW firms also consider trade secret law as a relevant instrument for the protection of innovations. More precisely, these firms make use of a complete range of instruments, including lead time, continuous innovation, and the linkages with firms endowed with complementary resources. This may also show the effect of large size, and therefore a greater enforcement power (see also the discussion of hypothesis 4).

Table 5.7 Instruments for the protection of innovation

	LEGAL	SECRET	LEAD	IMPROV	COOPAC	PERSON
Total[a]	2.87	2.37	3.73	4.16	2.75	3.14
Std. Dvt.	1.62	1.32	1.06	0.90	1.31	1.26
HW[b]	4.00	3.50	4.00	4.14	3.00	2.71
SW[c]	2.66	2.17	3.68	4.16	2.70	3.22
Chi-square	4.18	2.75	0.14	0.00	0.00	2.28
p-value	0.05	0.09	0.20	1.00	1.00	0.09

Notes
a.   Means of scores from 1 = not relevant to 5 = very relevant.
b.   HW = firms which manufacture hardware and software systems.
c.   SW = firms specialised in software and services.

By contrast, SW firms rely exclusively on dynamic appropriability – lead time, continuous innovation and the possession of skilled personnel, showing a weaker ability to enforce legal protection (including trade secret law). The reliance on dynamic appropriability as an alternative to legal protection was expected. Besides the uncertainty concerning legal protection, due to the relatively recent extension of copyright and patent laws to software activities, part of these results is explained by the structural difficulty of articulating the knowledge underlying software innovations and, more importantly, by the difficulty of separating the codifiable and protectable knowledge from the tacit knowledge that cannot be protected by property right law. The interviews carried out in 1997 show that legal protection (copyright) has increased its importance as an instrument for the protection of innovation in specialised firms. However, specialised software firms (SW) still assign smaller scores to legal protection compared with specialised firms. Finally, the follow-up interviews show that lead time (get to market first with an innovation) becomes the most powerful instrument to protect innovation, especially for specialised firms. Along with the rising importance of legal protection, this appears to be coherent with the increasing importance of major product innovations discussed above.

Firm size and specialisation

The analysis conducted so far shows that there are not significant differences between HW and SW firms with respect to the patterns of product innovation. Moreover, neither the firm specialisation nor firm size have any effect on the association between different types of product innovations and different opportunities to innovation. As discussed before, however, firm specialisation shows a significant influence on the range of instruments for the protection of innovation.

To complete the analysis of the differentiation between large and smaller firms, I divided the sample firms into two classes: small firms (up to 34 million dollars of annual revenue) and large firms (above 34 million dollars).[13] The study of association between firm size and the characteristics of product innovation (conducted with the chi-square statistic) shows that there are no significant differences between large and small firms.

By contrast, some differences emerge concerning the determinants of product innovations. Table 5.8 shows that large firms (which include the hardware firms in the sample) are more sensitive to technological opportunities from hardware (ADAPTA) and to the opportunities arising from product differentiation (DIFFER).

There are not statistically significant differences between large and smaller firms with respect to the protection of innovation. The chi-square test thus indicates that the responses reported in Table 5.7 were influenced by firm specialisation, rather than firm size.

These results overall indicate that firm size, by itself, accounts for a modest share of the variance in the types of and the incentives to product innovations in this industry. This gives some support to the hypothesis that *appropriability advantages* are counterbalanced by *flexibility disadvantages* associated with large size.

Finally, I looked at the differences in innovative strategies and incentives to innovation between producers of *software platforms* (that is, system software and application tools) and firms specialised in*software solutions* (application

13 In the first class there are 26 firms and in the second class there are 25 firms. This classification was adopted for convenience, that is, to have two classes with a similar number of firms.

Table 5.8 Incentives to product innovations and firm size

	ADAPTA	QUALIT	DIFFER
Firm size			
SMALL	3.08	3.80	3.00
LARGE	3.65	3.69	4.00
Chi–square	3.30	0.01	8.02
p–value	0.07	0.91	0.00

Notes
a.　Means of scores from 1 to 5.
b.　LARGE = over \$34 million of annual revenue.
c.　SMALL = up to \$ 34 million of annual revenue.

solutions, customised software and services). The chi-square test shows that there are not significant differences between these categories of firms.

3.3. Discussion of results

The study of association between the nature of product innovations, the determinants (incentives) to product innovations, firm size and firm profile in the software industry has been helpful to underline several important details that have not been sufficiently analysed in the literature on technological change, such as the role played by technological and market opportunities in product innovation and the differences between firms with different profiles of product specialisation. However, we should warn against generalisation of these results for the following reasons.

First, the analysis shows the links between incentives, or (subjectively) perceived opportunities to innovation, and the nature of innovation. We are unable to give a quantitative measure of market-pull or technology-push effects on the actual rate of product innovation. The use of data on patents or copyright as indicators of innovative performance would require further research effort. Moreover, it suffers from many limitations indicated by the results of this work and by previous studies.[14] Detailed case-studies and the analysis of specific product innovations could be used for future research on this issue.

Second, the analysis of these data gives support to the conclusion that the sample firms follow a pattern of incremental technological change. This

14 See Frumau (1992) for an attempt at using the INSPEC database containing bibliographic references from published literature on physics, engineering, computer science, and information technology.

result may reflect the product specialisation of the sample firms. However, this result has not significantly changed even when controlled for different firms' profiles (including the producers of software packages). The main factor that makes it difficult to generalise the conclusions from our results is the small size of the sample and the localisation of the sample firms in Europe, where few major software innovations have been developed.

Third, the innovative pattern described in this section could reflect a specific phase of the software industry evolution. In the past several major product innovations have occurred. Most of these innovations have arisen from advances in complementary technologies. For instance, the invention of the laser printer, led by Canon, has spurred the invention of new desktop publishing packages (for example, Aldus's Pagemaker). More generally, progress in semiconductors and computers, and major institutional changes (for example, unbundling) have represented important sources of 'creative disruption' for software.

The repetition of the survey in 1997, on a smaller scale, confirms the results of 1990. The small number of interviews conducted in 1997 does not allow any statistical analysis. However, these interviews indicate a greater emphasis on major product/service innovations. Moreover, software firms appear to be more confident of the effectiveness of lead time and copyright as instruments for the protection of innovation. This suggests that a process of maturation is occurring in this industry.

However, the rising importance of major product innovations, which is induced by factors discussed in this section, does not conform to the industry life cycle's predictions and makes this industry peculiar compared with other manufacturing sectors.

4. CHANGES IN THE ORGANISATION OF SOFTWARE PRODUCTION

4.1. Previous literature and research hypotheses

Attempts to quite rigorously define the main phases of software development activities have been made since the 1960s, as reported in many US Air Force and industry publications (Bohem, 1981, p. 35). The standard model of software production is known as the 'software lifecycle' or the 'waterfall' model. The main stages of this process are the following. The first is system analysis, which consists of the analysis of users' requirements. The second is overall system design and detailed system design, which represents the architecture of the system. The third is programming, including writing the source code by a high–level language and compilation of object code by translation of the source code into a binary code (readable by the machine). The object code can be generated automatically by programs called assemblers and compilers. Fourth is integration which aims to verify the compatibility of the single components and the performance of the whole system. The final step is implementation which includes system installation and users' training.

The product of each stage (called 'baseline') is submitted to verification and validation (testing). Once the system is in operation, it requires three types of maintenance: corrections of errors in performance, adaptation to external changes (in functional specification, or in hardware and software environment) and enhancement of system performance. Maintenance is the most labour-intensive and costly activity (up to 70 per cent of total costs) (Bohem, 1981; Gotlieb, 1985; Meyer, 1997). This model draws from manufacturing the fundamental idea that a complex system can be partitioned into simple, sequential tasks.

This division of labour brings about economies of specialisation and a better managerial control of production process. Like a traditional assembly line, the 'waterfall' model draws on a linear approach. However, it allows interactions and feed-backs among different stages (for example, design, coding and testing).

The application of engineering principles experienced in manufacturing industries to software development (including the 'waterfall' model) and the study of solutions to 'programming bottlenecks' have been recommended by computer specialists in various technical and scientific meetings. Two important conferences on software engineering were respectively held in 1961 at the MIT (Harvard University), and in 1968 at Garmisch (under NATO sponsorship), in response to several major software failures and errors in critical sectors (for example, banks), and to the problems with low productivity and inefficient programming management (Naur and Randall, 1969; Friedman, 1989, pp. 101–2).

The essence of the software engineering recipes debated during the 1960s was the following: modularisation and rigid specification of interfaces, standardisation of program structures, definition of the main sequences of a standard development process, introduction of rigid management and control of the process (Friedman, ibid., pp. 105–6).

Over time, software engineering has evolved as a distinct branch of the industrial engineering discipline. From a technological point of view, in the 1980s different approaches to software engineering emerged. First, CASE (computer-aided software engineering) and IPSE (integrated project support environment) tools, formal methods (mathematical methods used mainly for specification, testing and validation), KBS (knowledge-based systems, based on artificial intelligence principles), fourth generation (4GL) and object-oriented languages (OOL).

CASE tools aim at the automation or support of specific software development phases (for example, design). They aim to replace relatively unskilled work with automatic routines or to assist software engineers, within the framework of the traditional linear, 'waterfall' development model (for example, Synon's Synon/2 and Index Technology's Accelerator). IPSE techniques aim at integrating specific tools within development environments that set standard procedures and interfaces (for example, Softlab's Maestro and Hewlett-Packard's Softbench). A quite different approach to SE proposes structured methods of programming and mathematically-based methods for specification, design and construction of software systems. Commercially used formal methodologies are Yourdon (US) and SSADM (UK). More recently, object-oriented languages (OOL) have introduced a new approach to SE, which draws on the idea of modularity and re-usable standard components. Object-oriented tools (for example, Powersoft's Powerbuilder and Next Computer's Nextstep) aim to develop standard and re-usable components (objects) that can be utilised for packaging different application solutions (see *Financial Times*, 1994c, p. XIX).

Unlike CASE tools, IPSE tools and object-oriented programming induce some changes in the traditional sequential development model, such as 'rapid prototyping', the 'incremental development' and the 'advancemanship' approaches (Brooks, 1975; Bohem, 1981). For instance, recent object-oriented tools such as IBM's FlowMark and Intellicorp's Object Management Workbench explicitly aim to perform 'rapid application development' (Moad, 1995). Class libraries (collections of pre-written objects) are now available 'on the shelves' to make programming faster. Some class libraries are integrated in development environments. For instance, Microsoft Foundation Classes are integrated into Microsoft's Visual C++ and Object Windows Library is integrated in Borland International's C++ (Lindholm, 1994).

The evolution of software production technologies has favoured significant changes in the organisation of this activity. The adoption of software engineering techniques and improvements in the organisation of software development have shown positive effects on programmer productivity. For example, the introduction of the 'Chief Programmer Team' organisation by IBM in the 1970s led to an increase in programmer productivity from 219 instructions per month to 408. Moreover, the introduction of a formal structured programming approach accounted for an increase in productivity from 169 to 301 instructions per month.[15] In the 1980s the productivity gains from the adoption of CASE tools have also been estimated to be significant.

---

15 See Gotlieb (1985), p. 174. Other experiments conducted at IBM, such as the introduction of design and code inspections, are reported by Brooks (1975), Phister (1979) and Bohem (1981).

For instance, the Japanese NRI & NCC, a merged subsidiary of Nomura Securities, experienced an increase in programmer productivity from 1,000–1,500 lines of codes per month to 5,000 as a consequence of the use of CASE tools (*Datamation*, 1989, p. 14). Moreover, these tools and other SE tools have enabled Japanese firms to achieve very high level of program re-usability. In some cases, like Toshiba, the estimated reusability rate is about 65 per cent (Cottrell, 1994).

More recently, EDS (Electronic Data Systems) has compared the performance of two programming teams – one using object-oriented languages and the other not. The former developed its version of the same product with 10 person-months labour while the latter required 152 person-months. Moreover, the version developed by the object-oriented language had less than one-tenth the lines of code of the other version (Garber, 1993, p. 110).

Some large firms have pushed the process of rationalisation of the productive process very close to the manufacturing model. The literature has referred to this approach as the 'software factory', which is described as 'a deliberate attempt to transform software from an "unstructured service" to a "product" with a guaranteed level of cost and quality' (Cusumano, 1992, p. 467).

American firms such as IBM, Digital, TRW and System Development Corporation (SDC) led the first applications of the 'software factory' approach (or an integrated approach to software development) early in the 1970s, followed by Japanese ones.[16]

The following forces have led to the software factory approach especially in Japan. First, the possibility of re-using codes and other components across different projects was perceived by project managers as a major opportunity to reduce redundancies and costs. Second, the shortage of skilled personnel since the 1960s. In 1985 in Japan there was a shortage of 17,000 software engineers and 26,000 programmers (Dambrot, 1989, p. 16). Third, the engineers' and project managers' belief that 'software was not an unmanageable technology' (Cusumano, 1992, p. 475).

Different software factories have the following characteristics in common: an integrated set of development tools, standardised procedures and management practices, and a matrix organisation. In some cases there is a division of labour between corporate engineers, which perform critical design and project management, and subsidiaries or subcontractors, which specialise in programming. Some software factories, such as Toshiba, also have

16 However, only SDC explicitly referred to this approach as a 'factory approach'. Most firms preferred to refer to their experiences with software engineering techniques as integrated management of software development. For instance, IBM calls its software development laboratories or programming centres (Cusumano, 1991, p. 6).

developed an incentive structure (awards, controls and so on) to spur re–usability of components.

During the 1970s and the 1980s the Japanese integrated computer and software firms, such as Hitachi, Fujitsu and Toshiba, became the prototype of the 'software factories', while the US firms abandoned this approach. For example, SDC gave up the software factory approach because of the lack of portability of tools across projects, and the project managers' reluctance to rely on software developed by the factory (Cusumano, 1992, p. 466).

There are different opinions as to the similarities between the software factory approach and the manufacturing production. According to Cusumano (1991, 1992), this approach is similar to the experience of flexible production in industries such as automobiles. Unlike the automobile industry, however, software production converges to flexible production starting from the experience of the job-shop, craft-like approach, rather than mass production. Software factories rely on a medium level of skills, low volumes, medium variety, and a good mix of productivity and quality (Cusumano, 1992, Fig. 2, p. 477). This issue is discussed in more detail later.

The experiences described so far are limited to large software firms. These have greater resources (and incentives) to invest in software engineering and to impose a stronger managerial discipline to their software production compared to small firms. The latter organise their production on the basis of informal communication systems and a loose management style. The majority of small software firms are often described as relying on a job-shop, craft-like activity with little re-use of tools, methods and codes across projects. They are reported to employ highly skilled professionals whose productivity is very unpredictable. Also, productivity is reported to vary extensively from one project to another. One reason for poor productivity is the intensive use of old programs like Cobol which 'does not lend itself to efficient programming practices; indeed it encourage inefficiency' (Garber, 1993, p. 110). The adoption of new programming languages is constrained by the training (fixed) costs. Until recently an ordinary programmer might have needed between six to eighteen months to become proficient in object-oriented languages such as Smalltalk and C++ (Garber, ibid.). Another reason for the poor productivity is that, according to sociologists of organisations, software developers are creative craftsmen or professionals reluctant to adopt automation tools, structured methodologies and quality management systems (Quintas, 1993).

Thus, in spite of the expected productivity gains, until recently the diffusion of software engineering tools was limited. For instance, a survey conducted by the Software Engineering Institute at Carnegie Mellon University has showed that 74 per cent of software suppliers of the US Department of Defence employed an 'ad hoc, or possibly, chaotic process' in their software development activity.[17]

Before illustrating the empirical analysis, it is worth pointing out the research hypotheses arising from the discussion of the literature.

Hypothesis 1. The software industry is evolving from a job-shop, craft-like activity into an industry based on flexible production systems

Put in another way, this hypothesis is whether the 'flexible production system' represents a model for the European software firms. Moreover, assuming that a transformation of the software industry from a creative, craft activity to an industrial engineering discipline is occurring, it is important to understand how firms with different types of specialisation and size differ with respect to the organisation of production and R&D activities. This leads to another research hypotesis.

Hypothesis 2. The organisation of production and innovation activities in the software industry varies across firms of different size and specialisation

One should expect some differences across firms depending on the relatively high fixed costs associated with the use of software engineering techniques. Previous studies show that the costs for the implementation of new standards and training are one of the main reasons for the lack of adoption of CASE tools (Hayley, Fordonskyi and Puckett, 1992).

Market fragmentation and the small average size of software producers can explain the lack of automation and codification of software production. Firms that operate in small market niches (and small firms in general) may not have enough incentives to adopt development tools and management systems, because these techniques increase their fixed costs. By contrast, large and diversified firms can spread these costs over a large number of customers or applications. A second reason why one should expect significant differences across firms is linked to 'corporate culture'. For instance, hardware manufacturers are familiar with a formal organisation of production which draws on rigorous engineering principles. The experience of computer manufacturing can represent an important externality for their in-house software divisions. By contrast, software engineers and programmers of specialised software firms may find it difficult to give up their informal, creative corporate culture.

---

17 See Moad (1990). Similar results are indicated by Price Waterhouse 1990 DP review (see *Computer Weekly*, 1990).

4.2. The empirical results

This section analyses the patterns of process innovation in a period of software industry evolution characterised by the introduction of new software development tools (for example, OOL) and new organisation of IT resources (for example, client–server networks, team development or groupware, and Internet). The issues addressed in my analysis are the following. First, it aims to assess whether the introduction of new software engineering techniques (SE) concerns isolated phases of the software development cycle ('islands of automation') or involves the whole organisation of development activities ('flexible production system'). Second, the survey focuses on the determinants of process innovations, with the objective of highlighting the nature of the bottlenecks in the software development process. Third, the obstacles to the adoption of process innovations are illustrated. Finally, the differences between HW (integrated hardware and software) firms and SW (specialised software) firms and between large and small firms are studied. Table 5.9 illustrate the variables analysed in this section.

Characteristics of process innovations

Table 5.10 shows the use of different types of SE tools by the sample firms – CASE tools, structured methodologies integrated environments, and fourth generation languages (for example, object-oriented languages). The responses were checked by asking the interviewees to specify the type and, if possible, the name of the tools tried. Except for a few cases (classified as NONE), the tools utilised correspond to the definition of SE tools reported before. Eight firms did not answer this set of questions.

The majority of the firms from the sample make use of SE tools for the automation and support of specific development phases. A large proportion of firms do not use any kind of formal methodology (for example, Yourdon or SSADM), tools integrated in automatic support environments (IPSEs), or fourth generation programming languages (OOL) in their development activities.

However, there are some differences among firms. As expected, SW firms show a lower propensity to use SE techniques compared with HW firms. These differences can be explained by the high fixed costs of acquisition and learning, and by the fact that system engineering is still closer to the productive 'culture' of hardware engineers than software developers. Another result that has emerged from the survey concerns the origin of process innovations. Over 50 per cent of tools and methodologies utilised by our firms were developed in-house.

Table 5.9 Variables description

Characteristics of process innovations	
PHASES	New tools for specific phases of production
METH	New formal production methodologies
ENVIR	New tools integrated into IPSEs
4GL	4GL languages
NONE	No use of any new techniques
Determinants of process innovations	
EFFIC	Development efficiency
QUAL	Product quality
MAIN	Maintenance costs
REUS	Reusability of source codes and design
NEED	Speed of response to user's needs
FEASI	Development of new products
Obstacles to process innovations	
INC	Incompatibility with old methods
RELUCT	Programmers' reluctance
CUSTOM	Users' reluctance
TRAIN	High cost for programmers' re–training
DINVEST	High cost due to disinvestments
PROMAN	Project managers' learning time/costs
METRIC	Lack of metrics for testing new tools
NEW	Lack of information on new tools
WAIT	Future technological improvements, wait-and-see

As expected, large firms and firms specialised in system software and tools develop in-house over 60 per cent of their tools, while smaller firms and firms specialised in applications and services rely more on external sources (over 60 per cent).

These results confirm indirectly that many firms still rely on 'craft' or 'ad-hoc' methodologies, often developed in-house (except for a few firms that have developed methodologies and tools largely adopted by other firms).

However, they also indicate that significant research efforts are devoted to improving the organisation of tasks towards a more rigorous and predictable engineering discipline, as confirmed by other studies. The interviews made in 1997 reinforce the evidence of these efforts towards software engineering.

About 80 per cent of firms uses CASE tools for automating specific phases of the production process, especially overall system design, detailed system design and testing.

Table 5.10 Characteristics of process innovation in software[a]

	PHASES	METH	ENVIR	4GL	NONE	FIRMS
HW[b]	100[d]	50	17	25	0	6
SW[c]	51	23	18	1	20	39

Notes
a.   Percentage of firms that use different types of tools/methods.
b.   HW = firms which manufacture hardware and software systems.
c.   SW = firms specialised in software and services.
d.   Percentage values do not sum up because of multiple responses.

The same percentage of firms makes use of standard methodologies and 60 per cent of integrated development environments. Finally 90 per cent adopt fourth generation, object-oriented languages (see Appendix B).

In evaluating these data we should consider that the interviews of 1997 concern large firms. The average number of employees of the sample firms is about 6,780. There are three small- to medium-sized firms in the sample (between 60 and 430 employees). Except for the small one (60 employees), which has remained bounded to an informal production approach, the remaining two medium-sized firms have increased their use of standard methodologies and integrated development environments between 1990 and 1997. However, the information provided by these interviews is clear. The use of standard methodologies and integrated environments, which support fourth generation programming tools, has sharply increased in the last few years in large software firms.

The Determinants of process innovations

As discussed before, the specialised literature claims that bottlenecks in process technology drive the firm's attempts to adopt new SE tools. This survey gives some insight into the nature of these bottlenecks. Table 5.11 shows that the major determinants of process innovation are connected to the necessity of increasing the efficiency of the development activity, the quality and reliability of products, and the speed of response to users' needs (to improve the specification of users' requirements). The importance of product quality and speed of response to user needs indicates that, besides efficiency, quality management and flexibility of the development system are the most critical issues on which process innovation activity focuses.

Table 5.11 Determinants of process innovation

	EFFIC	QUAL	MAIN	REUS	NEED	FEASI
Total	4.15[a]	4.19	3.13	3.26	3.68	2.66
Std. Dvt.	1.16	0.98	0.96	1.42	1.25	1.40
HW[b]	4.40	4.21	2.75	3.57	4.00	2.57
SW[c]	4.05	4.15	3.38	3.23	3.77	2.68
Chi-square	0.11	0.00	0.00	0.27	0.00	0.07
p-value	0.75	1.00	1.00	0.33	1.00	0.49

Notes

a.   Means of scores from 1 = not relevant to 5 = very relevant.

b.   HW = firms which manufacture hardware and software systems.

c.   SW = firms specialised in software and services.

Chi-square tests show that there are no significant differences between integrated firms (HW) and specialised firms (SW) with respect to the perceived forces driving process innovation. Firm size and production profile also do not have significant effects upon the vision of the determinants of process innovations.

The 1997 interviews confirm this picture. The speed of response to users' needs becomes the major driving force while reusability of source code and design is more important than it used to be in the 1990 survey.

These results are associated with the progress in graphical interfaces and object-oriented tools which make programming easier compared with third generation tools (for example, C language). Moreover, the increasing portability of programs allowed by the new developing tools (including those supported by Java language) spurs customers to restructure their information systems, creating a new demand for applications written with new development techniques. Finally, the rising international competition in the software and services industry spurs firms to increase their efficiency (through a higher re-usability rate) and flexibility to changing users' needs.

The obstacles to process innovations

The specialised literature and some preliminary interviews with sectoral experts has suggested that there are several obstacles to the adoption of new SE techniques. In the US, SDC's attempts to adopt SE practices during the mid-1970s failed, as mentioned before, when system engineers had to develop new applications. Moreover, General Telephone and Electric (GTE) in 1980 was unsuccessful when it tried to put into practice a set of corporate standards, because of obstacles such as the variety of the firm's software activities, system engineers' preference for familiar tools and users' problems with the performance of the new standard process. Finally, NEC's Basic Software Division rejected an SE tool and methodology because of incompatibility with existing products and practices (Cusumano, 1991, pp. 32–7). Lack of metrics for testing the superior quality of the new tools and poor information about their quality were also pointed out by sector experts during pilot interviews as significant obstacles to the adoption of process innovations.

Table 5.12 shows that the most important obstacles for the sample firms overall are incompatibility with the old techniques, the difficulty for project managers to learn a new type of organisation of labour required by the new development tools, the lack of information on the new tools effectiveness, and the uncertainty of future technological progress in the field of software engineering that induces a wait-and-see behaviour in project managers (or chief programmers).

Overall, firm size and firm specialisation do not have a significant influence on the obstacles to the diffusion of new software engineering techniques.

The interviews made in 1997 indicate that the firm's perception of the obstacles to process innovation is much weaker than in the past. This should be explained by factors discussed before, including a decreasing uncertainty about the effectiveness of new development tools and the improved 'user-friendliness' arising from the introduction of graphical interfaces. The only obstacle which affects the adoption is represented by the high costs for programmers' re-training. Again, we should notice that these results can be affected by the large average size of the sample firms.

4.3. Discussion of results

What are the implications of the pattern of process innovation described in this section for the division of labour within software firms? And what will be the effects on the industry structure? – Does flexible production systems in software activities imply the convergence of firms towards a single model of product development or will there be a persistent variety of models?

The empirical results discussed above lend support to the hypothesis that this industry is evolving from an informal, craft activity towards a more systematic and scientific pattern of division of labour (hypothesis 1).

Table 5.12 Obstacles to the adoption of process innovations

	INC	RELUCT	CUSTOM	TRAIN	DINVEST
Total	3.33[a]	2.52	2.67	2.87	2.80
Std. dvt.	1.20	1.17	1.20	1.06	1.14
HW[b]	3.43	3.21	2.67	3.43	3.00
SW[c]	3.31	2.38	2.67	2.77	2.77
Chi-square	0.09	2.20	0.00	0.20	0.02
p-value	0.76	0.14	1.00	0.65	0.08

	PROMAN	METRIC	NEW	WAIT
Total	3.21	2.82	3.33	3.12
Std. dvt.	1.06	1.16	1.02	1.04
HW[b]	3.40	3.67	3.67	3.00
SW[c]	3.18	2.64	3.26	3.14
Chi-square	0.00	2.70	0.00	0.10
p-value	1.00	0.10	1.00	1.00

Notes
a.   Means of scores from 1 = not relevant to 5 = very relevant.
b.   HW = firms which manufacture hardware and software systems.
c.   SW = firms specialised in software and services.

The adoption of more formal, science-based methods for software development seems to be consistent with a more general change in the 'technology of technological change' as described by Arora and Gambardella (1994). However, there are obstacles to the adoption of 'scientific' methods of software production and innovation that reveal specific difficulties in transforming the tacit knowledge of system developers into a more codifiable and separable type of expertise. Moreover, there are within-industry differences across firms with respect to the organisation of production and innovation that are discussed in the following.

The organisation of innovative and production activities in this industry varies quite significantly across three types of firms: large established 'software factories' (including integrated hardware–software producers and some large specialised software firm), small established firms operating in market niches (many of our smaller firms specialised in application solutions and services), and entrepreneurial start-up firms. These differences give support to the hypothesis of structural differences across firms (hypothesis 2).

Table 5.13 summarises some characteristics of these classes of firms.

As mentioned above, the prototype of the large software factories are the Japanese software producers. The Japanese experience with software factories shows that a tight integration of development activities may increase productivity and flexibility, by the extensive re-use of common software components for different applications (Cusumano, 1991). However, this experience appears to be limited to large integrated firms which develop complex systems for specific applications – for example, real-time systems, on-line reservations and artificial intelligence. According to some critics, Japanese software factories rely on a rigid division of labour between specification, analysis and design on the one side, and programming activities on the other.

Specification, analysis and design are carried out by skilled system engineers and project managers, at the main contractor's firm, while programming (and some low level testing) is executed by unskilled workers on the basis of detailed designs provided by system engineers (Nakahara, 1993, pp. 27–9).

The main advantages of this type of organisation are specialisation and quality control. A major drawback is the lack of feedback between design and programming. While Japanese main contractors make use of SE technique, most smaller software houses in Japan carry out routine activities and rely on shop-floor, localised knowledge and trial and error.

Therefore, the efficiency and the relative flexibility of large firms seems to be achieved at the expense of the smaller firms' efficiency and innovativeness. More recently, the Japanese software factories have evolved into a more flexible type of organisation. Subcontractors have gradually learned the design activity and main contractors have reduced part of their detailed design activity. As a consequence, main contractors have begun to subcontract design activities along with programming. Moreover, for large projects main contractors usually set up on-site contract programming, and the programmers from subcontracting firms work together at the main contractor's development centre (cf. Nakahara, ibid.).

The largest US and European 'software factories' show a different approach: even when they have adopted SE techniques they have relied on a more flexible and horizontal type of division of labour, based on a less rigid separation of tasks between system designers and analysts, on the one hand, and programmers, on the other. Moreover, the decision to adopt standard CASE tools and other SE techniques in the US firms is more decentralised (Nakahara, ibid., p. 37).

Table 5.13 Trade-offs in software innovation management and a taxonomy of firms

Firm category	Technology	Market	R&D organisation
Large estabilished software firms (more than 500 employees)	Packaged and customised software	System software/ large applications	Chief technical officer (company project leaders)
	Product innovation led by adaptation to progress of hardware technology (integrated hardware–software firms)	Services	
	Software factories for customised systems and specific applications (real-time, on-line reservations)		R&D project organised by mkt/products Matrix organisation Multidisciplinary R&D teams
	Large use of system engineering tools (integrated hardware–software firms)		
	Legal protection and other instruments		
Small estabilished firms (less than 500 employees, more than 5 years old)	Packaged and custom. software	Mature market niches	R&D development teams below 60 employees organised by projects
	Incremental product innovation led by quality improvements and product differentiation		

Table 5.13 (continued)

Firm category	Technology	Market	R&D organisation
	Most use of methodologies and tools developed in-house	Small to large customers	Centralised, informal communication systems
			Project leaders
	Little use of legal protection		
Entrepreneurial start-ups (about five years old)	Product development activity focused on improvement of recent new products		
		New markets niches	Core developm. Team with few people, cross-functional skills
	No or little use of structured methodologies		
			Loosely organised 'inner' software development team
	Little effort to formal specifications, design documentation, testing		
			Informal communication and 'soft' deadlines
	Little use of CASE tools and 4GL tools		
			Cohesive units of motivated professionals
	Some code re-use for subsequent product improvements and feature proliferation		Rapid developement (under 2 years for new packs and 1 year for subsequent packages)
	Little use of legal protection (lead time more important)		

Source: Interviews, Cusumano (1991), Malerba and Torrisi (1993), Carmel (1993), Nakahara (1993)

Recently, many large US software firms have started separating these phases and have subcontracted the programming activities to smaller developers and less developed countries endowed with advanced system engineers skills (for example, China and India) (Narasimhan, 1993; Heeks, 1993).

My analysis shows that large software firms in Europe make use of more formal, structured methodologies and SE tools compared with the smaller ones. This is confirmed by the increased use of these tools in the last few years. Moreover, in Europe, large software firms organise their R&D activities around products/markets, rather than projects, make use of multidisciplinary teams and a matrix organisation (see Malerba and Torrisi, 1993). The application of principles drawn from 'flexible manufacturing systems' to software and the characteristics of the most recent SE approaches (for example, object-oriented languages and tools) should allow large firms to reconcile efficiency and flexibility. From this perspective, there is not much difference between software and other industries in terms of the economic implications of flexible manufacturing systems: large firms utilise SE tools to gain economies of scale and scope (Piore and Sabel, 1984; Hayes and Wheelwright, 1984; Jaikumar, 1986; Chandler, 1990; Womack et al., 1990; von Hippel, 1990b).

The other two classes of firm organise their innovative and production activities in a different way. They rely both on small teams of professionals and informal communication systems, and make no use of matrix organisations.

There are many small established software firms in Europe which have grown in small market niches following an 'ad hoc' organisational approach, using few development tools and structured methodologies. These firms mainly carry out modifications and improvements of their own products developed previously or develop routine programs and sub-systems on the basis of subcontracting agreements. These firms organise their R&D activities around projects, indicating a less formalised organisation compared with larger organisations centred on products/markets (Malerba and Torrisi, 1993). This class of firms is well represented in my survey by the smaller producers of applications solutions and services.

Finally, new start-ups specialise in one or few new products and carry out incremental product innovations. They also make little or no use of structured methodologies and development tools. They organise their development activities around cohesive 'core development teams' of few members endowed with cross-functional skills. Informal communication and 'soft' deadlines also characterise the organisation of software development in these entrepreneurial firms (Carmel, 1993). This class of firms is represented in my survey by a few firms specialised in development tools and artificial intelligence applications (expert systems), including the one interviewed again in 1997. Moreover, some large Japanese software factories are reported to organise their activities in a less structured and informal way (for example, 'special projects') when they focus on innovative design (Cusumano, 1992, p. 478).

Both the 'software factory' approach and the 'chaotic, craft' approach seem to be converging towards a 'flexible production' approach. This approach rests on the assumption that the management of software development, like other engineering activities, has to focus on the reorganisation of the development process to achieve the rising quality standards required by users. However, the differences among large firms and smaller firms mentioned before are likely to remain significant, showing a 'division of knowledge' between actors specialised in 'creative destruction' and actors focusing on systematisation, combination and 'creative integration' of different knowledge inputs.

Increasingly important components of this flexible approach are new development tools, which support the team development work (for example, Borland International's Delphi), and Internet, which favours the geographical decentralisation of software development activities. The interviews conducted in 1997 reveal that most firms normally make use of Internet-based tools in their development activities, claiming that these tools have changed substantially the organisation of their work.

5. CONCLUSIONS

This chapter investigates product and process innovation in the software industry. A survey of software firms was carried out in 1990. A set of sample firms were also interviewed in 1997. The analysis provides a quite comprehensive picture of the innovative activities in the software industry, including the type and the determinants of product innovations and process innovations, and the strategies for the protection of innovation. Various hypotheses have been tested on the basis of ideas and theories developed by the economics and management of technological change. The picture emerging from this study is that of an industry characterised by incremental product innovation and increasing focus on process innovation. The interviews carried out in 1997 show an increased effort towards major product innovations. Although the differences from the 1990 interviews are not statistically significant, this effort may reflect increased competition in the European software market, and new technological opportunities arising from the Internet and from the convergence among computers, telecommunications, and consumer electronics.

The major determinants of product innovations are new market opportunities, the need to improve product quality, and the opportunities arising from the advances in hardware technology. Ordered logit models were developed to analyse the effects of different incentives to engage in product innovations (market opportunities vs. technological opportunities) and the types of product innovations (major vs. incremental innovations). The estimation of multinomial logit models show that market opportunities have a positive effect on major innovations and a negative effect on incremental innovations. By contrast, technological opportunities (measured with the perceived opportunities from changes of hardware technology) have a significant positive effect on minor innovations (new features to existing products) and a negative effect on major innovations.

With respect to the protection of innovations, our results show that software firms overall rely mainly on dynamic appropriability (lead time, continuous innovation and the possession of skilled personnel) as opposed to legal protection (patents and copyright). Integrated hardware–software producers differ from specialised software firms in that they rely on a wide range of mechanisms for the protection of innovations, including legal protection.

In analysing the pattern of product innovation and appropriability, I controlled also for differences between firms in terms of size and production profile. The most marked differences are those between integrated hardware–software firms and specialised firms. These differences concern the integrated firms' propensity to use a wider range of instruments for the protection of innovation, including legal protection. However, legal protection, especially copyright, becomes more and more important also for the largest specialised software firms, as indicated by the 1997 interviews. These results depends on the declining uncertainty surrounding legal protection of innovation in the software industry.

With respect to process innovations, the analysis shows that the sample firms focus mainly on development tools for the automation of specific phases of the development cycle (CASE tools), and only a few firms have tried standard methodologies and development environments that integrate different tools. Moreover, specialised software firms show a smaller propensity to adopt software engineering tools as compared with integrated hardware–software producers. The picture arising from the interviews of 1997 appears significantly different. The use of integrated development environments and object-oriented tools is more diffused than it used to be in the past. This suggests that increased international competition, new opportunities offered by new development technologies, and the experience with the traditional software engineering tools (for example, CASE tools) have spurred large specialised software (and services) producers to adopt a more efficient and flexible system of production. It is important to notice, however, that this picture shows the experience of large software and services firms. Probably, many small firms still rely on traditional job-shop, craft-like production systems.

The major determinants of process innovations are linked to the need to increase efficiency and product quality, and to reduce the response time to user needs. Overall, there are no significant differences between firms of different size and specialisation with respect to the determinants of process innovation. The main obstacles to process innovations are linked to the incompatibility with the familiar techniques, the difficulty for project managers to learn new types of division of labour, and the lack of information on the new tools. These obstacles appear to be less important in the 1997 interviews for reasons discussed above.

Some implications for the changing organisation of software development activities were discussed in completing the analysis of process innovations, particularly the analogies with the 'flexible production system' experienced in manufacturing industries and the differences in the implementation of innovation strategies among different types of firms. The differences among different groups of firms, particularly among firms with different production profiles, indicate a high intra-industry heterogeneity of the firms' strategies and management of innovation which is likely to persist in the future. In particular, small firms and the most innovative firms will rely on informal, chaotic, and loosely managed organisation of production and R&D activities.

6. In-House Skills and External Sources of Innovation

1. INTRODUCTION

This chapter analyses the types of skills that are utilised by software firms in their innovative activities and the sources of technological change, including university, customers, and competitors. I propose a simple model for studying the association between skills and external sources of technological change. This model is based on the distinction between general-purpose (or generic) skills, which draw on scientific, abstract science, and context-specific (or application-specific) skills, which are linked to experience and knowledge of specific users' needs and applications.

As innovative activities require a wide range of know-how and capabilities, firms cannot rely only on their internal competencies, but have to establish linkages with external sources of knowledge and expertise. However, one can expect that the possession of different internal capabilities and knowledge will affect the firms' propensity or ability to resort to external sources of knowledge, and to select different types of external linkages. This may explain some infra-industry differences across firms in their networks with external sources of technological change.

Recent studies in the economics of innovation have pointed out the role played by different sources of innovation and the complementarity between internal and external sources of knowledge. These studies suggest that internal capabilities may provide firms with the ability to evaluate and absorb new advances in science and technology, and to set up linkages with other organisations. This literature provides useful theoretical and empirical insights into the role of capabilities and external linkages in firms' innovative activities. However, previous works have not provided a sound understanding of what types of internal competencies or skills make firms more *outward looking* and which ones reduce their incentives (ability) to set up links with external sources of technological change.

This chapter analyses this issue in the software industry. The topic is particularly important for the economics of innovation in this industry. For one thing, human capital is the most important factor of production and a major channel of technical progress in the software industry. Moreover, software firms employ a variety of skills, from mathematics to system engineering and experience with services, which may have different effects on the organisation of innovative activities and the firms' propensity to set up links with external sources of knowledge. Finally, as we learn from previous chapters, although software is a 'science-based' industry, well rooted in mathematics and computer science, software production is often a craft process based on experience and trial-and-error, rather than science and rigorous engineering. Therefore, it is interesting to study how software firms combine in-house 'general-purpose' and 'context-specific' knowledge with various types of knowledge accessible from external sources.

The chapter is organised as follows. Section 2 illustrates the results of previous works on firm capabilities and external sources of knowledge. Section 3 introduces the skills and capabilities utilised by software firms in innovative activities. Section 4 discusses the external sources of innovation. Section 5 discusses a theoretical framework and analyses the relationships between internal innovative skills and external sources of innovation. Section 6 closes the chapter.

2. PREVIOUS STUDIES ON FIRMS' CAPABILITIES AND EXTERNAL SOURCES OF KNOWLEDGE

There are different attempts to measure firms' innovative competencies in the economics and management of innovation. As discussed in Chapter 2, two main indicators have been proposed recently. A first indicator, based on the use of patents, has been utilised, among others, by Patel and Pavitt (1994) to map the competencies of large firms in different technological fields, with the aim to evaluate the evolution of their technological strategy. A second indicator for mapping the accumulation of technical competencies at the industry level has been utilised by Jacobsson and Oskarsson (1993). This indicator utilises data on the educational background of engineers and scientists employed in different Swedish industries.[1]

These indicators are particularly useful for inter-industry and inter-firm comparisons. Industry case-studies often require more qualitative and detailed indicators that rely on the collection of original information through interviews with firms and sectoral experts. The peculiarities of the software

---

1 Raffa and Zollo (1993) have utilised a similar indicator to measure the investment in human resources in Italian software firms. For a wider discussion of technological capabilities see Chapter 2.

industry make the use of indicators such as patented inventions particularly difficult. As discussed in earlier chapters, software immateriality makes it difficult to disentangle innovative and protectable expressions of original ideas from unprotectable ideas. This explains the negligible number of applications filed to the European Patent Office (EPO) by the largest US and European software firms between 1980 and 1993. Moreover, although the information arising from the number of engineers and scientists of different disciplines may be useful to understand the nature of firms' competencies, it does not tell whether these competencies are actually employed in the innovative activities or in other activities (for example, sales and post-delivery services).

An alternative indicator of how different skills are utilised in innovative activities is self-assessment of competencies through interviews with managers responsible for R&D projects. As with other indicators, the results based on self-assessment should be interpreted very carefully, especially in inter-firms and inter-industry comparisons of competencies.[2] In this work self-assessment is used to provide a qualitative assessment of the mix of innovative skills (for example, mathematics and computer science) in software firms, rather than to compare the level of competencies across firms or industries; other indicators would serve this function much better.

When products are complex and innovative activities require different types of scientific and technological knowledge, firms have to mix internal competencies, knowledge, and experience with external sources of knowledge, by establishing linkages with other organisations such as universities, specialised suppliers, and users (Teece, 1986).

Earlier studies have analysed the external sources of technological innovation and learning in several industries. A wide survey of sectoral studies concludes that:

> In most industries, no single firm commands a majority of the resources available for research, nor can any one firm respond to more than a portion of the needs or problems requiring original solutions. It is not surprising, therefore, to find that most of the ideas successfully developed and implemented by any firm come from outside that firm. (Utterback, 1974, p. 30)

The studies referred to by Utterback indicate that external sources of innovations account for over 55 per cent of the key ideas leading to product or process innovations overall, and 66 per cent in scientific and measurement instruments. Moreover, most ideas arise from the communication of a need and the subsequent search for technical solutions (problem solving). In most

---

2 The benefits and drawbacks associated with this indicator for the study of innovative activities at the firm level and the industry level, see Levin et al. (1987).

industries, such as instrumentation and machinery, classified as specialised suppliers, users and outside experts (for example, consultants) play an important role in the generation of new ideas and the suggestion of technical solutions (Utterback, 1971, Pavitt, 1984; and von Hippel, 1988).

Among external sources of innovation, the role played by universities and research institutes as a direct source of industrial innovation is controversial. In some cases, technical literature, a quite large proportion of which is produced by universities, represents a direct source of ideas for industrial innovations (see Utterback, 1971 and 1974). More often, scientific fields such as mathematics, applied mathematics and operational research, and computer science, seem to be indirectly relevant to industrial research (that is, in terms of education), rather than directly (new knowledge from academic research). Education, informal linkages and personal contacts represent major channels for communication of innovative ideas in several industries (see Nelson and Levin, 1986).

The effective combination, or integration, of internal and external sources of knowledge increases firms' competencies and innovative efficiency, thus representing a major determinant of sustained competitive advantage. Previous studies have showed that in-house research is a complement to, rather than a substitute for, external, contract research (Mowery, 1983; Arora and Gambardella, 1990). Internal capabilities are needed to evaluate and exploit the services of external research channels. As discussed in Chapter 2, there are also other factors that explain this complementarity, including the interdependencies between research and other activities (research output and manufacturing products are joint productions), the difficulty to codify and separate complex research tasks from the rest of in-house research activity, and agency problems arising from contractual uncertainty. Cohen and Levinthal (1989) and Rosenberg (1990) have further explored the nature of the interactions between internal and external research activities, by claiming that, besides innovation, firms' in-house research aims to accumulate absorptive capabilities. The latter are required for evaluating and 'inventing around' scientific and technological knowledge accessible from outside.

The effective combination of external knowledge and in-house unique technical and scientific capabilities relies on organisational competencies which are required to integrate different types of knowledge and information (see Aoki, 1990; Henderson and Clark, 1990; Teece et al., 1994; and Iansiti and Clark, 1995).

3. IN-HOUSE SKILLS AND EXTERNAL SOURCES OF INNOVATION: PRELIMINARY ANALYSIS

3.1 In-house skills

The project managers of the sample firms interviewed in 1990 were asked to evaluate the importance of different skills for their firms' innovative activities. The set of skills submitted to firms were selected on the basis of indications provided by industry experts and pilot interviews (see Chapter 5 and Appendix A for a description of the methodology and questionnaire).

The skills analysed include typical basic, general-purpose ones, that is mathematics and computer science, and context-specific types such as system engineering (a computer science-based competence that is employed in different critical activities, including users' needs analysis, design, and system integration), and experience with applications and post-delivery services, and marketing/sales skills.

Table 6.1 describes the skills analysed. Table 6.2 shows the importance of each skill. System engineering (SYST) and the experience with applications, post-commercialisation services, and ability of interacting with customers (SERV) are the most critical to innovative activities, followed by skills in computer science (COMP). Competencies in mathematics (MATH) and marketing skills (MARK) are less important for innovation compared with the other skills.[3]

There are no significant differences between integrated hardware–software firms (HW) and specialised software firms (SW) with respect to the importance assigned to different in-house capabilities, except for MATH skills, which are significantly more important for HW firms.[4] This indicates that their R&D activities are more formalised, and that more internal resources are devoted by these firms to basic research as compared with SW firms. Moreover, the possession of these skills may provide HW firms with an absorptive capability that can be utilised in a wider range of technologies, including hardware. HW firms rely more on in-house skills in computer science as compared with SW firms, because, as with mathematical skills, there are some economies of scope arising from the use of these skills in both hardware and software technology.[5]

---

3 This classification does not reflect the position of each skill in the organisational hierarchy (for example, programmers, analysts, chief team programmer and so on). For this reason programmers are not taken explicitly into account.
4 The chi-square value decreases to 2.1 at the 0.15 significance level after Yate's correction.
5 Chi-square after Yate's correction is 1.97 (*p*-value = 0.16).

Table 6.1 Variables desciption

Internal skills and capabilities	
MATH	Mathematics
COMP	Computer science
SYST	System engineering
SERV	Experience with applications/service
MARK	Marketing
External sources of innovation	
PUBL	Scientific/technical publications
FAIRS	Trade fairs
MEETING	Meetings and seminars
UNIV	Relationships with universities
HARDW	Relationships with hardware manufactures
COOPSW	Formal cooperation agreements with other software firms
INFORM	Informal relationships with other software firms
PROFES	Outside professional consultants
USERS	Innovative users
NEWPERS	Hiring of new scientific/technical personnel
IMITAT	Imitation of competitors
SALES	1989 revenues
DHW	Dummy for hardware firms

Table 6.2 Internal capabilities and skills

	MATH	COMP	SYST	SERV	MARK
Total[a]	3.00	3.73	4.03	3.91	3.06
Std. dvt.	1.30	1.26	0.95	0.89	1.41
HW [b]	3.83	4.17	4.50	3.50	3.33
SW [c]	2.78	3.67	3.93	4.03	3.08
Chi-square	3.60	5.08	0.43	1.61	0.09
p-value	0.05	0.02	0.50	0.20	0.76

Notes
a.   Means of scores from 1 = not relevant to 5 = very relevant.
b.   HW = firms which manufacture hardware and software systems.
c.   SW = firms specialised in software and services.

Moreover, there are no significant differences between firms with different specialisation (for example, producers of *software platforms* and firms specialising in *software applications*). Finally, firm size does not show any significant effects on the use of different skills.[6]

In the course of the field analysis, other skills that had not been taken explicitly into account in the survey were pointed out by the interviewees. These highlighted the importance of basic methods and skills to conceptualise and recognise problems, to interact with other people in a team, and to structure, edit, and communicate research results. The importance of these skills, often associated with the possession of an MBA degree, shows that, as discussed in Chapter 5, the organisation of R&D activities in software firms increasingly focuses on structured methodologies and more codified communication.

The follow-up interviews, conducted in 1997 with the project managers of ten firms included in the 1990 survey, do not change much the picture discussed above. Experience with service (SERV) is the most important skill (mean score = 4.25; sd = 1.09), followed by SYST (mean score = 4.06; sd = 1.01). MATH skill remains the least important skill in the sample firms' innovative activities, as illustrated in Appendix C. As discussed previously, the differences in average scores between 1990 and 1997 are not statistically significant.

3.2 External sources of technological change

This study compares different external sources of innovation at the firm level. The access to these sources may differ with respect to two dimensions:

a. the nature of linkages activated, which varies from informal exchange of know-how among scientists, engineers or managers to formal collaborative agreements;
b. the type of knowledge provided by the external sources, ranging from generic, scientific knowledge to context-specific, uncodified know-how.

The external sources of innovation analysed in this section are described in Table 6.1. Table 6.3 indicates that the main sources of technological change for the sample firms overall are innovative users and linkages with hardware manufacturers.[7]

---

6 As in Chapter 3, chi-square statistics used to test the difference between small firms (up to 34 million dollars of annual revenue) and large firms (above 34 million dollars), and that between firms with different specialisations.

7 In this context hardware manufacturers correspond to the computer divisions of integrated hardware software producers (HW). Therefore, project managers from the software divisions of HW firms gave a score to the importance of links with the computer division of their own company or other HW firms.

Table 6.3 Sources of technological change

	PUBL	FAIRS	MEETING	UNIV	HARDW	COOPSW
Total[a]	3.02	2.22	2.94	2.51	3.33	2.68
Std. dvt.	1.28	1.16	1.22	1.47	1.36	1.38
HW [b]	3.75	3.50	3.81	3.57	4.00	3.06
SW [c]	2.88	2.00	2.76	2.38	3.20	2.49
Chi-square	1.76	8.15	4.90	3.70	1.76	0.10
p-values	0.18	0.00	0.03	0.05	0.18	0.47

	INFORM	PROFES	USERS	NEWPERS	IMITAT
Total	2.56	2.42	3.56	2.91	2.09
Std dvt	1.18	1.22	1.22	1.19	1.20
HW[b]	2.69	2.50	3.38	2.19	3.00
SW[c]	2.63	2.38	3.59	3.10	1.83
Chi-square	0.06	0.15	0.24	3.40	4.40
p-values	0.79	0.69	0.62	0.06	0.03

Notes
a.   Means of scores from 1 = not relevant to 5 = very relevant.
b.   HW = firms which manufacture hardware and software systems.
c.   SW = firms specialised in software and services.

The importance of innovative users in the development of new software solutions sheds further light on the meaning of market opportunities in this industry. For many software firms, the exploration of these opportunities is not a process based on sophisticated and costly market research techniques. On the contrary, these opportunities are often indicated by innovative users. After all, most successful software products have been developed to meet the needs of specific users and then packaged for the market. This suggests that linkages with lead users reduce the need for searching new market opportunities. This does not mean, however, that all linkages with users are conducive to major innovation. In fact, except for innovative users, the majority of users are risk-averse and this is a major reason for the incremental pattern of innovation discussed in Chapter 5.

Linkages with users and hardware producers are important channels of innovation for firms of different size and specialisation. However, there are differences between HW and SW firms with respect to the importance assigned to external sources of innovation. HW firms rely on a wider range of external sources of innovation, as compared with specialised firms. HW firms have access to codified and relatively 'generic' channels of technological change, including scientific and technical publications, trade fairs, meetings and seminars, and universities (see Table 6.3). SW firms, by contrast, rely almost exclusively on informal, tacit, and context-specific channels of technical knowledge, including users and acquisition of new personnel.[8] HW firms do not rely on the hiring of new personnel probably because they carry out significant in-house training activities.

As discussed before, HW firms rely on a larger set of appropriability means, including copyright. Therefore, these firms show greater incentives to capture the technological opportunities arising from external sources of innovation and, at the same time, a larger ability to internalise the positive externalities generated by their in-house R&D activity.

HW firms' ability to set up links with a wide range of external sources of innovation can be explained by the fact that R&D activities in HW firms are more organised than those of the SW firms (see Chapter 5). HW firms may take advantage of their large size to reach a greater internal division of labour between scientists, marketing personnel, and software engineers, each of whom can focus on different external sources of knowledge. Moreover, HW firms' diversified 'knowledge capital' and customer base may require different types of technologies, especially in the field of software applications, where these firms show fewer in-house capabilities compared with specialised software firms. Finally, HW firms are likely to have a greater organisational ability to manage a variety of external links as compared with SW firms.

HW firms' greater propensity to set up links with universities apparently contradicts the results of previous studies showing that academic research is a more important source of spillovers for small firms as compared with their larger counterparts (Link and Rees, 1900; Acs et al., 1992). However, our analysis focuses on direct linkages with universities, while previous studies have analysed both direct and indirect links with academic research, such as the hiring of new personnel with a university degree, which is a significant source of innovation for many SW firms.[9]

There are some differences between firms specialised in *software platforms* (system software and development tools) and firms specialised in *software solutions* (application solutions, customised software and services). The former focus more on publications, fairs, meetings and universities as external sources of innovation, while the latter rely on lead users, the links with hardware manufacturers, and the acquisition of new personnel. The

8 However, only the acquisition of new personnel shows a statistically significant difference between HW and SW. Moreover, firms specialised in system software and tools show quite a specific pattern. For instance, for firms specialised in tools the modal score for universities is 5.
9 Another important difference with previous studies is that our analysis does not compare the innovative performance of different types of firms with the research expenditures or the scientific output of the university.

hiring of new personnel is particularly important for firms specialised in customised software and services. These differences show that there is a relationship between the nature of firms' competencies (measured by their product specialisation) and the types of channels firms choose to gain access to external knowledge. The following section studies more in detail this relationship by focusing on different types of skills used in the innovative activity.

Firm size does not show any significant effect on the propensity to search for external sources of technological change.

The follow-up interviews carried out in 1997 confirm that lead users represent the most important source of innovation for software firms. The relationships with hardware manufacturers are less important than in the 1990s survey, while formal and informal external relationships with other software firms and outside professional consultants become more important (see Appendix B).

4. THE ASSOCIATION BETWEEN INTERNAL SKILLS AND EXTERNAL SOURCES OF INNOVATION

4.1. Theory and research hypotheses[10]

Recent studies on the economics of innovation have shown that knowledge is not a homogenous good. At one end of the spectrum, knowledge can be abstract and codified or articulable, and therefore it can be easily transmitted across individuals and firms. At the other end, knowledge can be localised, context-specific, difficult to articulate and transfer across firms. This type of knowledge is person-embodied and can be in part transferred through personal, informal contacts, and training (Winter, 1987).

Even the skills and capabilities based on a formal, scientific background (for example, mathematics or physics) are, in part, tacit. As Nelson (1962) and other scholars have illustrated, the knowledge created during scientific activities is usually difficult to articulate and evaluate from outside (see Chapter 2). Also, the knowledge relative to complex processes is difficult to disentangle and transmit in separated batches because of the intricate interconnections among different parts and tasks of these processes. As a consequence, when knowledge is tacit, it is difficult to rely on any 'a priori' division of labour among tasks and capabilities. In the course of a scientific project or during the development of a complex software product there may

10 A different version of the model discussed in this section was published before by the author (see Malerba and Torrisi, 1992).

be numerous and unpredictable interactions between different tasks and the division of labour among these tasks evolves accordingly. However, the type of background (for example, formal education and training), learning by doing and 'learning to learn' bring about some degree of specialisation of skills and increase the opportunities for division of labour in innovative activities.

For the sake of simplicity, I assume that firms use two distinct types of skills or capabilities in their innovative activities: generic-abstract skills (general-purpose skills) and context or application specific skills (context-specific skills). This distinction draws on a distinction between general-abstract knowledge and context-specific knowledge discussed in Chapter 2.

General-purpose skills provide firms with absorptive capacity and ability to re-use local knowledge for different purposes, that is the ability to abstract knowledge from a specific context in order to allocate this knowledge to different uses.

Context-specific skills provide firms with the capacity to solve problems by way of trial-and-error, know-how, and experience. Although these skills are unlikely to lead to major technological changes, they may provide firms with the ability to address new questions to the sources of general-abstract knowledge, thus stimulating further basic research.

Given their complementarity, these two types of skills are jointly used in the innovative activities. However, their effects on the firms' ability or propensity to gain access to different external sources of innovation (for example, lead users and universities) are probably very different. For our purposes, it is useful to distinguish three possible effects of in-house skills. First, there is a positive absorptive effect, which relies on the ability to evaluate and use knowledge generated in a specific context in another context. Second, there is a positive complementary effect, which arises from the ability to point out the lack of in-house competencies and the need for external complementary ones. Third, there is a negative uncodifiability effect, which depends on idiosyncrasy and the difficulty to articulate, separate, and transfer localised (application or user specific) knowledge.

Table 6.4 shows the different importance of these effects between general–purpose skills and context-specific skills.

As Table 6.4 illustrates, general-purpose skills may have strong positive absorptive and complementary effects on the external sources of innovation. As mentioned before, general-purpose skills provide firms with the ability to evaluate knowledge from outside.

This ability, in turn, may favour the establishment of linkages with external sources of innovations (absorptive effect).

Table 6.4 Expected effects of different types of skills on external linkages

	Absorptive effect	Complementarity effect	Uncodifiability effect
General-purpose skills[a]	***	**	*
Context-specific skills[a]	*	**	***

Notes
a. * = not relevant, ** = relevant, *** = very relevant

More precisely, this type of skills may work as a bridge to external scientific knowledge (for example, from universities or consultants) that is required to understand and solve technical problems. Also, these capabilities may increase a firm's ability to highlight the lack of in-house complementary skills (complementary effect), such as technical or marketing ones, thus spurring on the search for these complementary skills through the set up of external linkages (for example, hardware manufacturers or software firms). By the same token, general-purpose skills may indirectly stimulate interactions with end users by indicating to system engineers and programmers significant complementarities with users' knowledge, or they may interact directly with users during of the innovative process. For instance, in the development of new artificial intelligence systems, the mathematics and human language experts have to interact with users, who possess the knowledge of the 'domain' (for example, medical diagnostics). However, except for the case of highly skilled users, the effect of general-purpose skills on the linkages with users should be less marked than the effects on other sources of innovation because of the 'distance' between these skills and the problems that users aim to solve. Finally, these skills should be highly flexible or reusable across different contexts (applications) in that they specialise in tasks (such as the generation of mathematical models for the simulation of complex decisional processes) which can be easily adapted for many different uses. Therefore, one should expect a weak uncodifiability effect (see Table 6.4).

Skills in mathematics (MATH) and computer science (COMP) are a fairly good proxy of general-purpose capabilities in the software industry, although computer science skills have a less generic nature compared with those in mathematics in that they draw on applied science and engineering rather than on basic knowledge (see Cohen and Levinthal, 1989).

The expected effect of context-specific skills on a firm's propensity to set up external linkages is ambiguous. On the one hand, these skills, as mentioned above, provide firms with a deep knowledge of technical and organisational problems. Therefore, they should blend with generic skills to highlight the lack of in–house complementary skills (complementary effect). On the other, these skills are based on tacit and uncodifiable know–how, compared with generic skills. Although there may be some informal exchange of know-how between technicians and engineers of different organisations, the knowledge underlying these skills and the type of activities in which they specialise are difficult to separate from their original context to be transferred or shared with external sources of innovation (uncodifiability effect). For example, the design of a system architecture and the combination of different component technologies are difficult to unbundle and transmit across firms. For this reason, software firms usually internalise system integration activity while other simpler and separable tasks (for example, detailed design and programming) are subcontracted. Finally, the close links with a specific application or users should reduce the monitoring and absorptive ability of context-specific skills (weak absorptive effect). The net effect of these skills on the firms' propensity to establish links with external sources of innovation is negative when the negative uncodifiability effect overcomes the positive complementary effect. Also, context-specific skills should favour linkages with similar sources of knowledge such as lead users. By definition, these skills are close to specific users and applications; therefore they are likely to increase a firm's ability to exploit the opportunities arising from these sources of knowledge.

The knowledge of applications and experience with users (SERV) represent, in theory, the most idiosyncratic and context-specific types of skills because they are bounded to the problems of specific users and applications.

Skills in system engineering (SYST) have some features in common with skills in computer science, but they tend to be closer to the needs of specific users.

The discussion of the differences among various innovative skills suggests the following hypotheses for the empirical analysis.

Hypothesis 1. Firms that rely on general-purpose skills, such as those in mathematics, for their innovative activities will be open towards a wide range of external sources of innovation, including sources of generic, codified knowledge, such as universities, and sources of more specific knowledge such as competitors.

Hypothesis 2. Firms relying on context-specific skills, such as the experience with particular applications, for their innovative activities will be less open towards external sources of innovation compared with firms relying on general-purpose skills. However, they will be more open towards context-specific sources of knowledge (for example, lead users).

4.2. Results and discussion

The research hypotheses introduced above have been tested with ordered logit models that describe the probability of establishing links with external sources of technological change as a function of different innovative capabilities. Although the data do not allow a causal link to be estabilished between the two sets of variables, my interpretation relies on the assumption that firm-specific skills and capabilities vary over a longer time horizon compared to the relationships with external sources of technological change. As a matter of fact, these relationships are often established to allow short-term transactions of intermediate goods (for example, technology) between different organisations. By contrast, the changes in the firms' core competencies occur in the long time because they require a complex process of selection and training. However, the analysis yields interesting results even if one considers the connection between the explanatory and response variables as an association rather than a causal relationship.[11]

The set of response variables includes five external sources of technological change:

a.   linkages with universities (UNIV);
b.   connections with hardware manufacturers (HARDW);
c.   cooperation agreements with software houses (COOPSW);
e.   informal relationships with software houses (INFORM);
d.   new ideas from innovative users (USERS).

The explanatory variables are the following: MATH, COMP, SYST, and SERV. Moreover, a dummy variable DHW and firms' 1989 revenues (SALES) are employed to control for, respectively, the effects of firm specialisation (HW firms vs. SW firms) and firm size.

As discussed before, data used for this analysis are multivariate ordinal observations rating along a five-point semantic scale. This justifies the use of ordered logit models (see Appendix D for an introduction to these models).

For the purposes here, the following equations corresponding to the five

---

11 The model specified is a reduced form. To specify the underlying structural form we should introduce a theory of firm behaviour.

dependent variables UNIV, HARDW, COOPSW, INFORM, and USERS, were estimated separately

$$L_i = f(S, z) \tag{6.1}$$

where L_i are the dependent variables (i=1,...5), S is the vector of internal skills and z is a vector which includes firm size (SALES) and the dummy variable DHW. Tables 6.5 to 6.9 show the results of logit analysis. The correlation coefficients among these variables and the explanatory variables are reported in Appendix C, Tables C.2 and C.3. The results of the logit regressions can be summarised as follows (see Tables 6.5 to 6.9).[12]

The effects of general-purpose capabilities

The results from logit regressions confirm that MAT and COMP skills have positive effects on the links with different types of external sources of innovation. Firms that rely on MAT skills in their innovative activities show a greater propensity to set up linkages with universities (UNIV) and informal links with other software firms (INFORM).[13] COMP skills have a positive effect on formal links with software firms (COOPSW). These results indicate the importance of the absorptive and monitoring capabilities associated with these skills. It is important to note that COMP skills have a negative effect on the logit of USERS. This result suggests that firm relying on general–purpose skills in their innovative activities may have a limited ability to develop the relationships with lead users, thus failing to capture the ideas and stimulation arising from this potential source of innovation.

The effects of context-specific capabilities

The logit estimates reported in the tables show that SYST and SERV skills have insignificant effects on the majority of linkages with external sources of innovation, including university and other software firms (the positive coefficients do not pass the t-test). Unlike the general-purpose skills, however, context-specific skills (SYST) have a strong positive effect on the links with the most context-specific external source of innovation (USERS).

As mentioned before, the context-specific skills have two expected contrasting effects on the linkages with external sources of innovation.

The results discussed so far indicate that the positive complementary effect is overcome by the negative context-specific effect, which generates an

---

12 The estimated coefficient of MARK is omitted because it interacts with other regressors.
13 The *t*-value is just below the threshold value (see Table 5.5).

Table 6.5 Ordered logit estimates for link with universities (UNIV)

Variables	Estimates		
CONSTANT	1.074	1.059	1.237
	(0.514)[a]	(0.506)	(0.589)
MATH	0.352	0.352	0.296
	(1.865)	(1.764)	(1.331)
COMP	0.115	0.112	0.106
	(0.474)	(0.464)	(0.439)
SYST	−0.092	−0.089	−0.148
	(−0.258)	(−0.248)	(−0.409)
SERV	−0.419	−0.425	−0.389
	(−1.267)	(−1.079)	(−0.981)
SALES	−	0.000	−
		(0.313)	
DHW	−	−	0.939
			(1.106)
Log. L.	−48.974	−48.925	−48.353
Cov (π, π^*)	0.632	0.697	0.654
	(0.000)	(0.000)	(0.000)
Observations	34	34	34

Notes
a.   Asymptotic *t*-values are in parentheses.

'inward looking' attitude in innovative activities.

These results overall indicate that a division of labour exists between different in-house skills. General-purpose skills specialise in creating links with a variety of external sources of innovation, including the sources of general-purpose, abstract knowledge (for example, university), but do not help firms to have access to more context-specific sources of knowledge. By contrast, context-specific skills enable firms to integrate the localised knowledge available from context-specific sources of innovations (for example, lead users) into their knowledge capital.

These results are robust when controlling for the effect of firm size (SALES) and specialisation (DHW). Thus, both large (integrated) firms and small (specialised) firms in the software industry resort to external sources of of knowledge for their innovative activities. The complexity and multidisciplinarity of knowledge underpinning software innovative activities force even the largest HW firms to rely on external sources of innovation. As discussed in Chapter 3, during the 1970s and the 1980s these firms reduced their commitment in software technology thus allowing the growth of an independent software industry.

Table 6.6 Ordered logit estimates for links with computer manufactures (HARDW)

Variables	Estimates		
CONSTANT	1.914	1.902	1.949
	(0.925)[a]	(0.922)	(0.940)
MATH	−0.088	− 0.087	−0.143
	(−0.331)	(−0.328)	(−0.507)
COMP	0.136	0.141	0.122
	(0.532)	(0.552)	(0.479)
SYST	0.272	0.278	0.225
	(0.814)	(0.832)	(0.657)
SERV	−0.351	−0.341	−0.283
	(−0.928)	(−0.907)	(−0.725)
SALES	−	−0.001	−
		(−0.794)	
DHW	−	−	0.564
			(0.636)
Log. L.	−52.300	−52.011	−52.083
Cov (π, π^*)	0.446	0.521	0.545
	(0.050)	(0.002)	(0.001)
Observations	34	34	34

Notes
a.   Asymptotic *t*-values are in parentheses

More recently, HW firms have re-focused their business activities towards the software sector. At present, however, HW firms can neither dominate all the relevant technologies nor possess the detailed information on the users' needs in the many software submarkets. The results discussed in this section does not contradict the analysis of Section 3, which shows HW firms relying on a wider set of external sources of innovations compared with SW firms. For the purposes here, I focus on external sources that do not show significant differences between HW and SW firms, except for UNIV, to which HW firms assign a greater importance compared with SW firms (see Table 6.3).

5. CONCLUSIONS

This chapter examines the relationship between firms' in-house innovative capabilities and external sources of innovation. The analysis of data collected in 1990 through interviews with 51 firms located in Europe shows that software firms rely on different in-house capabilities for their innovative

Table 6.7 Ordered logit estimates for formal links with software firms (COOPSW)

Variables	Estimates		
CONSTANT	−3.967	−4.214	−4.288
	(−1.735)[a]	(−1.828)	(−1.833)
MATH	0.173	0.154	0.022
	(0.636)	(0.558)	(0.078)
COMP	0.378	0.384	0.383
	(1.930)	(1.844)	(1.828)
SYST	0.131	0.151	0.498
	(0.345)	(0.399)	(0.012)
SERV	0.540	0.552	0.789
	(1.764)	(1.876)	(2.031)
SALES	−	0.005	−
		(1.536)	
DHW	−	−	1.516
			(1.648)
Log. L.	−48.362	−46.712	−46.956
Cov (π, π^*)	0.697	0.733	0.696
	(0.000)	(0.000)	(0.000)
Observations	34	34	34

Notes
a. Asymptotic *t*-values are in parentheses.

activities.

Overall, skills in system engineering, computer science and experience with applications are the most critical skills while those in mathematics are the least important.

Significant differences across firms emerge as a function of the firms' product specialisation. Integrated hardware-software producers (HW) rely more on mathematical skills for their innovative activities compared with specialised software firms (SW). Producers of system software and development tools also make use of computer and mathematics skills in their innovative activities.

Technological and economic change spur firms in innovative sectors to seek external sources of knowledge. The majority of software firms analysed in this work rely on leading users as a major source of innovation.

Like the use of internal capabilities, the access to external sources of innovation varies significantly across firms. HW firms show a greater propensity to establish linkages with various external sources of innovation, ranging from the typical sources of general-abstract knowledge (for example,

Table 6.8 Ordered logit estimates for informal links with software firms (INFORM)

Variables	Estimates		
CONSTANT	1.419	1.648	1.402
	(0.689)[a]	(0.784)	(0.682)
MATH	0.579	0.618	0.559
	(2.082)	(2.186)	(1.945)
COMP	−0.088	−0.093	−0.091
	(−0.363)	(−0.379)	(−0.377)
SYST	−0.104	−0.126	−0.117
	(−0.300)	(−0.355)	−(0.334)
SERV	−0.428	−0.428	−0.404
	(−1.620)	(−1.412)	(−1.424)
SALES	–	−0.006	–
		(−0.912)	
DHW	–	–	0.243
			(0.268)
Log L	−46.458	−46.308	−47.489
Cov (π, π*)	0.698	0.630	0.624
Observations	(0.000)	(0.000)	(0.000)
	34	34	34

Notes
a. Asymptotic *t*-values are in parentheses.

publications, fairs, meetings and linkages with universities) to the sources of context-specific knowledge (lead users). By contrast, SW firms rely more on links with HW firms and lead users as channels to new knowledge. Moreover, SW firms do not have strong direct links with universities, but have access to new knowledge and methodologies developed in universities, through the hiring of new skilled personnel.

Size does not show any significant effect on software firms' propensity to use specific types of internal skills or to gain access to external sources of innovations.

Ten follow-up interviews carried out in 1997 confirmed the analysis based on the 1990 survey. The new data indicate an increasing importance of system engineering and computer science as innovative capabilities, to the detriment of skills in mathematics. Compared to the 1990 survey, users are still the most important source of innovation. Also, relationships with other software firms and outside consultants gain importance compared with relationships with hardware manufacturers and general-abstract sources of knowledge (for example, university).

Table 6.9 Ordered logit estimates for ideas from lead users (USERS)

Variables	Estimates		
CONSTANT	−0.500	−0.565	−0.611
	(−0.241)[a]	(−0.269)	(−0.286)
MATH	−0.029	−0.057	−0.132
	(−0.110)	(−0.214)	(−0.484)
COMP	−0.514	−0.533	−0.513
	(−1.980)	(−2.037)	(−2.021)
SYST	0.791	0.827	0.692
	(2.050)	(2.069)	(1.721)
SERV	0.409	0.403	0.581
	(1.089)	(1.057)	(1.413)
SALES	−	0.004	−
		(1.467)	
DHW	−	−	1.141
			(1.134)
Log L	−46.210	−44.725	−45.540
Cov (π, π*)	0.724	0.767	0.739
	(0.000)	(0.000)	(0.000)
Observations	34	34	34

Notes
a.   Asymptotic *t*-values are in parentheses.

These results suggest that innovative activities of software firms during the 1990s have increasingly focused on development rather than basic research.

The next step of the analysis concerns the relationship between internal skills and external sources of innovation. For our purposes, a simple theoretical model is introduced. This model distinguishes between general–purpose skills (a fairly good proxy of which are skills in mathematics and computer science) and context-specific skills (system engineering and experience with the development of applications and services). According to this model, two research hypotheses are analysed. These concern the different effects of general-purpose and context-specific skills on the firms' propensity (ability) to establish links with other organisations. The empirical analysis, which is centred on the test of ordered logit models, shows that these two types of in-house skills have different effects on the firms' patterns of external linkages. The effects are robust also when controlling for other firm-specific variables (size and specialisation). Overall, firms which rely on general-purpose skills are open towards a wider range of external sources of innovation compared with firms which draw on context-specific skills. The latter enable firms to focus on 'localised' external sources of innovation such as lead users.

These results suggest the following policy implication. Considering the importance of links with external sources of knowledge for innovative performance and technological learning in this industry, software firms should invest more in general-purpose skills because these skills increase the ability to absorb knowledge from outside. However, this chapter indicates that software firms do not recognise the importance of general-purpose skills or have weak private incentives to invest in this type of skills. This raises two issues for public policy action. First, the public education system should contribute to the formation of these skills whose private production may be socially suboptimal. Second, public policies should inform firms, especially the small and medium-sized ones, about the potential returns of the investments in these skills in terms of a greater absorption capacity.

7. Conclusions

1. LEARNING FROM HISTORY AND STYLISED FACTS

This work draws on the history of software production and innovation and the 'stylised facts' collected from various sources. Some original data were collected to fill part of the gap in the evidence concerning the competencies used in innovative activities, the sources of innovation, and the 'division of knowledge' among software firms.

The analysis has benefited from suggestions found in the literature on technological change and market structure, on one hand, and the organisation and management of innovation on the other. A survey of the main theoretical issues is presented in Chapter 2. However, during the research questions emerged which were difficult to answer using the available stock of theories and models. It was necessary, on some occasions, to devise particular analytical frameworks and simple models to help to explore new research directions.

A main problem in the research process was to define the nature of software activities. The analysis of the specialised literature and interviews with sectoral experts confirmed that computer software and services are activities which have many similarities with other industrial engineering activities, including mechanical engineering. This, by itself, was a useful insight to direct empirical research and to develop an appropriate survey design. But what are the specific features of software activity that could be approached by the economic analysis?

Software is an intellectual, labour-intensive activity whose aim is the production of codified knowledge in the forms of methods and procedures or programs. The total software development costs are virtually all fixed costs relating to the activities of research and development, marketing and maintenance. However, the opportunities for increasing returns to scale in the production of software packages, which arise from the re-use of software programs and development methodologies, are limited by the fact that software has some characteristics of public goods. This has stimulated public support to industrial R&D and the extension of copyright to software innovation, especially in the US. The early public support has helped the US producers of software packages to exploit the opportunities for increasing returns arising from their large domestic market.

The economics of customised software (programs developed for specific customers) and services is quite different. This production shows higher marginal production costs which depend on the difficulty of re-using user-specific designs, source codes and methodologies. This difficulty in turn arises from the widespread use of job-shop, craft production techniques, especially in smaller software firms. Also, the knowledge of specific applications and user organisations is in part tacit and cannot easily be transferred to other contexts.

A further characteristic of software, especially customised software and services, is the great difficulty to define, 'ex ante', the product of the R&D activity. Like other industrial engineering activities, the development of a large, complex system requires continuous interaction with customers and involves many different actors: end users, system integrators and a series of specialised suppliers of different components. These interactions, particularly those between user and producer, make the outcome of development activities unpredictable. Moreover, the division of labour in software R&D activities tends to be an evolutionary one, in that it evolves during the R&D process with the acquisition of information and experience.

Finally, despite its 'revolutionary' effects on many different user sectors, software technology appears to evolve incrementally. However, there have been important discontinuities which have had 'competence-destroying' effects on established firms. For instance, firms that have grown in the 1960s and 1970s by developing software and services for large proprietary systems (mainframes and minicomputers) have been challenged by new 'open' platforms (computer architectures and operating systems) for personal computers and, more recently, by the client–server platforms and Internet-based development environments (for example, Java programming language and Hyper Text Markup Language, HTML). Some firms have been able to adapt their competencies to new platforms by developing new products, while others have lagged behind of technological change and went out of the market. These discontinuities have also created many windows of opportunities for new entries.

These characteristics of software development have evolved over time. Chapter 4 provides an historical reconstruction of this evolution which is based on various literature sources. At present, several users produce a significant amount of their software applications in-house. But the variety of complex technical and organisational problems that software products are required to solve, together with other economic and institutional factors, has brought about the vertical disintegration of software activities and the emergence of an independent software industry. At present specialised software firms account for about 70 per cent of total packaged software production in the US and Western Europe.

The analysis conducted in this chapter highlighted the main variables that have shaped the organisation of software activities since the 1950s.

First is the pervasiveness of software products which creates opportunities for technological convergence similar to those experienced by the machine tools industry in the last century. The possibility to use similar software programs and development tools in many different industries has brought about a rapid market growth. This is turn has spurred vertical disintegration and specialisation of software activities. Particularly, technological convergence has opened up many 'windows of opportunity' for firms specialising in specific applications. Think, for instance, of the variety of payroll or fiscal packages developed in many different countries or the plethora of other office automation programs developed for the requirements of specific organisations. Most of these products have been developed with a similar set of programming languages and have been based on similar 'platforms' (hardware, operating systems and development tools). However, due to the flexibility of software technology and the variety of users' needs, many of these products have quite unique, custom-specific features.

Another important factor that has helped lead to the changing organisation of software activities is the complementarity between hardware and software. The advances in hardware technology are an important stimulus to change. Software products have to adapt continuously to changes in hardware technologies and, on some occasions, the introduction of major innovations in computers (for example, personal computers) and electronic components (for example, integrated circuits and the microprocessor) have stimulated major breakthroughs in the software technology. The progress in electronic components and the related reduction of size and costs of computers have contributed to the rise and take off of many independent software firms, especially since the invention of microprocessor and personal computer.

Moreover, hardware manufacturers and scientific users have played a major role in the early software developments. During the 1940s and 1950s, scientists and engineers from universities, government agencies and hardware manufactures shared a *common set of rules, beliefs and expertise.* They played a role similar to that played by the Scientific and Technical Societies during the Industrial Revolution in the accumulation of a stock of knowledge and the diffusion of competencies which provided the basis for a new business activity.

Finally, an important institutional breakthrough in the industrial organisation of software activities came at the end of the 1960s when IBM, under the pressure of the US anti-trust, introduced a business practice consisting in selling software separately from hardware ('unbundling'). This also spurred on the development of an independent software industry and explains the declining proportion of hardware manufacturers in software production since then. More recently hardware firms have tried to re-enter software activities, particularly focusing on services and system integration, where established consulting firms (for example, Arthur Andersen and KPMG Marwick) and computer service providers (for example, EDS and Cap Gemini) also show a rising commitment. This produces further effects on the organisation of software activities.

These factors together have stimulated specialisation and the emergence of an independent software industry. The different combinations of these factors also account for major differences among countries. In particular, the largest European countries (Germany, France, the UK, and Italy) have lagged behind in the development of an independent software industry as compared with the US, with important consequences for the present (and the future) pattern of specialisation in the international market.

The following factors have accounted for the main differences between US and European experiences. First is the geographical proximity with leading hardware manufacturers. Second is the size of the domestic market. Third is the regulation of competition and the evolution of public policies focusing on IT, including the application of copyright to software and the public support for R&D in software technology, which varies significantly between Western Europe and the US.

US software producers have enjoyed the externalities arising from the interactions with the world leading hardware manufacturers located in the same country. These externalities have accrued in particular to software packages and operating systems, whose technology is closely related to progress in hardware. US producers of software packages have also benefited from a large and homogeneous domestic market, which has requested an increasing variety of software products. By contrast, in Western Europe cultural and linguistic differences are still responsible for a high level of market fragmentation.

Moreover, IBM's 'unbundling' affected the US market first, thus providing the domestic software firms with a lead time compared to their European competitors. Finally, as mentioned before, the US firms have benefited from an early, strong public support to software technology since the 1950s. The US government has supported industrial R&D in computers and software. For instance, the Semi-Automated Ground Environment (SAGE) project was carried out by MIT with the support of the US Air Force. During the 1950s and 1960s, the Advanced Research Project Agency (ARPA) and the National Science Foundation provided a significant financial support to the R&D in the field of software. The US government also helped the domestic industry through public procurements, which accounted for a large share of the domestic market until the early 1980s. Public procurements in the US have allowed the entry of new firms and favoured technological competition. Finally, the US copyright legislation was extended to software in 1980 (Software Amendment to the US Copyright Act of 1976).

In the European software industry the late and often inconsistent public support for software development has limited innovativeness and affected firms' specialisation. During the 1960s and 1970s, the national governments of the main European countries focused their actions (R&D subsidies and public procurement) to a few large 'national champions' specialised in electronics and computer hardware. Policies explicitly directed to software technology and independent software firms were inaugurated only in the 1980s, under the auspices of the European Commission Programmes (especially, Esprit and Eureka). European national policies have thus contributed to the fragmentation of the European market and have allowed little entry of new firms, especially in software. Moreover, the main European countries have lagged behind in legal protection of software innovation. The European Commission gave a directive concerning the application of copyright to software in 1991 and many European countries have assimilated the EU recommendations thereafter.

These factors explain why US firms were the first to enter the market of packaged software, pre-empting the entrance of European producers. The latter were spurred on to specialise in customised software (which often consists of adapting US packages to local markets) and professional services. Currently, the majority of the European software producers are small sized, specialising in small market niches, whereas US firms benefit from the increasing returns to scale in the production of software packages. Also, in customised software and services (for example, facility management and system integration) US hardware manufacturers and large computer service providers show strong competitive advantages.

The introduction of personal computers, the diffusion of LANs and increasing internationalisation of markets spurred major changes in the software industry in the 1980s. During this period, many new firms entered the market and most established firms undertook a major restructuring. In the 1990s the convergence between telecommunications and computer services, the rising importance of the domestic market, and the Internet have introduced new market opportunities and encouraged further changes in the organisation of the software industry.

The different historical evolution of software activities in the US and Western Europe explains some differences in the patterns of firms' growth and restructuring in recent years. To this end, I collected data on external growth (joint ventures, M&As and non-equity agreements) and internal corporate changes (creation or shutdown of subsidiaries and divisions, job cuts and so on) concerning 38 large US and European firms specialised in software and services in the period 1984–92. The main differences between US and European firms are the following. First, European firms relied more on international operations compared with US firms. This indicates the different size of their respective domestic markets. Second, US firms showed a larger share of research-oriented operations compared with their European counterparts. This difference reflects the specialisation of the US firms in software packages, whose production is more R&D-intensive compared with customised software and services.

Besides these differences, US and European firms show interesting similarities. All sample firms were subject to major restructuring during the period analysed. Most operations aimed to increase the scale of firms' activities either through internal growth and external growth (M&As, joint ventures and other collaborative agreements). Moreover, both the US and European firms relied mostly on external growth operations, which in many cases represented an efficient alternative to internal growth, by enabling software firms to grow fast in a rapidly changing economic environment.

2. THE PATTERNS OF PRODUCT INNOVATIONS

As discussed before, most European firms develop customised software and services. If European firms aim to survive the competition with the large US firms in this market segment, they have to direct their R&D efforts to improve their organisation and increase their rate of product/service innovation.

This study analyses the innovative activities of European software firms, ranging from the nature of product and process innovations to the in-house capabilities employed in innovative activities and the links with external sources of technological change. The analysis draws on data collected in 1990 through interviews with project managers of 51 firms. I also carried out follow-up interviews with ten of these firms in 1997 to take account of possible changes that may have occurred in the last few years. Two of these firms are integrated hardware-software firms. Chapter 5 focuses on the patterns of product and process innovations.

My analysis of European software producers confirms that the European software industry focuses on continuous, incremental product innovations. However, the interviews conducted in 1997 revealed an increased emphasis on major product innovations compared with the survey conducted in 1990. This is probably the result of recent changes associated with new Internet-based software platforms and the increased globalisation of markets, which have spurred European firms to introduce new products. This result is confirmed by the greater importance of copyright and lead time as instruments for the protection of innovation compared with 1990.

Moreover, the analysis aimed to study the firms' incentives to become involved in different types of product innovations. The different roles played by market opportunities and technological opportunities were explored by ordered logit models. The main results of this analysis can be summarised as follows.

New market opportunities stimulate the development of major innovations (new products for a new type of demand) and have a negative effect on minor innovations (new features in existing products). By contrast, technological opportunities arising from advances in hardware technology stimulate minor, continuous innovations in software products and make the development of major innovations unlikely. This reflects the fact that, despite its rapid change, the trajectories of hardware technology are quite well established. Therefore, software firms can anticipate technological opportunities arising from hardware and adapt their products incrementally. As mentioned before, technological breakthroughs of hardware technology have stimulated major changes in software in the past; but the results of my analysis reflect the recent evolution of software innovation. In the future, a major source of radical change for software firms may be the convergence of telecommunications, computers and consumer electronics. However, the most critical aspect of this process of convergence is more related to market differences and software than hardware technology. Technological convergence is a process which has started early in the 1980s with digitalisation of telephone networks, the development of computer-based communication and, more recently, the development of client-server computer architectures. The convergence of markets is a much slower process which is constrained by differences across users and distribution channels. The emergence of 'multimedia' markets depends mostly on the convergence of distribution channels and progress of software technology. As a matter of fact, many recent Internet-based multimedia services are based on the combination of traditional telephone networks and client–server computer communication networks architectures. The developers of Internet-based software and services are thus exploiting technological opportunities of hardware technologies that have been there for quite a long time. It is likely that new market opportunities will be perceived as an important source of major product innovations for software firms also in the future, because the convergence of many new markets will increase the possibility of experimentation and product variety.

A related aim of the survey was to analyse the differences among different types of software firms, particularly the differences between integrated hardware and software producers, on the one hand, and specialised software firms on the other. Also, the differences between producers of *software platforms* (system software and application tools) and *software solutions* (application solutions and services) and the differences between large and small firms were tested with respect to the types of product innovations carried out, the nature of the incentives to become involved in these innovations, and the mechanisms for the appropriation of innovations.

Concerning the characteristics of product innovations, there are no statistically significant differences between integrated hardware–software producers (HW firms) and specialised software producers (SW firms). The differences between large and small firms, and between firms of different production profiles, have also been shown not to be significant. This gives support to the hypothesis that the *appropriability advantages* of large, diversified firms are outweighed by the *managerial disadvantages* highlighted in the economics and management literature with respect to the incentives (ability) to undertake innovations.

Substantial differences emerged between HW firms and SW firms with respect to the appropriability mechanisms. The former show a greater propensity (ability) to resort to both legal protection (copyright, patents and trade secrets) and *dynamic appropriability* instruments (lead time and continuous product improvements). By contrast, the specialised software firms exclusively rely on dynamic appropriability mechanisms. Moreover, large firms, regardless of their specialisation, confirm their greater ability to enforce legal protection, particularly trade secrets, as compared with smaller firms. No significant results emerged between producers of *software platforms* and *software solutions*.

Finally, legal protection become increasingly more important for large SW firms, as indicated by the follow-up interviews made in 1997. This result is consistent with the increasing importance of major product innovations and the declining uncertainty surrounding the legal protection of software innovation in Europe after the EU directive of 1992.

3. PROCESS AND ORGANISATIONAL INNOVATIONS IN SOFTWARE ACTIVITIES

The history of software activities reveals that the efforts to introduce new development tools, structured methodologies, and managerial control of the development process have been a major concern for the community of software developers since the 1960s. Two important conferences on software engineering were held in the US at that time. They discussed the organisational changes in software R&D required by the recurring failures of critical software systems (for example, in banking). Software engineering has been spurred by these breakdowns and the low productivity of software activities. This discipline focuses on modularisation and rigid specification of interfaces, standardisation of program structures and the introduction of rigorous management and control systems.

The maturation of the software industry in the 1980s and the 1990s has brought about increasing emphasis on process and organisational innovations. These are also important for European software firms which, as mentioned before, specialise in customised software and services. These activities usually do not produce major technological breakthroughs, but require the use of quality control systems, service expertise and organisational skills which are important to adapt fast to the evolution of users' needs. The experience of large US and European computer service firms indicates that thet development of large software systems requires a rigorous organisational technology which is based on the use of standard tools and methodologies. This does not mean that the software development processes have to be standardised and divided into simple tasks in the same way as the 'scientific' production systems of the traditional manufacturing factories do. However, previous studies have showed that an incremental, evolutionary development approach, the use of fast prototyping and trial-and-error procedures may significantly improve the development of software systems. Adopting flexible development techniques enables software firms to increase the efficiency of their R&D and production activities.

The introduction of software engineering has been uneven among software producers, showing certain structural differences which have emerged in the analysis.

On the one hand, large integrated hardware–software producers in the US and Japan and some large system integrators (like SD-Scicon, Cap Gemini and Finsiel) have introduced significant process and organisational innovations (for example, the 'Chief Programmer Team' first introduced by IBM in the 1970s), which allow better control of development costs and time. In particular, the US and Japanese 'software factories' seem to have benefited from the introduction of 'strategic management and integration' of software activities in terms of increased productivity and flexibility. These experiences, however, are limited to large, complex systems, where a certain degree of division of labour in the R&D activities is required and the fixed costs of the automated systems can be spread over larger revenues. By contrast, previous studies indicate that there is a majority of small firms specialising in market niches (both packaged software and customised software) or in specific phases of the development cycle (for example, coding) that rely on job-shop, craft and ad hoc development techniques. As a consequence, the worldwide diffusion of software engineering practice is still modest, as reported by various market surveys.

This work does not aim to provide another quantitative assessment of the diffusion of software engineering, but it seeks to understand the nature of process innovations, their determinants, and obstacles within the firms. The survey results illustrated in Chapter 5 show that the majority of firms making use of new software engineering techniques aim to automate specific development phases (for example, CASE, computer-aided software coding tools) and make little use of formal methodologies (for example, Yourdon or SSADM structured methodologies) or 'fourth generation', 'object-oriented' development tools, which make software production similar to flexible manufacturing systems.

Also, SW firms show a lower propensity to resort to any type of software engineering tool as compared with HW firms (whose size is, on average, larger). This confirms the different behaviour and organisation of innovation among software producers. The integrated hardware and software producers show a particular involvement in the development of new integrated, flexible development environments. This shows the importance of these environments as a strategic component of the new IT platforms (hardware, operating systems and tools).

However, the evidence collected in 1997 shows that the differences between SW firms and HW firms are blurring. Specialised firms have increased their use of computer-aided software engineering (CASE) tools, object-oriented tools, formal methodologies and integrated project support environments (IPSE) compared with 1990.

The limited number of interviews does not allow us to reach any strong conclusions. Moreover, SW firms interviewed in 1997 are large and this reduces the expected differences with integrated firms. Many small firms interviewed in 1990 probably still rely on traditional job-shop, craft-like production systems. However, the comparison between 1990 and 1997 suggests that increased international competition, new opportunities offered by new development technologies, and the experience with the traditional software engineering tools (for example, CASE tools) have spurred large specialised software (and services) producers to shift from a job-shop production system to a more efficient and flexible production system.

Overall, among the major incentives to engage in process innovations there is the need to increase the efficiency of the development process and raise product quality. The flexibility of response to users' needs is another major determinant of process innovations. This result indicates that the new software development tools and methodologies are a source of a more flexible division of labour within the firm (despite the relatively high fixed costs associated with these new techniques). This gives support to the hypothesis that the new techniques (especially the 'object-oriented' tools) play, in the software industry, a role similar to that of flexible manufacturing systems in the manufacturing industries. The rank of the determinants of process innovation does not change significantly in 1997, except for the need to reduce the time of response to users' needs, which became the most important determinant of process innovations.

The analysis of the obstacles to process innovations shows that the major obstacles are incompatibility with familiar techniques, the difficulty for project managers to learn new types of organisation of work associated with the new techniques, lack of information on the new techniques, and uncertainty arising from expected significant changes in the existing new techniques. This picture has changed dramatically in 1997 compared to 1990. All obstacles to process innovations are less important than in the past. Software firms have probably improved their ability to use system engineering techniques. Also, in the last few years these techniques have improved their effectiveness and user-friendliness by incorporating graphical user interfaces (for example, Visual C++). Again, we should warn against the generalisation of this specific result for reasons discussed before.

Overall, the analysis of the software industry conducted in this work and other studies indicates the existence of several patterns of organisation of software activities. This intra-industry heterogeneity of firms' behaviour is reflected, in part, in the firm categories discussed so far, and can be summarised as follows.

There are three main categories of software supplier showing different patterns of innovation:

a.   Entrepreneurial start-up firms operating on the technological frontier;

b   Small and medium-sized software firms specialising in one or a few software products or services;

c.   Large firms offering system software or carrying out system integration activity.

The minority of small 'Schumpeterian' firms on the technological frontier (few of which populate the European markets) rely on unstructured and informal organisation of production and contribute to 'creative destruction' and *generation* of positive externalities in the innovative and competitive environment. Almost by definition, these firms make little use of system engineering techniques due to the difficulty of codifying their highly unpredictable activities. In a few cases, the commercial success of their products (usually software packages) account for their fast growth (for example, Borland, Oracle and Microsoft during the 1980s).

The majority of small and medium-sized firms (which represent the bulk of the European population) engage in minor or incremental product innovations and make only little use of automated tools and structured development methodologies. They also rely on a centralised, informal communication system of R&D management. A large proportion of these firms survive by specialising in small market niches (for example, accounting or technological applications for small customers) and do not grow very quickly. These firms, on the whole, play a significant role in the *diffusion* of software technology in different sectors.

Finally, established software firms include both large package developers and service suppliers, which have grown rapidly (for example, the present Microsoft and Cap Gemini), and integrated hardware–software firms. These firms show a converging pattern of innovation, despite their different backgrounds. They focus on system integration activity and their innovative activities are organised in accordance with formal methodologies and managerial systems. These firms increasingly rely on flexible systems of production and represent the locus of the *creative blending* or integration of different competencies and sources of knowledge spread in a variety of institutions. Most 1997 follow-up interviews were conducted with firms in this category.

4. FIRMS' INNOVATIVE SKILLS AND THE LINKS WITH EXTERNAL SOURCES OF TECHNOLOGICAL CHANGE

An increasingly important issue in the literature on innovation and industrial organisation is represented by the analysis of competencies and the external sources of the firms' technological change (universities, users, suppliers, competitors and so on).

This work suggests that innovative competencies at the firm level can be distinguished in *general-purpose capabilities*, which provide firms with the *ability to abstract* from a specific context and an *absorptive capacity*, and *context-specific capabilities*, which provide firms with a *trial-and-error ability* and the *ability to address new questions* to the sources of general-abstract knowledge. In the case of software activities, skills in mathematics and computer science represent, in theory, a fairly good indicator of *general-purpose* skills, while, at the other end of the spectrum, the skills based on experience accumulated in developing specific applications and services (and skills in system engineering) seem to be a good proxy for context-specific skills.

The analysis illustrated in Chapter 6 shows that the most important innovative capabilities for software firms are context-specific ones, while general-purpose capabilities are less important. In particular, the use of mathematical skills has declined between 1990 and 1997. By contrast, the importance of experience based on applications and marketing skills has increased over time.

Several external channels of technological change provide software firms with different, complementary knowledge and competencies. They range from the general-abstract knowledge provided by access to scientific and technological publications and the setting up of links with universities, to more context-specific knowledge arising from links with leading users. Lead users, the linkages with hardware manufactures and the access to scientific and technical publications are the most important sources of the firms' technological change. Interestingly enough, the sources of general-codified knowledge such as universities, publications and hardware manufacturers have reduced their importance between 1990 and 1997. On the contrary, the linkages with other software firms, external consultants, and users tend to become more important as a source of knowledge. This indicates that software firms are narrowing the scope of their innovative activities to improve their response to market opportunities and changes of users' needs. If we combine this result with the rising importance of software engineering techniques discussed above, European software firms seem to go in the direction of flexible manufacturing systems and a tighter managerial control of their innovative activities.

Significant differences emerged between SW firms and HW firms with respect to the propensity (ability) to gain access to external sources of innovation. HW firms show a propensity to gain access to a wider range of external sources of change, including the sources of general-abstract knowledge such as universities and scientific publications. If we compare this result with the wider range of appropriability mechanisms attempted by this category of firms relative to the specialised software firms, the integrated firms seem to be *net absorbers* of the positive externalities generated in the software industry. They absorb knowledge from a variety of different external sources and, at the same time, reveal a greater ability to protect their stock of proprietary knowledge from imitation. Moreover, the importance that this category of firms assigns to external sources of generic knowledge confirms the structured, formal division of labour of their R&D activities as discussed above. In particular, HW firms may take advantage of an internal division of labour between different in-house competencies which are dedicated to the setting up of links with different sources of external change (unlike SW firms, HW firms rely on mathematical skills in their innovative activities). The higher costs associated with this division of labour can be spread over a wider base of business activities (both hardware and software) as compared with specialised software firms. Therefore, a greater internal division of labour may increase the firm's 'absorptive' capacity. HW firms' greater propensity to gain access to a variety of external sources of innovation can also be explained by the recent evolution of software activities. During the 1970s and part of the 1980s, HW producers have reduced their involvement in software, particularly in application solutions. Late in the 1980s and in the 1990s, they have re-entered software activities, attracted by higher profits as compared with hardware. As mentioned above, they are focusing more on services and system integration than on packaged applications. Therefore, their competencies in many market segments remain relatively limited and need to be integrated with external sources of knowledge.

These differences between integrated and specialised firms are not affected by firm size, which does not show any significant effect on the incentives to search for or establish links with external sources of technological change. These results are confirmed by the evidence collected in 1997, even if the small sample does not allow us to test the differences between integrated and specialised software producers.

Finally, the work discusses the linkages between in-house competencies and external sources of change on the basis of a simple theoretical model. The main research hypothesis tested empirically is that different types of productive backgrounds and innovative competencies provide firms with different degrees of 'openness' towards different external sources of change.

General-purpose and context-specific capabilities may have three effects on the firm's incentive (ability) to set up links with external sources of change. First, a positive *absorptive effect* which draws on the ability to evaluate and re-use context-specific knowledge for different applications. Second, a positive *complementary effect* which relies on the ability to highlight the lack of in-house competencies. Third, a negative *uncodifiability effect* which relies on idiosycracy and the difficulty to articulate, divide and transfer localised knowledge.

This study argues that general-purpose skills have strong *absorptive* and *complementarity* effects on the firms' propensity to set up links with external sources of innovation. Also, these skills are expected to have a weak uncodifiability effect.

By contrast, context-specific skills are expected to have a *complementary effect*, similar to that of the general-purpose skills, and strong *uncodifiability effect*. Moreover, these skills should have a weak *absorptive effect*.

The test of this research hypothesis was carried out by testing logit models. Five equations corresponding to five different external links (links with universities, links with hardware producers, formal links with software firms, informal links with software firms, and links with leading users) were estimated separately. The main results of the analysis can be summarised as follows.

First, general-purpose skills (mathematics and computer science) make firms more open towards many external sources of knowledge under examination, except for the links with leading users. The effect of skills in computer science on the links with lead users is negative.

Second, context-specific skills (system engineering and experience accumulated in developing specific applications and servicing) have quite contrasting effects on the firms' propensity to set up external links with different sources of technological change. These skills show insignificant effects on the firm's propensity to set up links with most external sources of innovation, including universities and other software firms. However, they show a clear positive effect on links with lead users.

The results are robust when controlling for the effect of firm-specific characteristics (integrated hardware–software firms vs. specialised software firms) and firm size.

These results confirm that general-purpose skills provide firm's innovative activities with a greater 'outward looking' attitude compared with context-specific skills; and, probably, with a higher absorptive capacity. Moreover, and more interestingly, the analysis highlights a 'division of labour' between different types of skills working as interfaces with different types of external sources of knowledge. On the one hand, general-purpose capabilities are used to access the general, codified knowledge developed by universities and other software firms, through formal and informal linkages. On the other hand, context-specific capabilities address localised sources of knowledge such as lead users.

Our results suggest the following policy implications. Considering the importance of links with external sources of knowledge for innovation and technological learning in this industry, software firms should invest more in general-purpose skills because these skills increase the ability to absorb knowledge from outside. However, as our analysis indicates, software firms do not recognise the importance of general-purpose skills or have weak private incentives to invest in this type of skills. This raises two issues for public policy action. First, the education system should contribute to the formation of these skills whose private production is probably suboptimal from a social point of view. Second, public policies should inform firms, especially the small and medium-sized ones, about the potential returns of the investments in these skills in terms of a greater absorption capacity.

8. Appendices

APPENDIX A

Structure of the questionnaire

Section I. General information on the firm

- Annual revenues
- Employees
- Parent company
- Lines of business

Section II. Questions on the firm's product and process innovations
(multiple answers allowed, scores from 1 = not important to 5 = very
important)

- Measures of technological complexity
- Internal skills used in the innovative activities
- Characteristics of the firm's latest product innovations
- Determinants of product innovations
- Instruments for the protection of innovations
- Use of standard techniques, methods and organisational arrangements for
  software development
- Use of tools for quality assurance
- Type of new software engineering techniques in use (tools for the
  automation and support of specific phase of the software lifecycle,
  tools that support structured methods or development environments)
- Type of hardware utilised to develop software
- Type of programming language
- Type of CASE (computer-aided software engineering) or IPSE
  (integrated project support environment) tools utilised
- Use of tools for re-engineering of old software systems
- Origin of new tools, methods (developed in-house, acquired on the

market, developed in cooperation with third parties)
• Determinants of the firm's latest innovations
• Obstacles to the adoption of new software engineering techniques

Section III. Factors of competitive advantage and sources of innovation
(multiple answers allowed, scores from 1 to 5)

• Sources of the firm's technological change
• Main sources of competitive advantage
• Entry barriers into the firm's main business sector
• Barriers to diversification

Section IV. Technology and market scenarios
(open-ended answers)

• Importance of in-house production of hardware for software
  development
• Effects of technical advances in integrated circuits (specifically ASICs)
  on software activity
• Effects of the emergence of proprietary standards on innovative activity
• Probability that the software industry becomes more vertically integrated
  with hardware manufacturers

APPENDIX B

A comparison between 1990 and 1997 surveys (10 firms)

Means scores and standard deviations

Internal skills and capabilities	1990		1997	
	Mean	Std. dvt.	Mean	Std. dvt.
MATH	3.57	1.29	2.15	1.00
COMP	4.14	0.99	3.95	1.06
SYST	4.43	0.73	4.15	0.95
SERV	4.14	0.64	4.30	1.00
MARK	3.29	1.16	3.65	1.00
External sources of innovation				
PUBL	3.22	1.23	2.35	1.27
FAIRS	2.33	0.94	2.30	1.36
MEETING	3.10	1.37	2.50	0.67
UNIV	2.60	1.50	2.75	1.29
HARDW	3.40	1.20	3.15	1.23
COOPSW	3.10	1.37	3.35	1.38
INFORM	2.20	0.98	3.10	1.02
PROFES	2.90	1.45	3.28	1.13
USERS	3.60	1.11	3.95	0.72
NEWPERS	3.00	1.15	2.80	1.05
IMITAT	2.20	1.33	3.05	0.79

Characteristics of process innovation in software (percentage of responses)	1990	1997
PHASES	7	8
METH	4	8
ENVIR	3	6
4GL	2	9
NONE	0	0
FIRMS	10	10

Characteristics of product/service innovation				
	1990		1997	
	Mean	Std. dvt.	Mean	Std. dvt.
NEWPROD	2.90	1.45	3.75	1.17
NEWFEAT	3.30	1.10	4.20	0.64
ENHANCE	2.70	1.19	4.05	0.65
STAND	3.60	1.28	4.00	1.18
Determinants of product/service innovation				
NEWMARK	3.70	1.27	3.80	1.17
ADAPTA	3.78	1.23	3.60	1.28
QUALIT	3.78	0.79	4.35	0.74
DIFFER	3.50	0.50	3.95	1.01
Instruments for the protection of innovation				
LEGAL	3.30	1.73	3.50	1.43
SECRET	2.56	1.57	2.90	1.30
LEAD	3.70	1.27	4.60	0.66
IMPROV	4.30	0.64	4.35	0.55
COOPAC	3.50	1.12	3.45	1.35
PERSON	3.67	1.15	3.28	1.40
Determinants of process innovation				
EFFIC	4.40	0.66	3.95	0.79
QUAL	4.70	0.54	3.45	0.85
MAIN	4.33	0.94	3.40	1.11
REUS	3.50	1.28	3.85	1.18
NEED	4.00	1.10	4.60	0.66
FEASI	2.67	1.33	3.00	1.41
Obstacles to the adoption of process innovation				
INC	3.20	1.40	2.60	1.43
RELUCT	2.50	0.81	2.20	1.08
CUSTOM	3.20	1.40	2.30	1.27
TRAIN	2.50	1.20	3.25	1.08
DINVEST	2.50	1.20	2.85	1.42
PROMAN	3.38	0.86	2.90	1.30
METRIC	3.11	1.20	2.17	1.15
NEW	3.44	0.96	2.50	1.05
WAIT	3.22	0.79	2.94	1.34

APPENDIX C

Table C.1 Pearson's correlation coefficients

	ADAPTA	NEWMARK	DHW	SALES
ADAPTA	–	–	–	–
NEWMARK	0.088 (0.555)[a]	–	–	–
DHW	0.283 (0.053)	0.058 (0.698)	–	–
SALES	–0.160 (0.271)	0.098 (0.517)	0.451 (0.001)	–

Notes

a.   *p-* value in parentheses.

Table C.2 Pearson's Correlation coefficients

	COMP	DHW	MATH	SALES	SERV	MARK	SYST
COMP	–	–	–	–	–	–	–
DHW	0.204 (0.243)[a]	–	–	–	–	–	–
MATH	0.264 (0.134)	0.316 (0.064)	–	–	–	–	–
SALES	0.039 (0.826)	0.445 (0.008)	0.043 (0.802)	–	–	–	–
SERV	–0.168 (0.342)	–0.234 (0.183)	0.100 (0.573)	0.008 (0.963)	–	–	–
MARK	–0.031 (0.858)	–0.319 (0.066)	–0.446 (0.008)	–0.016 (0.927)	0.016 (0.928)	–	–
SYST	0.159 (0.368)	0.246 (0.164)	0.192 (0.274)	–0.004 (0.981)	0.035 (0.843)	–0.105 (0.551)	–

Notes

a.   *p*-value in parentheses.

Table C.3 Pearson's correlation coefficients

	COOPSW	INFORM	UNIV	USERS	HARDW
COOPSW	–	–	–	–	–
INFORM	0.436	–	–	–	–
	(0.010)[a]				
UNIV	0.266	0.446	–	–	–
	(0.128)	(0.008)			
USERS	0.181	–0.027	0.151	–	–
	(0.304)	(0.878)	(0.391)		
HARDW	0.328	0.164	0.169	–0.097	–
	(0.058)	(0.353)	(0.337)	(0.583)	

Notes

a.   *p*-value in parentheses.

APPENDIX D

Methodological notes

The multivariate ordinal variables analysed in this book require the use of ordered logit or probit models. These models draw on a latent regression which can be expressed as follows

$$y^* = \beta' X + \varepsilon \qquad \text{(A.1)}$$

where y^* is an unobserved continuous variable. In our case, y^* measures the propensity to engage in different types of product innovations (chapter 5) or to set up linkages with different external sources of technological change (Chapter 6). X is the vector of the explanatory variables. Each level taken by the observable y (in our case there are 5 levels) corresponds to a specific range of the latent variable

$$
\begin{aligned}
y &= 1 && \text{if } y^* \le 0, \\
  &= 2 && \text{if } 0 < y^* \le \alpha_1, \\
  &\quad . \\
  &\quad . \\
  &\quad . \\
  &= 5 && \text{if } y^* \ge \alpha_4.
\end{aligned}
\qquad \text{(A.2)}
$$

α_i are threshold parameters estimated along with βs (by maximum likelihood estimation). Assuming that disturbances are logistically distributed, we have the following probabilities

$$\begin{aligned} &\text{Pr}\,(y=1) = \Lambda(-\beta'X) \\ &\text{Pr}\,(y=2) = \Lambda(\alpha_1 - \beta'X) - \Lambda(-\beta'X) \end{aligned}$$

$$.$$
$$.$$
$$.$$

$$\text{Pr}\,(y=5) = \Lambda(\alpha_4 - \beta'X)$$

(A.3)

Where Λ is the logistic distribution and the μ_i must satisfy the condition

$$0 < \alpha_1 < \alpha_2 < ... < \alpha_4.$$

Ordered probit models arise from the assumption of normally distributed disturbance. As ordered logit and probit models yield similar results, the tables in Chapters 5 and 6 report only logit estimates.

The estimates are obtained by maximising the likelihood function. It is important to note that the marginal effects of the explanatory variables are different from the estimated coefficients. For continuous explanatory variables, the marginal effects are obtained by calculating the partial derivatives of the probability functions (A.3) with respect to each explanatory variable. As the derivatives depend on the level of x, they are calculated at the means appropriate values of x. Instead, the marginal effect of a binary explanatory variable X_k is calculated as follows

$$\text{Pr}(y = y_i \mid \overline{X}_{-k}, x_k = 1) - \text{Pr}(y = y_i \mid \overline{X}_{-k}, x_k = 0). \quad \text{(A.4)}$$

The correlation between observed and predicted logits and other standard statistics were calculated to measure the goodness of fit of the models.

Bibliography

Acs, Z.J., Audretsch, D.B. and Feldman, M.P. (1992), 'Real Effects of of Academic Research: Comment', *American Economic Review*, 82, pp. 363–7.

Agresti, A. (1990), *Categorical Data Analysis*, John Wiley & Sons, New York

Akerlof, G.A. and Dickens, W.T. (1982), 'The Economic Consequences of Cognitive Dissonance', *American Economic Review*, 72, pp. 307–19.

Antonelli, C. (1995), *The Economics of Localized Technological Change and Industrial Dynamics*, Kluwer, Dordrecht.

Aoki, M. (1986), 'Orizontal vs. Vertical Information Structure of the Firm', *American Economic Review*, December, pp. 971–83.

Aoki, M. (1990), 'Knowledge: Its Acquisition, Sharing and/or Asymmetry', in Aoki, M., Gustafsson, B. and Williamson, O. (eds), *The Firms as a Nexus of Treatises*, Sage Publications, London, pp. 26–51.

Arcangeli, F., Dosi, G. and Moggi, M. (1991), 'Patterns of Diffusion of Electronics Technologies: An International Comparison with Special Reference to the Italian Case', *Research Policy*, 20 (6), pp. 515–29.

Arora, A. and Gambardella, A. (1990), 'Complementarities and External Linkages: The Strategies of the Large Firms in Biotechnology', *The Journal of Industrial Economics*, June, 38, pp. 361–79.

Arora, A. and Gambardella, A. (1994), 'The Changing Technology of Technological Change: General and Abstract Knowledge and the Divion of Innovative Labour', *Research Policy*, 23, 523–32.

Arrow, J.K. (1962a), 'Economics Welfare and the Allocation of Resources for Invention', in Nelson, R. (ed.), *The Rate and Direction of Inventive Activity*, Princeton University Press, Princeton, NJ, 164–81.

Arrow, J.K. (1962b), 'The Economic Implications of Learning by Doing', *Review of Economic Studies*, 29, pp. 155–73.

Arrow, J.K. (1974), *The Limits of Organization*, W.W. Norton and Company, New York.

Arrow, J.K. (1984), *The Economics of Information*, Basil Blackwell, Oxford.

Arthur, W.B. (1989), 'Competing Technologies , Increasing Returns, and Lock-in by Historical Events', *Economic Journal*, 99 (394), pp. 116–31.

Asbrand, D. (1997), 'Outsourcing becomes strategic', *Datamation*, 7 July, p. 73 (www.datamation.com).

Ashworth, J. (1985), 'The Crisis Facing the UK Information Technology Industry', *Information Technology and Public Policy*, 3 (2), pp. 95–101.

Baba, Y., Takai, S. and Mizuta, Y. (1996), 'The Evolution of Software Industry in Japan: A Comprehensive Analysis', in Mowery, D. (ed.), pp. 104–30.

Babbage, C. (1832), *On The Economy of Machinery and Manufacturers*, Augustus, M. Kelly (2nd edn 1963).

Barras, R. (1986), 'Towards a Theory of Innovation in Services', *Research Policy*, 15 (4), pp. 161–73.

Becker, G.S. (1962), 'Investment in Human Capital: A Theoretical Analysis', *Journal of Political Economy* , 70, pp. 1–13.

Bohem, B.W. (1973), 'Software and Its Impact: A Quantitative Assessment', *Datamation*, May, pp. 48–59.

Bohem, B.W. (1981), *Software Engineering Economics*, Prentice-Hall, Inc., Edgewood Cliffs, New Jersey.

Brady, T. and Quintas P. (1991), 'Computer Software: The IT Constraint?', in Freeman, C., Sharp, M. and Walker, W., (eds), pp. 117–37.

Bresnahan, T. and Trajtenberg, M. (1995), 'General Purpose Technologies: Engines of Growth?', *Journal of Econometrics*, 65, pp. 83–108.

Bresnahan, T. and Gambardella, A. (1998), 'The Division of Inventive Labour and the Extent of the Market', in Helpman, E. (ed.), *General Purpose Technologies and Economic Growth*, MIT Press, Cambridge, MA, forthcoming.

Brooks, F.P. Jr. (1975), *The Mythical Man-Month*, Addison-Wesley Publishing Company, Reading, Mass.

Cantwell, J. (1989), *Technological Change and Multinational Corporations*, Blackwell, Oxford.

Carmel, E. (1993), 'Rapid Development in Software Packages Startups', Mimeo, Kogod College of Business Administration, The American University, Washington, DC, March.

Chandler, A.D. Jr. (1990), *Scale and Scope: The Dynamics of Industrial Capitalism*, Belknap Press, Cambridge, Mass.

Chapuis, J.R. and Joel, E.A. (1990) 'The Beginnings of the Computer Industry', in *Electronics Computers and Telephone Switching. A Book of Technological History*, North Holland Publishers, Amsterdam and New York, 2 (III), pp. 68–119.

Cohen, W.M. (1995), 'Empirical Studies of Innovative Activity', in Stoneman, P. (ed.), pp. 182–264.

Cohen, W.M. and Klepper, S. (1992), 'The Anatomy of Industry R&D Intensity Distributions', *American Economic Review*, 82 (4), pp. 773–99.

Cohen, W.M. and Levin, R.C. (1989), 'Empirical Studies of Innovations and Market Structure', in Schmalensee, R. and Willig, R. (eds), pp. 1059–107.

Cohen, W. and Levinthal, D. (1989), 'Innovation and Learning: The Two Faces of R&D', *The Economic Journal*, 99, pp. 569–96.

Computer Weekly (1990), *Computer Weekly Guide to Resources*, Computer Weekly Publications, Sutton.

Cottrell, T. (1994), 'Fragmentated Standards and the Development of Japan's Microcomputer Software Industry', *Research Policy*, 23 (2), pp. 143–74.

Cusumano, M. (1991), *Japan Software Factories. A Challenge to the U.S. Management*, Oxford University Press, New York.

Cusumano, M. (1992), 'Shifting Economies: From Craft Production to Flexible Systems and Software Factories', *Research Policy*, 21, pp. 453–80.

Dambrot, S.M. (1989), 'Japan Prepares for Software Crisis', *Datamation*, May 1, pp. 13–16.

Dasgupta, P. and Stoneman, P. (eds) (1987), *Economic Policy and Technology Performance*, Cambridge University Press, Cambridge.

Dasgupta, P. and Stoneman, P. (1987), 'Introduction', in Dasgupta, P. and Stoneman, P. (eds), pp. 1–5.

Dasgupta, P. (1987), 'The Economic Theory of Technology Policy: An Introduction', in Dasgupta, P. and Stoneman, P. (eds), pp. 7–23.

Dasgupta, P. and David, P. (1986), 'Information Disclosure and the Economics of Science and Technology', in Feiwle, G. (ed), *Essays in Honour of K. Arrow*, Macmillan, London.

Dasgupta, P. and Stiglitz, J. (1980), 'Industrial Structure and the Nature of Innovative Activity', *Economic Journal*, 90, pp. 266–93.

Datamation, (1982), 'Datamation 100', June 15.

Datamation, (1985), 'Datamation 100', June 15.

Datamation, (1989), 'Datamation 100', June 15.

Datamation, (1990), 'Datamation 100', June 15.

Datamation, (1991), 'Datamation 100', June 15.

Datamation, (1992), 'Datamation 100', June 15.

Datamation, (1993), 'Datamation 100', June 15.

Datamation, (1994), 'Datamation 100', June 15.

Datamation, (1995), 'Datamation 100', June 15.

Datamation, (1997), 'Datamation 100', June 15.

David, P.A. (1985), 'CLIO and the Economics of QWERTY', *American Economic Review*, 75, pp. 332–7.

David, P.A., Mowery, D. and Steinmueller, E. (1988), 'The Economics Analysis of Payoffs from Basic Research. An Examination of the Case of Particle Physics Research', *CEPR Discussion Paper*, No. 122, Center for Economic Policy Research, Stanford University, CA, January.

Dorfman, N.S. (1987), *Innovation and Market Structure. Lessons from the Computer and Semiconductor Industries*, Ballinger, Cambridge, MA.

Dosi G. (1982), 'Technological Paradigms and Technological Trajectories: A Suggested Interpretation of the Determinants and Directions of Technical Change', *Research Policy*, 11 (3), pp. 147–62.

Dosi, G., Freeman, C., Nelson, R., Silverberg, G. and Soete, L. (eds) (1988), *Technical Change and Economic Theory*, Pinter, London.

Dunning (1988), 'The Eclectic Paradigm of International Production: A Restatement and Possible Extensions', *Journal of International Business Studies*, Spring, 19, pp. 1–31.

Duysters, G. (1996), *The Dynamics of Technical Innovation. The Evolution and Development of Information Technology*, E. Elgar, Cheltenham.

Dutton, J. and Thomas A. (1985), 'Relating Technological Change and Learning by Doing', *Research on Technological Innovation, Management and Policy*, 2, pp. 187–224.

EEC (1991) *L'industrie Europeenne de L'electronique et de L'informatique*, Bruxelles, March.

EEC (1992), *ESPRIT Results and Progress 1991/92*, the Commission of the European Communities, DGXIII, Brussels.

EITO (1993), *European Information Technology Observatory 1993*, EITO, Frankfurt.

EITO (1995), *European Information Technology Observatory 1995*, EITO, Frankfurt.

EITO (1996), *European Information Technology Observatory 1996*, EITO, Frankfurt.

EITO (1997), *European Information Technology Observatory 1997*, EITO, Frankfurt.

Eurostat (1995), *Report of the Eurostat Pilot Project to Investigate the Possibilities to Measure Innovation in the Service Sectors*, Eurostat, Luxembourg.

Evangelista, R. and Sirilli, G. (1995), 'Measuring Innovation in Services', *Research Evaluation*, 5 (3), pp. 207–15.

Evans, R. (1991), 'Esprit Evades the Soft Option', *International Management*, February, pp. 58–61.

Farrell, J. and Saloner, G. (1985), 'Standardization, Compatibility, and Innovation', *Rand Journal of Economics*, 16 (1), pp. 70–83.

Fertig, R.T. (1985), *The Software Revolution: Trends, Players and Market Dynamics in Personal Computer Software*, Elsevier, Amsterdam.

Financial Times (1994a), 'Future Strength Open Systems is the Key to Business', Financial Times Survey, Information and Communications Technology, March 16, p. IV.

Financial Times (1994b), 'History Often Repeats Itself', Financial Times Survey, Information and Communications Technology, March 16, p. XIII.

Financial Times (1994c), 'Rise of Object-Oriented Technology', Financial Times Survey, Information and Communications Technology, March 16, p. IV.

Flamm, K. (1988), *Creating the Computer*, The Brookings Institution, Washington, DC.

Freeman, C. (1982), *The Economics of Industrial Innovation*, 2nd edn, Pinter, London.

Freeman, C. and Perez, C. (1988), 'Structural Crises of Adjustment: Business Cycles and Investment Behaviour', in Dosi, G., Freeman, C., Nelson, R., Silverberg, G. and Soete, L. (eds), pp. 38–66.

Freeman, C., Clark, J. and Soete, L. (1982), *Unemployement and Technical Innovation: A Study on Long Waves in Economic Development*, Pinter, London.

Freeman, C., Sharp, M., and Walker, W. (eds.) (1991), *Technology and the Future of Europe*, F. Pinter, London.

Friedman, A. (1989), *Information Systems Development: History, Organisation and Implementation*, Wiley, Chichester.

Frumau, C.C.F. (1992), 'Choices in R&D and Business Portfolio in the Electronic Industry: What the Bibliometric Data Show', *Research Policy*, 21, pp. 97–124.

Gambardella, A. and Torrisi, S. (1998), 'Does Technological Convergence Imply Convergence in Markets? Evidence from the Electronics Industry', *Research Policy*, forthcoming.

Garber, J.H. (1993), 'Working faster', *Forbes*, April 12, p. 110.

Georghiou, L., Guy, K., Quintas, P., Hobday, M., Cameron, H. and Ray, T. (1991), *Evaluation of the Alvey Programme for Advanced Information Technology*, HMSO, London.

Geroski, P.A. (1992) 'Vertical Relations between Firms and Industrial Policy', *The Economic Journal*, 102, pp. 139–47.

Gotlieb, C.C. (1985), *The Economics of Computers: Costs, Benefits, Policies, and Strategies*, Prentice-Hall, Inc., Englewood Cliffs, New Jersey.

Granstrand, O. and Sjolander, S. (1990), 'Managing Innovation in Multi-Technology Firms', *Research Policy*, 19, pp. 35–60.

Greene, W.H. (1997), *Econometric Analysis*, Prentice-Hall, 3rd edition, Upper Saddle River, NJ.

Grindley, P. (1996), 'The Future of the UK Software Industry: Limitations of Independent Production', in Mowery, D. (ed.), pp. 197–239.

Grossman, S. and Hart, O. (1986), 'The Costs and Benefits of Ownership: A Theory of Lateral and Vertical Integration', *Journal of Political Economy*, 94, pp. 691–719.

Hagedoorn, J. (1993), 'Understanding the Rationale of Strategic Technology Partnership:Interorganisational Modes of Cooperation and Sectoral Differences', *Strategic Management Journal*, 14, pp. 371–85.

Hayley, K., Fordonski, J. and Puckett, B. (1992), 'What CIOs need to Do Now' *Datamation*, July, 15, pp. 83–5.

Hayes, R.H. and Wheelright, S.C. (1984), *Restoring Our Competitive Edge: Competing Through Manufacturing Concepts and Situations*, Wiley & Sons, New York.

Heeks, R. (1993), 'Software Subcontracting to the Third World', in Quintas, P., (ed.), *Social Dimension of Software Engineering: People, Processes, Policies and Software Development*, Ellis Horwood, Chichester, pp. 236–47.

Henderson, R.M. and Clark, K.B. (1990), 'Architectural Innovation: The reconfiguration of Existing Product Technologies and the Failure of Established Firms', *Administrative Science Quarterly*, 35, pp. 9–30.

Hirschman A.O. (1970), *Exit, Voice and Loyalty*, Harvard University Press, Cambridge, Mass.

Holmstrom, B. (1989), 'Agency costs and Innovation', *Journal of Industrial Behaviour and Organisation*, 12, pp. 305–27.

Holmstrom, B. and Tirole, J. (1989), 'The Theory of the Firm', in Schmalensee, R. and Willig, R. (eds), pp. 61–133.

Iansiti, M. and Clark, K.B. (1995), 'Integration and Dynamic Capability: Evidence from Product Development in Automobiles and Mainframe Computers', *Industrial and Corporate Change*, 3, pp. 557–605.

IDC (1990), European Software and Services. Review and Forecast, International Data Corporation, European Research Centre, Paris.

IDC (1994), Worldwide Software Review and Forecast, International Data Corporation, Framingham, Mass.

Irvine, J. and Martin, B. (1980), 'The Economic Effects of Big Science: the Case of Radio-Astronomy', in *Proceedings of the International Colloquium on Economic Effects of Space and Other Advanced Technology*, ESA SP 151, European Space Agency, Paris.

Itoh, H. (1987), 'Information Processing Capacities of the Firm', *Journal of the Japanese and International Economies*, 1, pp. 299–326.

Itoh, M. et al. (1991), *Economic Analysis of Industrial Policy*, Academic Press, San Diego.

Jacobsson, S. and Oskarsson, C. (1993), 'Educational Statistics as an Indicator of Technology Activity', *Research Policy*, 24, pp. 127–36.

Jaffe, A.B. (1989), 'Real Effects of Academic Research', *American Economic Review*, 79 (5), pp. 957–70.

Jaikumar, R. (1986), 'Postindustrial Manufacturing', *Harvard Business Review*, September, pp. 301–8.

Johannessen, K.S. (1988), 'Rule Following and Tacit Knowledge', *Artificial Intelligence and Society*, Vol. 2, pp. 287–301.

Kamien, M.I. and Schwartz, N.L. (1982), *Market Structure and Innovation*, Cambridge University Press, Cambridge, Mass.

Katz, M.L. and Shapiro, C. (1986), 'Technology Adoption in Presence of Network Externalities', *Journal of Political Economy*, 94, pp. 822–41.

Kelly, T. (1987), *The British Computer Industry. Crisis and Development*, Croom Helm, London.

Khazam J. and Mowery D. (1994), 'The Commercialization of RISC: Strategies for the Creation of Dominant Designs', *Research Policy*, 23 (1), January, pp. 89–102.

Kicherer, S. (1990), *Olivetti. A Study of the Corporate Management of Design*, Trefoil Publications, London.

Klepper, S. (1997), 'Industry Life Cycles', *Industrial and Corporate Change*, 6 (1), pp. 145–81.

Kline, S.J. and Rosenberg, N. (1986), 'An Overview of Innovation', in Landau, R. and Rosenberg, N. (eds), *The Positive Sum Strategy. Harnessing Technology for Economic Growth*, National Academy Press, Washington DC, pp. 275–305.

Koike, K. (1987), 'Skill Formation Systems, A Thai–Japan Comparison', *Journal of the Japanese and International Economies*, 1, pp. 408–40.

Kuznets, S. (1966), *Modern Economic Growth: Rate, Structure and Spread*, Yale University Press, New Haven.

Levin, R.C., Klevorick, A.K., Nelson, R.R. and Winter, S.G. (1987), 'Appropriating the Returns from Industrial Research and Development', *Brookings Papers on Economic Activity*, No. 13.

Lindholm, E. (1994), 'Snap-On Code', *Datamation*, 1, February, 1994, pp. 63–5

Link, A.N. and Rees, J. (1990), 'Firm Size, University Based Research, and the Returns to R&D', *Small Business Economics*, March, 2, pp. 25–32.

Lundvall, B.A. (1988), 'Innovation as an interactive process: From User Producer Interaction to the National System of Innovation' in Dosi, G., Freeman, C., Nelson, R., Silverberg, G. and Soete, L. (eds), pp. 349–69.

Machlup, F. (1980), *Knowledge: Its Creation, Distribution, and Economic Significance*, Princeton University Press, Princeton, NJ.

Maddala, G.S. (1983), *Limited-Dependent and Qualitative Variables in Econometrics*, Cambridge University Press, Cambridge.

Malerba, F. (1992), 'Learning by Firms and Incremental Technical Change', *Economic Journal*, 52, pp. 845–59.

Malerba, F., Torrisi, S. and von Tunzelmann, N. (1991), 'Electronic Computers' in Freeman C., Sharp, M. and Walker, W. (eds), pp. 95–116.

Malerba, F. and Orsenigo, L. (1996), 'Schumpeterian Patterns of Innovation are Technology–Specific', *Research Policy*, 25 (3), 451–78.

Malerba, F. and Torrisi, S. (1992), 'Internal Capabilities and External Networks in Innovative Activities. Evidence from the Software Industry', *Economics of Innovation and New Technology*, 2, pp. 49–71.

Malerba, F. and Torrisi, S. (1993), 'Software', *Research and Technology Management in Enterprises: Issues for Community Policy*, Sectoral Report, Monitor-SAST, Project No. 8, Brussels, March.

Malerba, F. and Torrisi, S. (1996), 'The Dynamics of Market Structure and Innovation in the Western European Software Industry', in Mowery, D. (ed.), pp. 165–96.

Mansfield, E. (1968), *Industrial Research and Technological Innovation: An Econometric Analysis*, Norton, New York.

Merges, R. and Nelson, R. (1990), 'On the Complex Economics of Patent Scope', *Columbia Law Review*, 90, pp. 839–906.

Meyer, B. (1997), *Object-Oriented Software Construction*, Prentice-Hall, 2nd edition, Upper Saddle River, NJ.

Miles, I. (1993), 'Services in the New Industrial Economy', *Futures*, 25 (6), 653–72.

Miller, R., Hobday, M., Leroux-Demers, T., Olleros, X. (1993), 'Innovation in Complex Systems Industries: The Case of Flight Simulation', *Industrial and Corporate Change*, 4, pp. 363–400.

Moad, J. (1990), 'The Software Revolution', *Datamation*, 15, February, pp. 22–30.

Moad, J. (1995), 'Object Methods Tame Reengineering Madness', *Datamation*, 15, May, pp. 43–8.

Mowery, D. (1983), 'The Relationship Between Intrafirm and Contractual Forms of Industrial Research in American Manufacturing, 1900–1940', *Explorations in Economic History*, 20, pp. 351–73.

Mowery, D. (ed.) (1988), *International Collaborative Ventures in US Manufacturing*, Ballinger Publishers, Cambridge, Mass.

Mowery D. (ed.) (1996), *The International Computer Software Industry: A Comparative Study of Industry Evolution and Structure*, Oxford University Press, Oxford.

Nakahara, T. (1993), 'The Industrial Organisation and Information Structure of the Software Industry: A US–Japan Comparison', *CEPR Discussion Paper*, No. 346, Center for Economic Policy Research, Stanford University, Stanford, CA, May.

Narasimhan, R. (1993), 'Software Industry: A Developing Country Perspective', in UNIDO, *Software Industry. Current Trends and Implications for Developing Countries*, General Studies Series, United Nations Industrial Development Organisation, Vien.

National Research Council (1991), *Intellectual Property Issues in Software*, National Academy Press, Washington, DC.

Naur, P. and Randall, B. (1969) (eds), *Software Engineering: A Report on a Conference Sponsored by the NATO Science Committee*, Scientific Affairs Division, NATO, Brussels, January.

Nelson, R.R. (1962), 'The Link between Science and Invention: the Case of the Transistor', in Nelson, R. (ed.), *The Rate and Direction of Inventive Activity*, Princeton University Press, New Jersey.

Nelson, R.R. (1982), 'The Role of Knowledge in R&D Efficiency', *Quarterly Journal of Economics*, 97, pp. 453–70.

Nelson, R.R. (ed.) (1993), *National Innovation Systems. A Comparative Analysis*, Oxford University Press, Oxford.

Nelson, R.R. and Winter, S. (1982), *An Evolutionary Theory of Economic Change*, The Belknap Press of Harvard University Press, Cambridge, Mass.

Nelson, R.R. and Levin, R. (1986), 'The Influence of Science, Universitity Research and Technical Societies on Industrial R&D and Technical Advance', *Policy Discussion Paper*, No. 3, Research Program on Technological Change, Yale University Press, New Heaven.

OECD (1985), *Software: An Emerging Industry*, ICCP Series, No. 9, Organisation for Economic Cooperation and Development, Paris.

OECD (1992), *OECD Proposed Guidelines for Collecting and Interpreting Technological Innovation Data – Oslo Manual*, Organisation for Economic Cooperation and Development, Paris.

OECD (1997), *Information Technology Outlook*, Organisation for Economic Cooperation and Development, Paris.

Panzar, J.C. (1989), 'Technological Determinants of Firms and Industry Structure', in Schmalenses, R. and Willig, R. (eds), pp. 4–59.

Patel, P. and Pavitt, K. (1994), 'Technological Competencies in the World's Largest Firms: Characteristics, Constraints and Scope for Managerial Choice', *STEEP Discussion Paper*, SPRU, University of Sussex, No. 13, May.

Pavitt, K. (1984), 'Sectoral Patterns of Technical Change: Towards a Taxonomy and a Theory', *Research Policy*, 13 (6), pp. 343–73.

Pavitt, K. (1991a), 'What Do We Know about the Usefulness of Science? The Case for Diversity', in Hague, D. (ed.), *The Management of Science. Proceedings of Section F (Economics) of the British Association for the Advancement of Science*, MacMillan, Basingstoke, pp. 21–46.

Pavitt, K. (1991b), 'Key Characteristics of the Large Innovating Firm', *British Journal of Management*, 2 (1), pp. 533–45.

Pavitt, K., Robson, M. and Townsend, J. (1987), 'The Size Distribution of Innovating Firms in the UK: 1945–1983', *Journal of Industrial Economics*, March, 35, 291–316.

Perry, M.K. (1989), 'Vertical Integration: Determinats and Effects', in Schmalensee, R. and Willig, R. (eds), pp. 183–255.

Phister, M. (1979), *Data Processing Technology and Economics*, 2nd edn Digital Press, Santa Fe, New Mexico and Santa Monica, Mass.

Piore, J., Sabel, C.F. (1984), *The Second Industrial Divide: Possibilities for Prosperity*, Basic Books, New York.

Polanyi, M. (1962), *Personal Knowledge: Towards a Post–Critical Philosophy*, Harper, Torchbooks, New York.

Polanyi, M. (1967), *The Tacit Dimension*, Doubleday Anchor, Garden City, New York.

Prahalad, C.K. and Hamel, G. (1990), 'The Core Competence of the Corporation', *Harvard Business Review*, May–June, pp. 79–91.

Predicasts (1984–1992), *Predicasts F&S Index – United States*, Annual Edition, Predicasts Inc., Cleveland Ohio.

Predicasts (1984–1992), *Predicasts F&S Index – International*, Annual Edition, Predicasts Inc., Cleveland Ohio.

Predicasts (1983), *Predicasts Company Thesaurus*, Company Section, Annual Edition, Predicasts Inc., Cleveland Ohio.

Quintas, P. (ed.) (1993), *Social Dimension of Software Engineering: People, Processes, Policies and Software Development*, Ellis Horwood, Chichester.

Raffa, M. and Zollo, G. (1993), 'Technical Skills and Small Innovative Firms in Northern and Southern Italy', *International Contributions to Labour Studies*, 3, pp. 101–27.

Reinganum, J.F. (1983), 'Uncertain Innovation and the Persistence of Monopoly', *American Economic Review*, 47, pp. 341–8.

Ryle, G. (1949), *The Concept of Mind*, Hutchinson, London.

Rosenberg N. (1976) *Perspectives on Technology*, Cambridge University press, Cambridge.

Rosenberg, N. (1982), *Inside the Black Box: Technology and Economics*, Cambridge University Press, Cambridge.

Rosenberg (1990), 'Why do Firms do Basic Reasearch (with Their Own Money)?', *Research Policy*, 19, pp. 165–74.

Rosenbrock H.H. (1988), 'Engineering As An Art', *Artificial Intelligence & Society*, 2, pp. 315–20.

Rosenbrock, H.H. (1990), *Machines with a Purpose*, Oxford University Press, Oxford.

Rothwell, R. (1983), 'Firm Size and Innovation: A Case of Dynamic Complementarity', *The Journal of General Management*, 8 (3), pp. 5–25.

Rothwell, R. and Zegreld, W. (1982), *Innovation and the Small and Medium Sized Firms*, Pinter, London.

Rullani, E. and Vaccà, S. (1987), 'Scienza e tecnologia nello sviluppo industriale', *Economia e politica industriale*, 53, pp. 3–41.

Salter, W.E.G. (1966), *Productivity and Technical Change*, 2nd edn, Cambridge University Press, Cambridge

Schmalensee, R. and Willig, R.D. (eds) (1989), *Handbook of Industrial Organisation*, North Holland, Amsterdam.

Schumpeter, J. (1934), *The Theory of Economic Development*, Harvard University Press, Cambridge, Mass.

Schumpeter, J. (1942), *Capitalism, Socialism, and Democracy*, Harper, New York.

Semich, J.M. (1993), 'Software's Big 100', *Datamation*, 15, September, pp. 38–44.

Simon, H.A. (1972), 'Theories of Bounded Rationality', in MacGuire, C.B. and Radner, R. (eds), *Decision and Organization*, North Holland, Amsterdam, pp. 161–76.

Simon, H.A. (1979), 'Rational Decision Making in Business Organizations', *American Economic Review*, 69, 493–512.

Smith, A. (1776), *An Inquiry into the Nature and Causes of the Wealth of Nations*, W. Strahan and T. Cadell, London (bicentennial ed. Clarendon Press, Oxford, 1976).

Sommerville, I. (1982), *Software Engineering*, Addison-Wesley, Wokingham.

Steinmueller W.E. (1996), 'The U.S. Software Industry: An Analysis and Interpretative History', in Mowery, D. (ed.), pp. 15–52.

Stigler, G. (1951), 'The Division of Labour is Limited by the Extent of the Market', *Journal of Political Economy*, LIX (3), pp. 185–93.

Stiglitz, J.E. (1987), 'Learning to Learn, Localized Learning and Technological Progress', in Dasgupta, P. and Stoneman, P. (eds), pp. 125–53.

Stoneman, P. (ed.) (1995), *Handbook of the Economics of Innovation and Technological Change*, Basil Blackwell, Oxford.

Swann, P. and Gill, J. (1993), *Corporate Vision and Rapid Technological Change. The Evolution of Market Structure*, Routledge, London and New York.

Teece, D.J. (1986), 'Profiting from Technological Innovation: Implications for Integration, Collaboration, Licencing and Public Policy', *Research Policy*, 15, pp. 285–305.

Teece, D.J. (1988), 'Technological Change and the Nature of the Firm', in Dosi, G., Freeman, C., Nelson, R., Silverberg, G. and Soete, L. (eds), pp. 256–81.

Teece, D.J., Rumelt, R., Dosi, G. and Winter, S. (1994), 'Understanding Corporate Coherence: Theory and Evidence', *Journal of Economic Behaviour and Organisation*, 23, pp. 285–305.

Torrisi, S. (1994), *The Organization of Innovative Activities in European Software Firms*, D-Phil dissertation, SPRU, University of Sussex, Brighton, September.

Torrisi, S. (1998), 'Firm Specialisation and Growth. A Study of the European Spftware Industry', in Gambardella, A. and Malerba, F. (eds), *The Organisation of Innovative Activity in Europe*, Cambridge University Press, Cambridge, forthcoming.

Tucker, J.M. (1997), 'A juggling act between old and new', *Datamation*, 7 July, pp. 61–6 (http://www.datamation.com).

Tushman, M.L. and Anderson, P. (1986), 'Technological Discontinuities and Organisational Environments', *Administrative Science Quarterly*, 31 (3), pp. 439–65.

Usher, A.P. (1971), 'Technical Change and Capital Formation', in Rosenberg, N. (ed.), *The Economics of Technological Change. Selected Readings*, Penguin Books, Harmondsworth (original edition 1955), pp. 43–72.

Utterback, J.M. (1974), 'Innovation in Industry and the Diffusion of Technology', *Science*, 183, 15, February, pp. 658–62.

Utterback, J.M. (1971), The Process Innovation, A Study of the Origination and Development of Ideas from New Scientific Instruments, *IEEE Transactions on Engineering Management*, EM-8.

Utterback J.M. and Abernathy W.J. (1975), 'A Dynamic Model of Process and Product Innovation', *Omega*, 3 (6), pp. 424–41.

von Hayek, F. (1948), *Individualism and Economic Order*, University of Chicago Press, Chicago (reprinted in 1980).

von Hippel, E. (1988), *The Sources of Innovation,* Oxford University Press, New York.

von Hippel, E. (1990a), 'The Impact of «Sticky» Information on Innovation and Problem-Solving', *Alfred P. Sloan School of Management Working Paper*, 3147-90-BPS, MIT, Cambridge, Mass, April.

von Hippel, E. (1990b), 'Task Partitioning: An Innovation Process Variable', *Research Policy*, 19, pp. 407–18.

Williamson, O.E. (1975), *Markets and Hierarchies: Analysis and Antitrust Implications*, Free Press, New York

Winter, S.G. (1987), 'Knowledge and Competence as Strategic Assets', in Teece, D.J. (ed.), *The Competitive Challenge: Strategies for Industrial Innovation and Renewal*, Ballinger, Cambridge, Mass., pp. 159–84.

Winter, S.G. (1993) 'On Coase, Competence and the Corporation', in Williamson, O.E. and Winter, S.G. (eds) *The Nature of the Firms*, Oxford University Press, New York, pp. 179–95.

Womack, P.J., Jones, T.D. and Roos, D. (1990), *The Machine that Changed the World*, Macmillan, New York.

Young A. (1928), 'Increasing Returns and Economic Progress', *The Economic Journal*, 152, XXXVIII, pp. 527–42.

Zanfei, A. (1993), 'Patterns of Collaborative Innovation in the US Telecommunications Industry after the Divesture', *Research Policy*, 22 (4), pp. 309–25.

Subject Index